Parties and Voters at the 2013 German Federal Election

The 2013 federal election in Germany took place amidst considerable uncertainty over the EU's economic crisis. Financial rescue packages for several countries required the provision of huge sums. Some EU-members barely avoided the economic abyss. Germany, however, was spared much of the hardship as her economy produced record-levels of employment, exports boomed, and German state coffers began to see a budget surplus. Against this backdrop, this book examines the choices offered to voters by parties, and publics' decision calculus. How did Germany's voter evaluate economic conditions and the Euro crisis? For example, is there a demand for a new party representing the rising EU-skeptical sentiments? How did long-term developments such as the weakening party–voter ties affect the election outcome? What programs did parties offer to voters in the election? The book brings together several leading experts of German and European politics to address these questions.

This book was originally published as a special issue of *German Politics*.

Robert Rohrschneider is Sir Robert Worcester Professor of Political Science at the University of Kansas, USA. His current research focuses on political representation in advanced industrial democracies.

Rüdiger Schmitt-Beck is Professor of Political Science and Political Sociology at the University of Mannheim, Germany. He is chairperson of the German Society for Electoral Research (DGfW) and one of the principal investigators of the German Longitudinal Election Study (GLES).

T0347511

Parties and Voters at the 2013 German Federal Election

Edited by
Robert Rohrschneider and Rüdiger Schmitt-Beck

Routledge
Taylor & Francis Group

LONDON AND NEW YORK

First published 2018
by Routledge

2 Park Square, Milton Park, Abingdon, Oxfordshire OX14 4RN
52 Vanderbilt Avenue, New York, NY 10017

Routledge is an imprint of the Taylor & Francis Group, an informa business

First issued in paperback 2019

British Library Cataloguing in Publication Data
A catalogue record for this book is available from the British Library

ISBN 13: 978-1-138-56680-4 (hbk)
ISBN 13: 978-0-367-89240-1 (pbk)

Typeset in Times New Roman
by RefineCatch Limited, Bungay, Suffolk

Publisher's Note
The publisher accepts responsibility for any inconsistencies that may have
arisen during the conversion of this book from journal articles to book chapters,
namely the possible inclusion of journal terminology.

Disclaimer
Every effort has been made to contact copyright holders for their permission to
reprint material in this book. The publishers would be grateful to hear from any
copyright holder who is not here acknowledged and will undertake to rectify
any errors or omissions in future editions of this book.

Contents

CONTENTS

Citation Information

The chapters in this book were originally published in *German Politics*, volume 26, issue 1 (March 2017). When citing this material, please use the original page numbering for each article, as follows:

Introduction
Introduction: Parties and Voters at the 2013 German Federal Election
Robert Rohrschneider and Rüdiger Schmitt-Beck
German Politics, volume 26, issue 1 (March 2017), pp. 1–11

Chapter 1
Social Cleavages and Electoral Behaviour in Long-Term Perspective: Alignment without Mobilisation?
Martin Elff and Sigrid Roßteutscher
German Politics, volume 26, issue 1 (March 2017), pp. 12–34

Chapter 2
An 'Angela Merkel Effect'? The Impact of Gender on CDU/CSU Voting Intention between 1998 and 2013
Marc Debus
German Politics, volume 26, issue 1 (March 2017), pp. 35–48

Chapter 3
Another Dog that didn't Bark? Less Dealignment and more Partisanship in the 2013 Bundestag Election
Kai Arzheimer
German Politics, volume 26, issue 1 (March 2017), pp. 49–64

Chapter 4
Merkwürdig oder nicht? What Economic Voting Models and the 2013 Bundestag Elections Have to Say about Each Other
Katsunori Seki and Guy D. Whitten
German Politics, volume 26, issue 1 (March 2017), pp. 65–82

Chapter 5

Party Positions about European Integration in Germany: An Electoral Quandary?
Robert Rohrschneider and Stephen Whitefield
German Politics, volume 26, issue 1 (March 2017), pp. 83–103

Chapter 6

Instrumental and Expressive Coalition Voting: The Case of the FDP in the 2009 and 2013 German Federal Elections
Sascha Huber
German Politics, volume 26, issue 1 (March 2017), pp. 104–123

Chapter 7

The 'Alternative für Deutschland in the Electorate': Between Single-Issue and Right-Wing Populist Party
Rüdiger Schmitt-Beck
German Politics, volume 26, issue 1 (March 2017), pp. 124–148

Chapter 8

If You Don't Know Me by Now: Explaining Local Candidate Recognition
Heiko Giebler and Bernhard Weßels
German Politics, volume 26, issue 1 (March 2017), pp. 149–169

Chapter 9

Correct Voting at the 2013 German Federal Election: An Analysis of Normatively Desirable Campaign Effects
Ben Christian
German Politics, volume 26, issue 1 (March 2017), pp. 170–186

For any permission-related enquiries please visit:
http://www.tandfonline.com/page/help/permissions

Notes on Contributors

Kai Arzheimer is Professor of Political Science and Head of the German Politics and Political Sociology unit at the University of Mainz, Germany. He has published widely in the field of political parties, electoral behaviour and quantitative methods.

Ben Christian is MA candidate at the Faculty of Social Sciences at the University of Mannheim, Germany.

Marc Debus is Professor of Comparative Government at Mannheim University, Germany. His research interests include political institutions, in particular, multilevel systems and their effects on the political behaviour of voters and legislators, party competition, coalition politics and decision making within parliaments and governments.

Martin Elff is Professor of Political Sociology at Zeppelin University, Germany. His research interests are in comparative politics, political behaviour and political methodology. He has published on various topics within these fields in journals such as *Electoral Studies*, *German Politics*, *Perspectives on Politics* and *Political Analysis*.

Heiko Giebler is a Research Fellow at the WZB Berlin Social Science Center, research unit 'Democracy and Democratisation', and he is working in the German Longitudinal Election Study (GLES). His research focuses on electoral behaviour, political parties, political elites and applied quantitative methods.

Sascha Huber is Lecturer in Political Science at the University of Mannheim, Germany. His research mainly focuses on voting behaviour, decision making, survey research and experimental methods.

Robert Rohrschneider is Sir Robert Worcester Professor of Political Science at the University of Kansas, USA. His current research focuses on political representation in advanced industrial democracies.

Sigrid Roßteutscher is a Full Professor at the Faculty of Social Sciences at the Goethe University Frankfurt/Main, Germany. Her research interests are on religion and politics, social capital and political participation, particularly electoral participation. She is author and editor of numerous publications including *Voters on the Move or on the Run?* (2014; with Bernhard Weßels, Hans Rattinger and Rüdiger Schmitt-Beck); *Social Capital and Associations in European Democracies: A Comparative Analysis* (2007; with William A. Maloney).

NOTES ON CONTRIBUTORS

Rüdiger Schmitt-Beck is Professor of Political Science and Political Sociology at the University of Mannheim, Germany. He is chairperson of the German Society for Electoral Research (DGfW) and one of the principal investigators of the German Longitudinal Election Study (GLES).

Katsunori Seki is a Post-Doctoral Researcher at SFB 884 'Political Economy of Reforms', University of Mannheim. Germany. His research focuses on electoral accountability, elections in nondemocratic settings and legislative politics.

Bernhard Weßels is Senior Researcher at the WZB Berlin Social Science Center, research unit 'Democracy and Democratisation', and Professor of Political Science at Humboldt-Universität zu Berlin, Germany. His main areas of interest are comparative political behaviour, attitudes and elections, interest intermediation and representation.

Stephen Whitefield is Professor of Politics in the Department of Politics and International Relations, and Rhodes-Pelczynski Fellow in Politics in Pembroke College, University of Oxford, UK. His research has focused on public opinion in post-Communist Europe and, with Robert Rohrschneider, on party competition across Europe as a whole.

Guy D. Whitten is Professor and College of Liberal Arts Cornerstone Fellow in the Department of Political Science at Texas A&M University, USA. His research interests are political economy, public policy, political methodology and comparative politics. Much of his published research has involved cross-national comparative studies of the influence of economics on government popularity and elections.

Introduction: Parties and Voters at the 2013 German Federal Election

ROBERT ROHRSCHNEIDER and
RÜDIGER SCHMITT-BECK

Introducing the special issue, section (1) provides an overview of the election campaign, (2) discusses major aspects of the election's outcome and (3) highlights the broader theoretical implications of the contributions to the special issue to the research literature.

The 2013 Federal Election indicates a considerably growing volatility of the German electorate. Smaller parties, partly founded just shortly before the election, gained substantial support from an increasingly dealigned electorate. For the first time ever, the FDP, which was represented in every Bundestag since 1949, failed to clear the 5 per cent threshold and did not gain any seats in the Bundestag. For the second time in short order a Grand Coalition became thus the most viable option for the formation of a government. However, this time the Social Democrats entered the collaboration with the Christian Democrats clearly as a smaller partner. All this (and more) signals the greater mobility and willingness of the electorate to defect from the pillars of the established party system. With these features, the German context seems to reflect broader trends that occur in many European democracies. Most electorates in Western Europe clearly experience weakening partisan loyalties among voters; and in newer democracies in Central-Eastern Europe, partisan loyalties are still forming so that, on the whole, the patterns in the 2013 election fit a more general assessment that established parties are losing their grip on electorates.[1]

THE CAMPAIGN CONTEXT

The 2013 Federal Election took place amid the sovereign debt crisis which in turn was a result of the greatest economic crisis that had gripped Europe since the Great Depression. Rescue packages for several countries involved hundreds of billions of Euros; some countries were near or even reached financial collapse, and unemployment rates in many European states soared to unprecedented levels. Europe, it appeared on the eve of the Federal Election, had reached a point where it would have been only too natural to debate the future of the EU, the fiscal implications and the expense of the integration project among publics and established elites in

Germany. Except this did not happen: while many countries suffered from Europe's economic malaise, Germany's economy was the exception proving the rule with unemployment at a long-time low, inflation rates also very low and Germany's tax coffers bursting at the seams. Any visitor to Germany during the campaign was impressed by its economic prowess and its capacity to weather the economic storm, at least for the time being. Europe's economic malaise, it appeared, had spared 'fortress Germany'.

Against this backdrop, it seems only logical that the election campaign was generally considered uneventful if not outright boring.[2] Like its predecessor in 2009, the 2013 campaign went over the stage without rhetorical sabre-rattling and big drama, and it did not focus on Europe. In fact, compared to 2009 it offered even fewer highlights and tension. This had several reasons. One of them was that most observers and voters had long since been aware that the next Federal Chancellor would yet again be the leader of the CDU and incumbent since 2005, Angela Merkel; an assumption backed by opinion polls. The remaining question was who would serve as the Union's junior partner in the next government. Neither parties nor voters seemed to prefer an unusual coalition (like a black–green or a 'Jamaica' coalition), so only two options appeared realistic as prospects. The current junior coalition partner – the FDP – was eager to continue the government with the Christian Democrats which also preferred the black–yellow coalition, although with a remarkable lack of enthusiasm. The only alternative that seemed realistic was a Grand Coalition with the SPD. However, the Social Democrats (SPD) were extremely reluctant to endorse a Grand Coalition with the CDU/CSU before the election because the last one (2005–09) had ended with their worst election result since the founding of the Federal Republic. But during the campaign, opinion polls indicated that the red–green coalition it instead aimed for was unlikely to become a viable option for the Social Democrats. As both the SPD and the Greens ruled out the possibility of a coalition with the Left on the federal level, it was clear that a Grand Coalition was the only conceivable power perspective for the SPD even if it insisted on denying this option.[3]

Another reason for the attenuated course of the election campaign was the campaign strategy of 'asymmetric demobilization'[4] that was applied by the CDU for the second time after its inception in 2009. Characteristic of this strategy was its lack of assertiveness, and its strict avoidance of statements that might draw attacks from competitors. Instead of controversial political claims the campaign focused on promises of costly 'election gifts', for instance increasing pensions. This was facilitated by the fact that Germany's economy in 2013 was an isle of the blessed when compared to many neighbouring states that struggled economically. The country could, for instance, enjoy the fruits of decreased unemployment rates which resulted from the *Agenda 2010* reform package initiated by the red-green government under Chancellor Gerhard Schröder (SPD) a decade earlier.[5] Other economic indicators recovered also quickly so that Germany was in the black while the dominating colour of budgets in the rest of the Euro zone was red. Even the objective of a balanced federal budget seemed to be within reach. This does not mean that Germany was left completely untouched by the crisis. As a major guarantor for voluminous bailout and rescue packages in support of heavily indebted countries of the Euro zone, Germany was enmeshed in the crisis. Yet, strangely, during the campaign the Euro crisis was the big elephant in the room. As most parties supported the government's policy course in parliament[6] they played it safe by avoiding the topic in their campaigns, presumably for fear of toxic fallout at the ballot box.

VOLATILE ELECTORAL BEHAVIOUR AND PARTY SYSTEM CHANGE

Although – or because – its campaign seemed lacklustre, if only by dint of avoiding the most pressing issue on European governments' agenda, the 2013 election registered the highest amount of volatility in voters' choices ever. Already the 2009 election had surpassed the high point of electoral volatility which until then had been held by the second Federal Election that took place in 1953 (8.5 on the Pedersen volatility index), but 2013 saw a further increase, to 13.0. Never before had the vote shares of the parties shifted as much from one election to the next as they did between 2009 and 2013. Other indicators for the fragmentation of the party system remained at high levels, although not quite as extreme as in 2009.[7] The significant increase of electoral mobility that had already characterised the 2009 election and further intensified in 2013 considerably transformed the German party system and may lead to further changes in the future.

For no other party was the outcome of the election more dramatic – and traumatic – than for the FDP. After having continuously held seats in the Bundestag since 1949 and having achieved its best election result ever in 2009, the FDP lost more than two-thirds of its previous vote share and failed to pass the 5 per cent threshold of the electoral system. For the first time ever it lost all its seats and disappeared from the Bundestag. To be sure, this result did not come without forewarning. Although the black–yellow coalition had in 2009 presented itself as a 'desired marriage' the reality of governmental cooperation spoke a different language. Discord among the parties quickly surfaced, and a massive loss of sympathy and competence attributions among voters was the immediate consequence. However, while the Christian Democrats succeeded to slowly regain popularity among voters during the electoral cycle the FDP never recovered. When the 2013 campaign started the Liberals already looked back at a succession of defeats at state elections, and had to face a tough uphill struggle, going against extremely bad voter evaluations.[8] Importantly, the FDP did not benefit from voters' positive assessment of the government's performance and the good economic situation.[9] Its partisan base in the electorate had always been slim, but now it had almost completely dissolved.[10] Even repeated changes in the party leadership could not stop the decline. Presumably as a consequence, more voters now preferred a Grand Coalition than a continuation of the black–yellow coalition, in stark contrast to 2009.[11] During the campaign media polls raised serious doubts whether the FDP could make it across the 5 per cent threshold at the federal level, and a week before the Federal Election the Bavarian state election confirmed voters' doubts by catapulting the FDP out of the state legislature. Adding insult to injury, the CDU/CSU refused to support the campaign for tactical votes that the FDP immediately launched in response to this event. The road was thus paved for an unprecedented electoral debacle.

While the FDP experienced the hardest fall in its history, the CDU/CSU could record the greatest gain of votes ever achieved at a Federal Election. It missed the absolute majority of parliamentary seats by only a few votes and thus the possibility of forming the first single-party government in the history of the Federal Republic. Compared to the SPD, the Christian Democrats could benefit from a larger partisan base which was more willing to cast their ballot for their party.[12] In addition, the CDU/CSU benefited enormously from the popularity of their Chancellor candidate Angela Merkel, on which they had resolutely tailored their campaign, while the candidacy of her challenger Peer Steinbrück of the SPD was ill-starred right from his nomination a year before the election.[13] Another success factor was the superior problem-solving competence voters accorded the CDU/CSU with regard to the issues they considered most pressing.[14] Nonetheless, even under these unusually favourable conditions the Christian Democrats did not achieve a vote share comparable to those regularly obtained between the 1950s and 1980s. Their large seat share was to a significant part due to the fact that in 2013 more votes than ever were not counted because they went to parties not surpassing the 5 per cent threshold.[15] No less than one voter out of seven cast their ballot for a party that did not gain any seats in the Bundestag.

Among them was a new party – the *Alternative for Germany* (Alternative für Deutschland, AfD) – which came close to clearing the 5 per cent hurdle with a vote share of 4.7 per cent, nearly outperforming the FDP. The AfD had been founded just half a year before the election. Never before since 1949 had a new party achieved such a good result at a Federal Election when participating for the first time. At its inception the AfD presented itself as a single-issue party with the mission to point at the elephant in the room: it made its marks primarily by criticising the Euro rescue policy enacted by the government with support by the SPD and the Greens.[16] Partially at the expense of the FDP, the AfD succeeded to transform the concerns of some voters on the perspectives of Germany as a member of the European currency union into ballots in its favour. Therefore, to some extent its electoral success was a consequence of the hesitation of the other parties to discuss openly the problems of the Euro crisis during the election campaign. However, the AfD also gained a sizable number of votes from people who wanted to express their resentments against immigrants at the ballot box. It thus benefited from the fact that in Germany there was hitherto no right-wing populist party comparable to the Austrian FPÖ, the French Front National or the Dutch PVV.

The success of the AfD signals that Germans are increasingly willing to experiment with their votes by considering supporting parties outside the mainstream of those with decades-long presence in the federal parliament. Partisan dealignment is one of the long-term developments behind this trend. It also made itself felt during the electoral cycle at state elections and in the polls. Most notably this concerned the Pirate Party which between 2011 and 2012 gained enough votes at several state elections to win parliamentary seats and according to polls also enjoyed considerable support at the federal level.[17] In the end, this was a straw fire, and at the Federal Election the Pirates obtained only some 2 per cent of the votes. Still, although in hindsight this episode was not more than a flash in the pan, it illustrates the considerable mobility of today's voters.

The Greens were probably the party most immediately threatened by the Pirates. During the electoral cycle they had at first been quite highly ranked in the voters' favour, but they had no stamina in the end. In light of the nuclear accident in the Japanese Fukushima, they had rapidly gained popularity and managed to win for the first time the leadership in a state government at the state election in Baden-Württemberg in 2011.[18] But afterwards their popularity took a nosedive and in the end the Greens did not succeed to reach the two-digit result at the Federal Election that they had hoped for.[19] This was also true for the Left that stagnated at less than 10 per cent, but is now, after the formation of the current Grand Coalition, the leading opposition party in the federal parliament. It has a relatively stable base of voters at its disposal and has the appearance of a classical cleavage party with regard to the regional cleavage between new and old states as well as the socio-economic cleavage. On that dimension of partisan conflict, it stands in direct competition to the SPD which tries to compete with the Left on such classical social democratic issues like social, labour and economic policy.[20]

A parameter of utmost significance with regard to voting behaviour, the party system and the perspectives of government in Germany is the Social Democrats' (and Greens') refusal to cooperate with the Left in a red–red–green coalition, even when vote shares would numerically allow for a combined majority. Just like in 2009, the run-up to the Federal Election 2013 has once more made it clear to the SPD that it is difficult to run an election campaign without a plausible coalition scenario, especially in an age when news media increasingly rely on horse race journalism.[21] The Left showed some willingness to cooperate with the Social Democrats on the federal level, but many of its political statements particularly on foreign affairs clearly foiled this possibility. Moreover, voters held strong reservations about this option.[22] In the end, voters' increasing mobility in conjunction with the constraints on the parties' room to manoeuvre led for the second time within a few years to a situation where a Grand Coalition was considered the best solution. Facing a disappointing election result with only very little improvement compared to the disastrous result of the 2009 election, the Social Democrats reluctantly agreed to enter their third governmental cooperation with the Christian Democrats (after 2005 and 1966).[23] Since 2009, vote shares for the SPD dropped even below those it received in the pre-Godesberg elections in the 1950s. The historically low results in recent elections call into question the Social Democrats' ability to function as a leading challenger of the Christian Democrats. This, in turn, seriously undermines the traditional German model of party competition, which centred on the two major 'Volksparteien' as equally viable aspirants for alternating leadership in the federal government.

All told, and paradoxically, the fragmentation of the party system at the 2013 Federal Election thus led to a concentration of political power at the federal level. Grand Coalitions are special in several respects.[24] First of all, they almost by necessity appear to be a sub-optimal solution typically only resorted to in cases where no alternative seems feasible. Their formation can be interpreted as voter deception because denying the possibility of a Grand Coalition is a standard element of the large parties' campaign inventories, in order not to undermine their followers' mobilisation. Therefore, the legitimacy of a Grand Coalition is always doubtful. Such alliances of major parties normally competing with each other are typically considered temporary. Their continuation is not wanted by any of the partners. Moreover, Grand Coalitions weaken the logic inherent to the rivalry between government and opposition in parliamentary democracies, since the opposition is often too weak to be considered an alternative government in waiting. They thus undermine a central mechanism of democratic accountability. In fact, the Bundestag opposition that was instituted in 2013 is even smaller than at the time of the previous Grand Coalition between 2005 and 2009. The Left is the strongest opposition party by a small margin, and together with the Greens it controls only one-fifth of all seats in the Bundestag. Responding to these circumstances, the government parties were willing to strengthen some parliamentary minority rights, but the opposition is denied its potentially most powerful control instrument, abstract judicial review by the Federal Constitutional Court, because even together the two parties have too few mandates to reach the necessary quorum (whose reform would require a change of the constitution).[25] Moreover, even within the Grand Coalition there is some imbalance. The centre of gravity has clearly shifted to the Chancellor's party since the Christian Democrats have achieved a much better result than the SPD. While the Social Democrats had still been almost on a par with their partner in the 2005 Grand Coalition, they are now clearly junior as measured by the number of seats in the Bundestag. Within the electorate, the asymmetry of the party system, that is, the relative vote shares of the CDU/CSU and the SPD, has in 2013 returned to the level of the 1950s.[26]

From the perspective of government *effectiveness*, however, the Grand Coalition almost appears like a necessary outcome of the 2013 Federal Election, and in that respect points towards a further diffusion, rather than a concentration of power. Due to its institutional structure, in particular the balance of power in its multi-level system of governance, the Federal Republic has been characterised as an informal 'Grand Coalition State'.[27] The only alternative to a Grand Coalition that during the election campaign had appeared realistic, the continuation of the cooperation of CDU/CSU and FDP, would – in the counterfactual case of obtaining a joint majority of seats – have had to face considerable limitations of their political scope of action because of the constellation of seats in the Federal Council (Bundesrat). Indeed, a black–yellow coalition could have relied only on a handful of the 69 votes in the assembly of states. Strikingly, due to the colourful coalition landscape that has emerged in the states during recent years, even a Grand Coalition is not in a position to govern with blinkers on. For those policies that require the support of the Federal Council it needs to strike bargains with governments that also include a party from the Bundestag opposition, most notably the Greens. As it seems, Germany's mobile voters are about to turn the country from a 'Grand Coalition State' into an 'Oversized Grand Coalition State'.

THEORETICAL ISSUES

Against this backdrop, the contributions to this special issue analyse the 2013 Federal Election but the relevance of topics reaches beyond Germany. To illustrate this, Table 2 shows the general topics addressed in this volume, the articles examining a topic and the general research question underlying each article. This discussion thus structures the volume but also highlights the broader theoretical implications of the articles.

The first topic analyses a long-standing theme in the literature on partisan dealignment and realignment – the relevance of *social cleavages* in advanced democracies which have structured advanced industrial societies – including Germany – for much of the twentieth century, as well as *partisan change* relating to them. Given

TABLE 1
RESULTS OF 2013 GERMAN FEDERAL ELECTION (PER CENT)

	First votes				Second votes				Bundestag seats	
	Total	West	East	Change from 2009	Total	West	East	Change from 2009	Seats won	Change from 2009
CDU/CSU	45.3	46.4	40.5	+5.9	41.5	42.2	38.5	+7.8	311	+72
SPD	29.4	31.5	19.6	+1.5	25.7	27.4	17.9	+2.7	193	+47
The Left	8.2	4.7	24.4	−2.9	8.6	5.6	22.7	−3.3	64	−12
Bündnis 90/Greens	7.3	7.8	4.7	−1.9	8.4	9.2	5.1	−2.3	63	−5
FDP	2.4	2.5	1.8	−7.1	4.8	5.2	2.7	−9.8	0	−93
AfD	1.9	2.1	0.9	+1.9	4.7	4.5	5.9	+4.7	0	
Pirate Party	2.2	2.1	2.6	+2.1	2.2	2.1	2.4	+0.2	0	
Other parties	3.3	2.9	5.5	+0.4	4.0	3.8	2.8	0.0	0	

Source: Bundeswahlleiter.

the historical relevance of social cleavages and partisanship in Germany, but also recent controversies over the precise nature of their current importance, this symposium includes two articles centring on this topic. One article, by Elff and Roßteutscher, examines the degree to which the two large political parties – the SPD and CDU/CSU – were able to mobilise their potential supporters during the 2013 election. It turns out that the decline in electoral support for the Social Democrats is not just due to vote defections to other parties but to its inability to get its potential

TABLE 2
GERMAN POLITICS TOPICS AND THEORETICAL ISSUES ADDRESSED IN THE SPECIAL ISSUE

Topic	German politics	General theory
Social divisions	Cleavage base of mainstream parties (Elff/ Roßteutscher)	Cleavage-voting vs mobilisation of core voters
	Decline of party base (Arzheimer)	Partisan dealignment in advanced democracies
Campaign effect	Campaign effects on determinants of vote choice (Christian)	Does correct voting increase throughout a campaign?
	Why did the FDP fail to clear the 5 per cent threshold? (Huber)	Expressive vs instrumental coalition preferences
	Determinants of Support for AfD (Schmitt-Beck)	The representation of Euro-scepticism and xenophobia
Voter–elite linkages	Did Angela Merkel disproportionately attract female voters? (Debus)	Does a female lead candidate help a conservative party to narrow the gender gap?
	Economic voting (Seki and Whitten)	Dynamic clarity of responsibility
	Do German voters recognise district candidates and why? (Giebler/Weßels)	Interplay between voter perceptions, candidate efforts and context on candidate awareness
Party stances on European integration	Have the SPD and CDU/CSU responded to the rise in EU-scepticism? (Rohrschneider/Whitefield)	Do mainstream or extreme parties offer EU-critical choices to voters?

supporters to turn up at the ballot box in the first place. In contrast, the CDU/CSU has been considerably more successful in mobilising its own supporters, thus securing a strong showing at the end of the election day. In theoretical terms, the study suggests that the behaviour of parties may contribute as much to the vibrancy – or decline – of a cleavage as changes in the characteristics of voters. Consistent with this interpretation, the second study on this topic suggests that the decline of partisanship may have come to a halt by 2013 (Arzheimer). It not only shows that voters identify with a party at roughly the same levels as in previous elections but also indicates that each of the main left-of-centre variety of parties – the SPD, Greens and the Left – are able to count on a loyal clientele. Together, the observed relevance of social divisions and partisanship may indicate that their decline is glacial and their diminishing effect may be felt mainly in the long run (as Dalton and others have argued).

A second topic examines *campaign effects* throughout the 2013 contest. While we know that campaigns matter for the mobilisation of supporters, the decision making of voters and the crystallisation of beliefs, Christian's article addresses a novel aspect: do voters increasingly vote 'correctly' as a result of their exposure to the flow of campaign information? The article builds on the US-based literature that identifies those factors that predispose voters to endorse a specific party which is then 'abandoned' for one reason or another (termed 'incorrect' voting). But it also moves beyond it by showing the dynamic properties of correct voting throughout a campaign: as Election Day comes closer voters increasingly tend to prefer the party that with regard to its platform and leading candidate best articulates their prior views. This clearly suggests that campaigns can live up to their democratic potential by informing voters about the choices on offer and enabling them to select the party that is 'appropriate' for them. A second article also points to effects of the election campaign (Schmitt-Beck). The study examines the success of the Alliance for Germany (AfD), initially a Euro-sceptic party but one that increasingly advocated anti-immigrant policies, to a minor extent already in the 2013 campaign, and more clearly in the more recent 2014 election to the European parliament, as well as several state elections. The results point to the success of the party to appeal to Euro-sceptic voters early on. More importantly, though, the study indicates that the AfD's strong outcome at the polls was already at the Federal Election mainly a result of its appeal to late-deciders that were sensitive to anti-immigrant overtones in its campaign rhetoric and chose the party primarily to express xenophobic sentiments. The study anticipates the break-up of the AfD in 2015 into a newly founded liberal–conservative bourgeois party (labelled ALFA) and the original AfD, now more unambiguously leaning towards right-wing populist stances on migration and nationalism. A third study on campaign effects reveals a seeming paradox (Huber). On one hand, most voters preferred a CDU/CSU-FDP coalition after the election. On the other hand, many voters who preferred this coalition – including FDP identifiers – failed to support the FDP during the 2013 election, in contrast to 2009 when those preferring a black–yellow government supported the liberal party to a greater degree. This study points to the fact that the emphasis of the CDU/CSU on 'keeping' its voters at bay by not defecting to the FDP may well have doomed the FDP to spend the post-2013 legislative period in the extra-parliamentary arena.

A third general topic concerns the analysis of *voter–elite linkages*. One article examines the influence of economic perceptions on voter support for the governing parties

(Seki and Whitten). It shows that the clarity-of-responsibility hypothesis is not only applicable across countries but equally applies to variation in governing responsibility within countries over time. In Germany, this means that a context where one party controls both chambers of government allows voters to attribute responsibility for economic outcomes unambiguously to one party whereas divided control of these chambers obfuscates the attribution of responsibility and thus lowers the extent of economic voting. Another article examines whether the CDU/CSU chancellor Angela Merkel as a female lead candidate mattered to voters (Debus). Comparing the influence of lead candidate gender over time since 1998, however, the study finds little evidence of a gender influence in the last five Federal Elections. A final study examines voters' awareness of the candidates that compete for the district vote (Giebler and Weßels). It develops a model that accounts for voter perceptions of candidates, the efforts of candidates themselves and the properties of districts. The study shows that only a fully specified model taking into account a range of factors from all levels can properly capture the way that parties and voters interact.

A final article examines *party stances* about European integration (Rohrschneider and Whitefield). Given the importance of this issue for the election, the article asks whether the two mainstream parties have muted the historically supportive stance towards European integration. It shows that especially the Union has lowered its support when compared to the 2009 election whereas the SPD was nearly as supportive now as it had been in the previous election. It is important to recognise, however, that both mainstream parties remain staunchly pro-EU (except for the CSU) when comparing the position of both parties to those of their relatives from the same party family in other West European countries. Among the smaller parties, the Greens continue to endorse European integration as an idea although they also critique the current policies of the EU. In contrast, the Left has been and remains a critic of the idea of Europe's integration as well as its implementation.

DISCLOSURE STATEMENT

No potential conflict of interest was reported by the authors.

NOTES

1. See, for example, Russell J. Dalton and Martin Wattenberg (eds), *Parties Without Partisans: Political Change in Advanced Industrial Democracies* (Oxford: Oxford University Press, 2000); Russell J. Dalton and Steven Weldon, 'Partisanship and Party System Institutionalization', *Party Politics* 13/2 (2007), pp.179–96; Geoffrey Evans and Nan Dirk de Graaf (eds), *Political Choice Matters* (Oxford: Oxford University Press, 2013).
2. See Mona Krewel, 'Die Wahlkampagnen der Parteien und ihr Kontext', in Rüdiger Schmitt-Beck, Hans Rattinger, Sigrid Roßteutscher, Bernhard Weßels, Christof Wolf et al., *Zwischen Fragmentierung und Konzentration: Die Bundestagswahl 2013* (Baden-Baden: Nomos, 2014), pp.35–45.
3. See Thomas Schubert, 'Politikfloskeln oder Bündnissignale? Koalitionsaussagen zwischen Wahlkampfstrategie und Bündnispolitik', in Eckhard Jesse and Roland Sturm (eds), *Bilanz der Bundestagswahl 2013* (Baden-Baden: Nomos, 2014), pp.75–93.
4. Günter Bannas, 'Mit den Ideen der anderen', *Frankfurter Allgemeine Zeitung*, 10 June 2013, p.1.
5. See Frank Bandau and Kathrin Dümig, 'Administering the Inherited "Employment Miracle": The Labour Market Policy of the Second Merkel Government', *German Politics* 23/4 (2014), pp.337–52.
6. See Hubert Zimmermann, 'A Grand Coalition for the Euro: The Second Merkel Cabinet, the Euro Crisis and the Election of 2013', *German Politics* 23/4 (2014), pp.322–36.
7. See Jan Erik Blumenstiel, 'Merkels Triumph und der Alptraum der FDP: Das Ergebnis der Bundestagswahl 2013', in Schmitt-Beck et al., *Zwischen Fragmentierung und Konzentration*, pp.101–17.
8. See Ina Bieber and Sigrid Roßteutscher, 'Dominante Union und taumelnde FDP: Zur Ausgangslage der Bundestagswahl 2013', in Schmitt-Beck et al., *Zwischen Fragmentierung und Konzentration*, pp.19–33; Aiko Wagner, 'Leistungen von Regierung und Parteien', in Schmitt-Beck et al., *Zwischen Fragmentierung und Konzentration*, pp.239–52.
9. See Markus Steinbrecher, 'Wirtschaftliche Entwicklung und Eurokrise', in Schmitt-Beck et al., *Zwischen Fragmentierung und Konzentration*, pp.225–38.
10. See Anne Schäfer and Rüdiger Schmitt-Beck, 'Parteibindungen', in Schmitt-Beck et al., *Zwischen Fragmentierung und Konzentration*, pp.203–11.
11. See Sascha Huber, 'Koalitions- und strategisches Wählen', in Schmitt-Beck et al., *Zwischen Fragmentierung und Konzentration*, pp.293–311.
12. See Schäfer and Schmitt-Beck, 'Parteibindungen'.
13. See Bieber and Roßteutscher, 'Dominante Union und taumelnde FDP'; A. Wagner, 'Spitzenkandidaten', in Schmitt-Beck et al., *Zwischen Fragmentierung und Konzentration*, pp.267–79; Harald Schoen and Robert Greszki, 'A Third Term for a Popular Chancellor: An Analysis of Voting Behaviour in the 2013 German Federal Election', *German Politics* 23/4 (2014), pp.251–67; Ulrich Rosar and Hanna Hoffmann, 'Einflüsse der Bewertung der Kanzlerkandidaten Steinbrück und Merkel auf die Wahlchancen der Parteien bei der Bundestagswahl 2013: War er der Falsche, war sie die Richtige?', in Karl-Rudolf Korte (ed.), *Die Bundestagswahl 2013. Analysen der Wahl-, Parteien-, Kommunikations- und Regierungsforschung* (Wiesbaden: Springer VS), pp.119–39.
14. See Thomas Plischke, 'Politische Sachfragen', in Schmitt-Beck et al., *Zwischen Fragmentierung und Konzentration*, pp.253–65.
15. See Oscar Niedermayer, 'Aufsteiger, Absteiger und ewig "Sonstige": Klein- und Kleinstparteien bei der Bundestagswahl 2013', *Zeitschrift für Parlamentsfragen* 45/1 (2014), pp.73–93; Viola Neu, 'Hidden Champions oder eweige Verlierer? Die "sonstigen" Parteien bei der Bundestagswahl', in Jesse and Sturm (eds), *Bilanz der Bundestagswahl 2013*, pp.295–313.
16. See Robert Grimm, 'The Rise of the German Eurosceptic Party Alternative für Deutschland, between Ordoliberal Critique and Popular Anxiety', *International Political Science Review* 36/3 (2015), pp.264–78.
17. See Bieber and Roßteutscher, 'Dominante Union und taumelnde FDP'.
18. See Oscar W. Gabriel and Bernhard Kornelius, 'Die baden-württembergische Landtagswahl vom 27. März 2011: Zäsur und Zeitenwende?', *Zeitschrift für Parlamentsfragen* 42/4 (2011), pp.784–804.
19. See Bieber and Roßteutscher, 'Dominante Union und taumelnde FDP'; Lothar Probst, 'Bündnis 90/Die Grünen – historische Chance verpasst? Personal, Organisation, Programmatik, Koalitionsstrategie, Wahlergebnis', in Jesse and Sturm (eds), *Bilanz der Bundestagswahl 2013*, pp.255–76.
20. See Krewel, 'Die Wahlkampagnen der Parteien und ihr Kontext'.
21. See Frank Esser and Katharina Hemmer, 'Characteristics and Dynamics of Election News Coverage Coverage in Germany', in Jesper Strömback and Lynda Lee Kaid (eds), *The Handbook of Election News Coverage Around the World* (New York: Routledge, 2008), pp.298–307.
22. See Huber, 'Koalitions- und strategisches Wählen'.
23. See Manuela S. Blumenberg and André Förster, 'Die Regierungsbildung', in Schmitt-Beck et al., *Zwischen Fragmentierung und Konzentration*, pp.341–53; Roland Sturm, 'Die Regierungsbildung

nach der Bundestagswahl 2013: lagerübergreifend und langwierig', *Zeitschrift für Parlamentsfragen* 45/1 (2014), pp.207–30.

24. See Christof Egle and Reimut Zohlnhöfer, 'Die Große Koalition – eine "Koalition der neuen Möglichkeiten"?', in Christof Egle and Reimut Zohlnhöfer (eds), *Die zweite Große Koalition. Eine Bilanz der Regierung Merkel 2005–2009* (Wiesbaden: VS, 2010), pp.11–25; Wolfgang C. Müller, 'Warum Große Koalition? Antworten aus koalitionstheoretischer Sicht', *Zeitschrift für Staats- und Europawissenschaften* 6/3 (2008), pp.499–523.

25. See Blumenberg and Förster, 'Die Regierungsbildung'.

26. See Blumenstiel, 'Merkels Triumph und der Alptraum der FDP'.

27. Manfred G. Schmidt, 'Germany: The Grand Coalition State', in Josep M. Colomer (ed.), *Comparative European Politics* (New York: Routledge, 2008), pp.58–93.

Social Cleavages and Electoral Behaviour in Long-Term Perspective: Alignment without Mobilisation?

MARTIN ELFF and SIGRID ROßTEUTSCHER

On the occasion of the Federal Election 2009, Germany experienced a drastic decline in turnout. In 2013, the most recent Federal Election, turnout was thus a political issue hotly debated in the media and the Social Democrats ran an explicit non-voter campaign. Nevertheless, turnout rates remained at a low level, and the election resulted in the second lowest turnout in the entire history of post-war Germany. At the same time the SPD, one of the traditionally cleavage-based parties in Germany, suffered equally dramatic losses in terms of electoral support in 2009 from which it did not recover in the succeeding election. While the sudden decline of the vote share of a cleavage-based party may cast doubt on previous findings of a relative stability of cleavage voting in Germany, the almost parallel decline in turnout points to a blind spot in the cleavage voting literature. This research has focused exclusively on the role of social cleavages in shaping choices between parties, and thus has neglected the possibility that cleavages erode due to a decline in electoral mobilisation of cleavage groups. The present article looks at the long-term and short-term changes in party choice and turnout in the social groups that traditionally formed the constituency of the main cleavage parties, the SPD and the CDU/CSU. In doing so, the article also examines whether and how these changes in party vote and electoral participation are related to cohort and period effects. Empirically, we show that a decline in the support for the SPD among the working class consists of both long-term and short-term components, but it does not lead to vote defection yet mostly to abstention from voting. Further it shows that the CDU/CSU is unaffected by the mobilisation problems that plague Social Democracy in Germany. However, first long-term effects are visible across birth cohorts. Younger core religious groups are increasingly opting for other parties.

INTRODUCTION

Throughout the last decade, Germany has experienced a dramatic decline in electoral turnout. Never has turnout declined between two subsequent Federal Elections as much as between 2005 and 2009, thus in 2009 reaching an unprecedented low point of 70.8 per cent.[1] Four years later, during the 2013 election campaign, turnout was therefore hotly debated. It was the topic of numerous TV talk shows and discussion rounds and *Bild*, Germany's most widely circulated tabloid, published an entire special issue on non-voting distributed for free to 41 million German households a day before Election Day. During the last days of the campaign the SPD issued posters that explicitly targeted non-voters and asked for their vote. Yet, the outcome of all these efforts was marginal: turnout increased by 0.7 percentage points and the 2013 Election showed the second lowest participation rate since 1949, topped only by the preceding 2009 Election. Moreover, turnout is not evenly distributed across the population. Electoral abstention is particularly high among younger individuals from lower educational backgrounds. Moreover, the gap between individuals with low and with high levels of education increased dramatically. On the occasion of the Federal Election 2013, those younger than 36 years old with a high level of education reported a turnout of above 90 per cent while reported turnout of those with a lower level of education was less than 50 per cent, a gap of almost 50 percentage points.[2] Decline in turnout and in political equality are not restricted to Germany. Similar patterns are visible in most established democracies of Europe. In a clear majority of countries the lowest turnout rate ever materialised during the last decade. However, both the decline and the amount of the social disparity in voting are particularly pronounced in Germany.[3] There is, moreover, a clear trend of rising inequality in voting. During the 1980s turnout was similarly high among those with high and low education. The 1990s witnessed a strengthening of the relation between electoral participation and educational level and social class, particularly among young citizens. This process continued into the first decade of this century at an accelerated pace, resulting in dramatic differences in turnout related to education, income or class.[4]

For decades the changing role of the traditional cleavage structure and its impact on electoral behaviour has been debated in Germany and elsewhere. The point of departure of this debate is the notion that the cleavage structure, which originated from the double processes of state-formation and industrialisation in nineteenth-century Germany, led to a long-term stability of the patterns of voting behaviour in Germany.[5] Both cleavage-based parties, the SPD and the CDU/CSU, could rely on large segments of voters – workers in the case of the SPD, Catholics and devout Christians in the case of the CDU/CSU – to ardently support them. However, from the 1970s onwards the apparently 'frozen' cleavage structure began to melt. The emergence and persistent success of the Green Party signalled the opening of a new cleavage which cut across the old left–right divide.[6] Yet, it is contested whether this reflects just a numerical decline of traditional cleavage groups or also a qualitative change in the linkage between cleavage parties and their previous strongholds. One line of reasoning focuses on quantitative decline and sees the causes of the decline of the traditional cleavage structures in the diminishing of traditional core groups. It is argued that, because of the tertiarisation of the economy and the secularisation of society, the numbers of workers, on the one hand, and church affiliated Catholics, on the other, are in decline, leading to a decline in cleavage voting.[7] Another perspective claims that because of qualitative changes, that is, increasing social mobility, or ongoing individualisation processes, a more profound change occurs than a mere numerical shrinking of core cleavage groups. Moreover, enduring economic growth and the expansion of the welfare state have increasingly blurred differences between the working and middle classes, concerning both incomes and lifestyles. Such changes found their manifestation in terms such as the 'affluent worker'[8] or the 'embourgeoisement' of the working class.[9] Hence, the old social milieus erode and thus the linkage between cleavage parties and their former electoral strongholds. Equivalent changes affected the voter reservoir of the Christian Democratic Party. Fewer and fewer Germans were part of one of the two major Christian churches. The Catholic Church, in particular, suffered from a massive decline of active church involvement.[10] In 1980, 45 per cent of the German electorate were members of the Catholic Church; 20 per cent went to church on a regular basis. Roughly three decades later, the proportion of Catholics fell below 30 per cent and less than 10 per cent of the electorate attends church services regularly.[11] While empirical research has confirmed the significance of numerical decline, very little evidence concerning a qualitative change in the linkage between cleavage party and its core voter groups has emanated until very recently.[12]

More recent research on Germany, however, seems to contradict these findings concerning the stability of cleavage voting. Longitudinal analyses of the German general social survey series (ALLBUS) from 1980 to 2010 show that non-voting increased especially among workers, the SPD's core clientele.[13] Others, by contrast, find evidence for a clear period effect. While the percentage of workers who abstained from elections was stable (and low), it shows a sudden and stark increase in the 2009 Election.[14] While the results based on ALLBUS analyses suggest a gradual but ongoing process of milieu dissolution, evidence based on German election studies rather points to a failed mobilisation of workers specifically during the last two election campaigns. It is this double puzzle that this article wants to address: first, is the impression of stability still correct if we take non-voting into focus? Second, is cleavage decline an ongoing social process transmitted via cohort exchange or, rather, a result of failing mobilisation strategies?

Hence, the article is organised as follows: after discussing the conceptual background (subsequent section), we focus on the latest Federal Election in 2013 and show how the cleavage structure currently relates to party choice and electoral abstention. In a second step of the analysis we turn to a longitudinal perspective by employing election studies since 1994 in order to compare how findings concerning the present relate to previous elections. Finally, we focus on the core cleavage groups – workers and regular churchgoers – and turn to multivariate analyses. In this last step of the analysis we examine whether changes in cleavage voting and electoral abstention are mainly caused by long-term processes, that is, are transmitted via cohort exchange, or rather due to short-term campaign effects, that is, related to period effects.

MOBILISING CLEAVAGE STRUCTURES

The traditional literature on cleavage voting has a blind spot. It exclusively focuses on individuals' choices between parties and ignores the possibility that one of these choices might be electoral abstention. However, Germany and most other European countries experience shrinking turnout rates. Hence, those who exclude non-voters from the analyses may miss an essential part of the picture. If the loyalty of voter segments to certain parties decreases or if parties no longer direct programmatic appeals to their (former) core constituency, vote defection, that is, the vote for another party, is only one option. It is also possible that disaffected members of this core constituency react by abstention. In other words, both eroding party loyalties caused by changes in the social structure of society and absent mobilisation by political parties might result in decreasing turnout. It is the aim of this article to contribute to the debate on the stability of cleavage voting by taking non-voting systematically into account.[15]

Why should party mobilisation matter? The classic literature on cleavage structures claims that there were certain historical moments when alignments between particular parties and particular voter groups emerged. But such linkages only survive across time and generations if the basic conflict that once founded the voter–party alignment is regularly political reinvigorated.[16] However, because the mobilisation of loyal voters (i.e. Catholics, church attendants or workers) no longer suffices to guarantee electoral victory, the nature of campaigning has changed significantly. If campaigns had the purpose of mobilising 'faithful supporters by activating their partisan predispositions'[17] in the past, this was clearly no longer enough to win elections. Contemporary forms of electioneering had to persuade new voters beyond the pool of the older core clienteles. The less relevant the 'old' core became for securing electoral success, the more important were strategies to attract 'new' voters. Scholars coined different phrases for this new form of campaigning: some speak of 'targeting', others of 'chasing' strategies.[18] As Lane and Ersson formulated: '[p]arties want two things that contradict each other: On the one hand they want stable support from loyal voters, but on the other they also wish to attract new voters'.[19] No doubt, if the CDU/CSU would only mobilise church-attending Catholics or the SPD the (unionised) working class, both would be 10-per cent-parties. But if parties emphasise persuasion and recruitment over activation, chasing over mobilisation, they might, unwillingly, alienate their last reliable strongholds.[20] With a focus on left parties, Przeworski and Sprague formulated the 'dilemma of electoral socialism', that is, the recruitment of new voter segments might be sanctioned by losses among the former core electorate.[21] Parties thus face a dilemma: if they target (remaining) core voters too openly they might fail in attracting new voter segments – segments which are increasingly necessary and decisive for winning elections. However, the politicisation of the linkage between party and core clientele is essential.[22]

Historically, parties mobilised the link through either the activation of classical linkage organisations or issue campaigns. An organisational-based politicisation of conflicts is an important pre-condition of cleavage voting.[23] Traditionally, this politicisation unfolded through an intimate collaboration with the cleavage parties' linkage organisations, that is, the (Catholic) Church and the trade unions. However, these alliances are fragile. Since the Second Vatican Council the Catholic Church defines itself as a civil society actor who no longer wants to issue vote suggestion to the church members.[24] As a result of Chancellor Schröder's labour market reforms, the trade unions, on the other hand, adopted a rather ambivalent, partly even critical stance towards the SPD.[25] Moreover, with regard to the activation of the alignments between voter segments and parties, political issues played a prominent role.[26] Typically for the Christian Party–voter alignment were themes around marriage and family, abortion, gene technology or homosexuality but also issues of law and order and other traditional conservative values. For the socio-economic cleavage mobilising issues are about social security, taxation of the wealthy, shorter working hours or higher wages. Issue mobilisation of core voters historically played a core role in previous campaigns of both the SPD and the CDU/CSU. Both parties framed their political programme to mobilise their most loyal voter segments.[27] For the reasons spelled out above, contemporary campaigns are devoid of such outspoken issue mobilisation. How will this impact the link between party and (former) core clientele?

Until very recently, analyses concerning the link between cleavage structures and party vote provided clear evidence for the stability of cleavage voting, in Germany and elsewhere. In a nutshell, there is a numerical decline of core cleavage groups. However, those who remained within the cleavage structure are continuously loyal to their party.[28] Most recent evidence however points to the fact that the story of stability is no longer valid. Elff and Roßteutscher find that the Federal Election of 2009 is a watershed with regard to the socio-economic cleavage: there are massive losses of the SPD coupled with an immense increase of non-voting among the working class and lower service professions, that is, the former core clientele of the Social Democrats. This pattern re-emerged unchanged on the occasion of the Federal Election 2013. Moreover, looking at the 2013 Election, there is hardly any relevance of class membership for SPD support. However, class is a highly significant predictor of turnout.[29] By contrast, the religious cleavage is indeed characterised by stability. Religious denomination and church attendance are still powerful predictors of a Christian Democrat vote. The authors interpret the observed increase in non-voting among the core voter segment of the SPD as a result of the absence of explicit mobilisation efforts along traditional working class themes. In fact, since Schröder's agenda of labour market reforms, the so-called Hartz IV reforms, the SPD explicitly targeted the 'new' middle classes. Yet, there is a further puzzle to solve: due to the numerical decline of core Christian Democrat voter segments, we assume that there is also little activation on the basis of core themes in contemporary campaigns of the CDU/CSU. In other words, there might not only be a 'dilemma of electoral socialism' but also a dilemma of electoral Christian Democracy. If this assumption is correct, why do we observe stability in one case and decline and electoral abstention in the other?

One possible explanation could be that even devout Christians and Catholics do care less about their traditional themes. Indeed, Wolf and Roßteutscher found that during the last three decades, the religious and the secular had become more similar with regard to traditional policy issues such as attitudes towards gender roles, abortion, immigration, but also political orientations such as self-positioning on the left–right scale, preferences for hierarchy and order or attitudes towards re-distribution. Thus, religiosity is a much less powerful predictor of traditional conservative opinions than in the past. There are two exceptions to the rule: attitudes towards homosexuality which present a last vivid dividing line between religious and secular groups and – surprisingly – electoral participation.[30] However, the discrepancy between religious and secular groups concerning turnout increased because non-voting is increasingly frequent among the non-religious while there is little change among the religious.[31] If it were the case that individuals from the working class did not change their issue positions, it might explain why one party, the SPD, is sanctioned for lacking issue mobilisation, while the other party camp, the CDU/CSU, is not. In other words, there might be an increasing gap between the issue positions of the SPD and her former core clientele, while CDU/CSU and their voter clientele have both become more secular.

Hence, targeting secular voter groups does little harm to the link with core religious voter groups who are themselves secularising.

In this contribution, however, we want to follow another line of research. Recent publications showed that there is a clear temporal dynamic in party vote and turnout with regard to the socio-economic cleavage. However, it is unclear whether the impact of time is linear, or rather a period effect. Non-voter research, based on general social surveys such as the ALLBUS, tends to find evidence for an ongoing, and gradual impact of time, that is differences in turnout between high and low social status/high and low educational background continuously increase over time.[32] In contrast, recent research on the basis of election studies depicts the Federal Election 2009 as a turning point. Until then, there was stability in electoral participation among the core clientele of the Social Democrat Party. In 2009, however, the SPD suffered massive losses in the support by the working classes, mirrored by a similarly stark increase in non-voting by workers and members of the low service classes.[33] Temporal variation is thus uncontested, but it is unclear whether its effect is gradual or impacts through particular moments, that is, is in fact a period effect. Whether the religious cleavage is unconcerned by such temporal processes, is by now fully unclear. It is thus a major aim of this article to disentangle cohort and period effects.

SOCIAL CLEAVAGES AND VOTING IN THE FEDERAL ELECTION OF 2013

Before we present the result of our analysis of stability or change in the role of social cleavages for vote choice and turnout, we first look whether and how social cleavages still shape electoral behaviour at present. For this purpose we rely on data from the GLES 2013 pre- and post-election studies which consist of face-to-face interviews of a probability sample of the German population.[34] The dependent variable in this section is the party vote intention (in the pre-election study) or reported party vote (in the post-election study), where we, in contrast to most previous research, include the intention to abstain or the report not to have voted, along with the parties chosen, as a valid response category. The relevant independent variables in this section are social class, religious denomination and church attendance. While respondents' religious denomination and church attendance can be directly obtained from their statements in the corresponding questionnaire items, social class has to be reconstructed from other variables. In line with a standard approach to social stratification, social class is reconstructed from respondents' reported own occupations or, if they are not economically active, the occupations of their spouses or partners. The GLES studies use a full ISCO-88 encoding for occupations and also contain information about the number of employees supervised if respondents or their partners are self-employed or have an occupation that involves the supervision of others. This allows us to use Ganzeboom's schema of recoding occupational information into EGP classes.[35]

Do social cleavages still matter? Figure 1 illustrates the voting behaviour of citizens from different social classes. Documented are the percentages of respondents from the 2013 GLES election study concerning party choice and turnout – along with 95 per cent confidence intervals and broken down for West and East Germany. For two reasons we decided to treat East and West Germany separately. First,

FIGURE 1
CLASS AND ELECTORAL BEHAVIOUR ON OCCASION OF THE BUNDESTAG ELECTION OF
2013

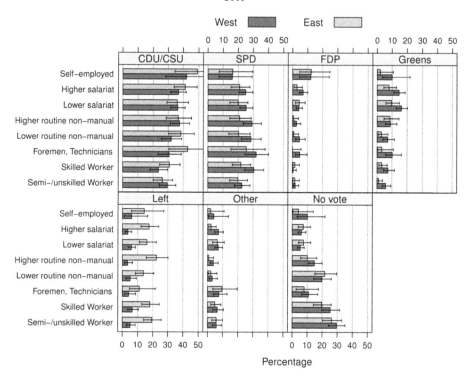

because the historical trajectories of cleavage voting are clearly different: after World War II in the West, the cleavage structure was essentially re-established. In the East, by contrast, the SPD was forced to merge with the Communist Party and became quickly marginalised within the emerging one-party system. Hence, in the East voting along cleavage lines was impossible for another four decades. After the collapse of state socialism and the subsequent re-unification of both parts, it became clear that – during the first elections at least – cleavages played no role for explaining party choice. However, more recently evidence indicated that there is re-alignment, particularly concerning the religious–secular cleavage.[36] Yet, considering the long-term interruption it is plausible to expect that cleavage voting in the East is even less stable than in the West. Second, and related to this, there are – because of the electoral strength of the Left Party (LINKE) in the East, the successor party of the State Socialist Party, the SED – two different party systems as the Left Party, a competitor to the Social Democrats, is still relatively insignificant in the West of Germany. Therefore, Figure 1 reports findings for both German regions separately.

From this figure one can derive some striking conclusions. First of all, looking at the SPD and the CDU/CSU, patterns hardly conform to traditional notions of class voting. In West Germany, skilled workers, foremen and technicians seem to be still a relative stronghold of Social Democracy, but the SPD is far from reaching a majority in these groups (roughly 30 per cent SPD vote). Hence, this support is only marginally, that is, less than 10 per cent, higher than in the two salariat classes. Moreover, the SPD's support among the semi- and unskilled workers is not higher than in the salariat classes and even lower than the support for its major 'bourgeois' rival, the CDU/CSU – a really alarming result for a workers' party. Moreover, in East Germany the CDU/CSU is stronger than the SPD in core working class groups, that is, among foremen, technicians, skilled and semi- or unskilled workers. Strikingly, the socialist LINKE, which also considers itself as a working class party, is not particularly strong among the traditional industrial working class. Rather, it is at least as much a party of the salariat and the higher ranks of routine non-manual occupations as it is a party of skilled or unskilled labour (in East Germany, there are almost no class differences concerning Left Party vote). That being said, there are still some patterns that conform to traditional class politics: the parties of the 'bourgeois' camp, the CDU/CSU and the FDP, find the highest level of support among the self-employed and in the higher salariat class. Not surprisingly, the support for the Greens does not conform to any pattern of traditional class politics.

While the choice between parties reflects only weak traces of traditional class politics, electoral abstention shows a quite marked class-related pattern: the tendency towards abstention is strongest among semi-, unskilled and skilled workers and the lower ranks of routine non-manual occupations, while all other (higher) occupational classes vote at a much higher rate. In fact, among West German skilled and semi- or unskilled labour percentages of non-voting rival the percentages of votes for the CDU/CSU and surpass even the support for the SPD.

Figures 2 and 3 illustrate the impact of denominational and religious–secular differences on voting and both lead to the conclusion that the corresponding cleavages appear still intact. From Figure 2 one can conclude that support for the CDU/CSU is strongest among Roman Catholics, somewhat less strong among the small group of members of Protestant free churches and considerably less strong among mainline (mostly Lutheran) Protestants.[37] It is weakest among respondents without religion or with a non-Christian religion. Figure 3 shows that support for the Christian parties increases monotonously with the frequency of church attendance. The pattern of support for the other parties by and large mirrors the pattern of support for the Christian parties. It is lower among Roman Catholics and higher among the non-religious. This mirroring pattern extends also to the propensity of non-voting, which is higher among the non-religious than among Protestants and Catholics and monotonously decreasing with church attendance.

To sum up our findings regarding cleavage-related patterns of voting in 2013: denominational and religious–secular differences exert a continuing impact on voting, quite in line with the earlier findings of Elff and Roßteutscher, while class differences have almost vanished. Instead, there are striking class differences in terms of non-voting. Apparently, the role of class for voting has (further) declined relative to Elff and Roßteutscher's earlier findings, or at least it has undergone a notable transformation. This poses the question about the nature of this change: is it a consequence of an ongoing, secular trend, or is it an expression of short-term, potentially reversible fluctuations? This question is systematically addressed in the following section.

FIGURE 2
RELIGIOUS ADHERENCE AND ELECTORAL BEHAVIOUR ON OCCASION OF THE
BUNDESTAG ELECTION OF 2013

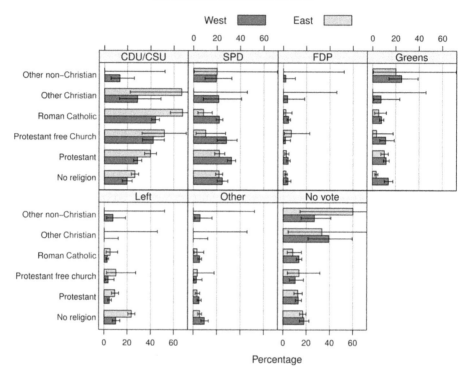

CHANGE IN THE ELECTORAL BEHAVIOUR OF CORE CLEAVAGE GROUPS

In the current section we look at the nature of the changes that led to the situation of 2013. For this purpose we make use of the academic Bundestag election studies from 1994 to 2013,[38] and proceed in two steps. The first step is more descriptive, where we look at the distribution of vote choices at the Bundestag elections from 1994 to 2013 broken down by social class, religious denomination and church attendance. In the second step we focus on the traditional social bases of the two camps of cleavage-based parties and use multinomial logit modelling to disentangle the various factors of change of party choice and voting abstention *within* these core groups.

The Development of the Relation between Social Cleavages, Voting and Electoral Abstention

Figure 4 illustrates the development of electoral behaviour in German Federal Elections since 1994, broken down by social class. Social class is based here on the so-called main occupational category variable present in all election study data sets from 1994, in contrast to ISCO88 occupational codes that are available only in the GLES modules of 2009 and 2013. For ease of exposition and analysis, we use a simpler class schema than above, with only five categories that represent combinations

FIGURE 3
CHURCH ATTENDANCE AND ELECTORAL BEHAVIOUR ON OCCASION OF THE BUNDESTAG
ELECTION OF 2013

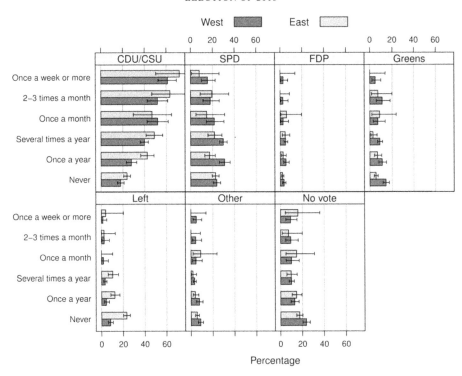

FIGURE 4
CLASS AND ELECTORAL BEHAVIOUR IN GERMAN FEDERAL ELECTIONS 1994–2013

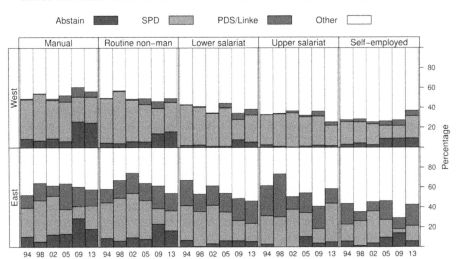

of the Goldthorpe occupational class categories: manual workers; routine non-manual workers; the lower salariat; the upper salariat; and the self-employed. What the figure makes strikingly clear, is that the large amount of abstention among the manual working and routine non-manual classes that we observed in the previous section is a relatively recent phenomenon that emerged in 2009, the election that marked the dramatic losses of SPD votes and an equally dramatic decline in turnout. In East Germany, the surge in abstention appears to have receded to some degree, however.

The sudden increase of abstention in 2009 does not seem totally unique to the manual and routine non-manual classes, because the West German lower salariat also shows such a jump, yet a much smaller one. The other two classes also show an increase in abstention, yet these increases are very modest, from extremely low levels of abstention to low levels of abstention in West Germany. These increases are a bit more marked in East Germany, yet one should be careful not to over-interpret these East–West differences, since the East German subsamples are smaller than the West German ones, so that the observed changes might also be sampling fluctuations. In addition, these increases do not constitute a sudden rise in 2009, but a more gradual development.

The increase in abstention is accompanied throughout by equally large if not higher losses by the SPD. In the manual working class, and to a lesser degree in the routine non-manual classes, the SPD losses are so similar in magnitude to the increases in abstention that the sum of the percentages of SPD votes and of abstention hardly changes at all. This strongly suggests that the loss in votes the SPD suffered in 2009 was a consequence of a withdrawal of former SPD voters from the elections. However, we cannot prove this interpretation, because that would require appropriate panel data.[39]

Over the long haul, but also in the short-term perspective between 2005 and 2009 in West Germany, there are no indications of a realignment of the manual and routine non-manual working classes to the camp of the 'bourgeois' classes. Rather, the summed percentages of the non-socialist parties (even if we include the Greens here) do *not* increase in the manual working class and in the West German routine non-manual working class between 1994 and 2013. Besides, it is also worth noting that the SPD neither in the short nor in the long run is able to make inroads in social groups beyond the manual and routine non-manual working classes, and thus is not able to compensate for the losses suffered in their former core constituency group. *If* the losses in the working classes were the consequences of a reorientation of the SPD towards the middle classes, as an attempt to deal with what Przeworski and Sprague call the 'dilemma of electoral socialism',[40] then it failed utterly.

In a manner similar to Figure 4, Figure 5 illustrates the development of electoral behaviour in Germany from 1994 to 2013 broken down by religious denomination. The figure makes clear that the increase in abstention occurs mainly among voters without religious denomination, while there is little difference between Protestants and Catholics in this regard. The relative advantage that the CDU/CSU enjoys among Catholics in comparison to Protestants and the unaffiliated remains unaffected. Figure 6, which depicts the development of electoral behaviour broken down by church attendance, shows also how stable the relation between church attendance and support for the CDU/CSU is, while the increase in abstention has a *negative* relation with

FIGURE 5
RELIGIOUS DENOMINATION AND ELECTORAL BEHAVIOUR IN GERMAN FEDERAL
ELECTIONS 1994–2013

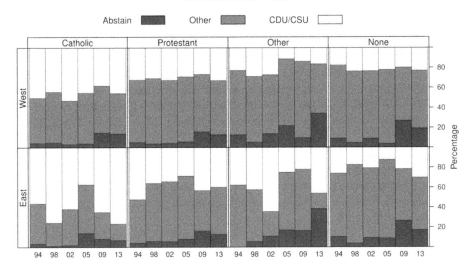

FIGURE 6
CHURCH ATTENDANCE AND ELECTORAL BEHAVIOUR IN GERMAN FEDERAL ELECTIONS
1994–2013

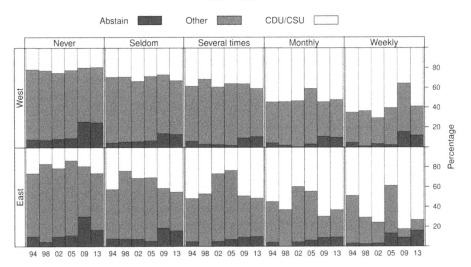

church attendance: the increase in abstention in 2009 is lower the higher the frequency of church attendance.

All the figures discussed so far show that, when abstention increases it does not cut into the support for the Christian Democrats, but mainly into the support for the SPD. Thus, whatever brought about the drop in turnout in 2009, it left the CDU/CSU unscathed.

Factors for the Development of Abstention and Defecting Votes in Core Cleavage Groups

In the previous subsection we uncovered a sharp increase in electoral abstention among the manual working class that accompanies an equally sharp drop in SPD support. This sudden change may suggest that there are mostly short-term factors at work. Nevertheless, there may also be long-term changes at work behind the scenes. It is now well known that turnout has a strong habitual component, which means that people who have abstained from the first election they were eligible to will tend to abstain from the following elections.[41] As a consequence, cohorts defined by year of birth may differ in their tendency to participate in elections. Another implication is that changes as sudden as they appeared in 2009 may be particularly pronounced in the birth cohort that entered the electorate at that time. In order to work out the effects of habitualisation it is necessary to examine cohort effects together with other potential factors affecting voting behaviour that may also change with the year of birth. Such factors are in particular church attendance and church membership.

To disentangle the short-term from long-term effects on electoral choice and abstention we fit multinomial logit models for the core groups of the class cleavage and the religious–secular cleavage, that is, for the manual workers on the one hand and for people attending church at least several times a year on the other.[42] For ease of interpretation of results, we collapse some of the party categories of the voting variable. For the analysis of the long- and short-term effects within the manual working class, the voting variable is reduced to the four categories 'Abstain', 'SPD', 'PDS/Linke' and 'Other (non-socialist) parties'. The independent variables in the corresponding multinomial logit model are the election year (which we treat as categorical), the year of birth, a dummy for those who entered the electorate in 2009, church attendance and religious denomination. Since the coefficients of multinomial logit models are difficult to interpret, we refrain from discussing their sample estimates and instead discuss the implications of the estimated models with respect to the proportions of the response categories. For reference, the coefficient estimates are reported in the Appendix of this article (Table A).[43] The estimates were computed separately for West Germany and East Germany, to take into account the different trajectories of cleavage voting and shapes of the party system in the two regions of the country.

Figure 7 shows how the percentages of abstaining from a Federal Election, of voting for the SPD, of voting for the PDS/Linke and of voting for another (non-socialist) party is affected by the year of election, the year of birth, church attendance and religious denomination within the manual working class in West Germany and East Germany, as implied by the model estimates. These quantities are marginal predictions, often referred to as 'predictive margins'.[44] For each pane in the figure they are obtained by (1) varying one predictor of interest (e.g. the year in the top-left pane and religious denomination in the top-right pane of Figure 7a) for *all* respondents while keeping the other covariates at their sample values, (2) computing the model predictions about vote probabilities for each respondent and each of the values of the predictor of interest and (3) averaging the model predictions over all respondents for each specific value of the predictor of interest. This procedure thus differs from King et al.'s

FIGURE 7
FACTORS OF CHANGE IN ELECTORAL BEHAVIOUR WITHIN THE WORKING CLASS –
MULTINOMIAL LOGIT MODEL PREDICTIONS

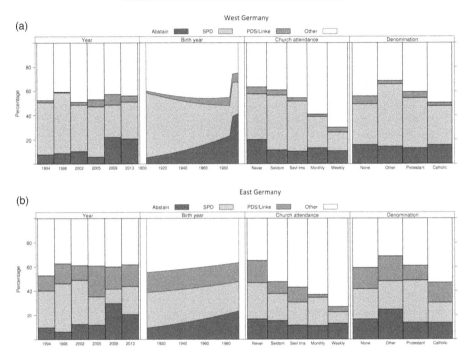

'Clarify' approach[45] by not just fixing the other covariates to their respective sample mean or sample mode.

As Figures 7a and 7b show, the short-term increase in abstention within the manual working class does not disappear, when year of birth, church attendance and religious denomination are taken into account; neither does the drop in support for the Social Democrats. We also find a gradual increase in electoral abstention by year of birth in West Germany, which accelerates with the cohort that entered the electorate in 2009. Consistent with the previous discussion of Figure 6 we find that the support for the SPD decreases with church attendance (likely in favour of the Christian Democrats) and is smallest among Catholics. The fact that the support for the SPD appears so small among those without religious denomination is because we simultaneously also control for birth cohort and church attendance. Hence, the effect of being a member of a later-born cohort and never going to church is already subtracted from the effect of not being a member of a church.[46] It is also worth noting that social cross-pressures, coming from being a member of the working class *and* being a regular churchgoer, do not seem to depress turnout, since turnout does not increase with church attendance here. Instead, abstention is still highest among those who state *never* attending church.

In the same way as Figure 7 illustrates an analysis of the core constituency of the Social Democrats, Figure 8 illustrates an analysis of the core constituency of the Christian Democrats, those who state attending church at least several times a year. For the

FIGURE 8
FACTORS OF CHANGE IN ELECTORAL BEHAVIOUR AMONG CHURCHGOERS
–MULTINOMIAL LOGIT MODEL PREDICTIONS

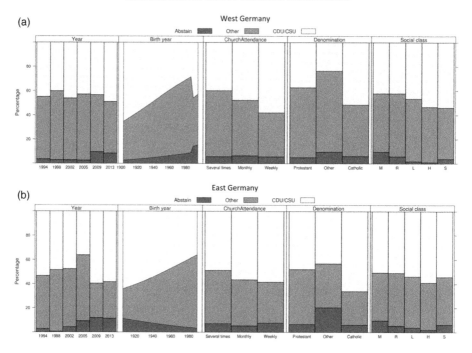

Abbreviations: M = 'Manual workers'; R = 'Routine non-manual workers'; L = 'Lower salariat'; H = 'Higher salariat'; S = 'Self-employed'.

analysis of the electoral behaviour of this group we also simplified the dependent variable, this time into three categories: 'CDU/CSU'; 'Abstain'; and 'Other (non-Christian Democrat) party'. The multinomial logit model for this analysis contains the election year, the year of birth, social class and religious denomination as independent variables. It also contains church attendance as a further control variable, because the core constituency of the Christian Democrats, as defined here, is not homogenous with respect to church attendance. One could of course also have used a more restrictive definition of this core constituency group, more homogenous in terms of church attendance. However such a group might have been too small to allow obtaining stable results, especially in East Germany. Yet, an exclusion from the analyses of those who attend church less often than monthly, did not lead to substantially different results from those that we report in the following. Again, we refrain from discussing coefficient estimates of the multinomial logit model, which can be found in the Appendix (Table B), and focus on the implied distribution of voting behaviour instead.

If one compares the rate of electoral abstention shown in Figure 7 with electoral abstention in Figure 8, it becomes clear that abstention is lower among churchgoers, with class held constant, than abstention in the manual worker class, with church attendance held constant. This finding reinforces the conclusion that church attendance, in a manner of speaking, 'protects' from a tendency to abstain from elections. Nevertheless, we also find a (much more moderate) increase in abstention in 2009. This increase however does *not* affect the support for the Christian Democrats, but rather the category of 'other' parties (most likely the SPD). For East Germany we find, after controls are applied, even an increase in CDU-support from 2005 to 2009. Looking at birth cohorts we see however a decrease in CDU-support (again after holding all other predictors in the model constant), which in West Germany seems to be partially undone by the entrance of a new birth cohort into the electorate in 2009. Curiously, in East Germany abstention seems to decrease with birth cohort as does CDU-support. Other than that, Figure 8 provides few surprises. The effects of church attendance, religious denomination and social class are similar to those found in Figures 2, 3 and 7. It is noteworthy however, that class differences among churchgoers with respect to CDU/CSU-support and abstention are smaller than the effects of church attendance in the manual working class. Thus one could argue that the effect of church attendance 'dominates' the effect of social class. To summarise the findings provided by Figure 8: the social base of the support for the CDU/CSU appears more stable in the short term than the social base of the support for the SPD. However, in the long-term the CDU/CSU might have to face an erosion of its support beyond the consequences of a shrinking of the proportion of churchgoers, since we find a marked cohort effect moving away from the Christian Democrats.

DISCUSSION

In this article we argued that it is essential for valid interpretations concerning the stability or instability of cleavage voting to take non-voting systematically into account. Citizens who are dissatisfied with 'their' party have two natural options: they can defect to a different party, or they can abstain from elections. In times of decreasing turnout rates, we argued, it is no longer acceptable to ignore the latter option. The article took a very recent piece of evidence as its point of departure: the decline of turnout among the core clientele of the SPD, the working class. However, the nature of this trend is unclear. Research on turnout tends to find a continuous increase across age cohorts in vote abstention among resource-poor individuals, that is, individuals from the working class, and individuals poor on income and education. In contrast, non-voting has shown a sudden increase at specific elections, that is, in particular on the occasion of the 2009 Federal Election. It is this double puzzle that this article wanted to tackle: first, is the previous impression of stability no longer true for the socio-economic cleavage but until now confirmed for the religious cleavage, still correct if we take non-voting systematically into focus? Second, is cleavage decline an ongoing social process transmitted via cohort exchange or is it, rather, a result of failing mobilisation strategies.

Looking at the socio-economic cleavage, there are clearly both processes at work. However, party defection and vote abstention are not just two sides of the same coin, but driven by different processes. With regard to non-voting among workers, there are clear period effects: the probability of non-voting is much higher during the last two elections than at the four preceding elections. Moreover, there is also a strong cohort dynamic, that is, each younger cohort of workers shows a higher probability of non-voting than its predecessor cohort. Of those born before World War II, the probability of non-voting was less than 10 percentage points, whereas among the youngest cohorts the probability of non-voting increased above 30 percentage points. Looking at party defection, the story to tell is completely different. Period effects are less significant and tend to indicate that during the two most recent elections there was less defection than on the occasions of the 2002 and 2005 elections. Moreover, looking at birth cohorts there is, if at all, a modest tendency towards declining defection rates. In short, the socio-economic cleavage suffers from abstention and not from vote defection. Both long-term social dynamics and the effects of particular election campaigns contribute to the rising number of non-voters among the former core clientele of the SPD.

In political discourse the present-day weakness of the Social Democrats is often explained by reference to Schröder's labour market reforms and the explicit electoral campaigns targeting the 'new' middle classes. As a result, it is said, the Social Democrats alienated the trade unions, the previous core linkage organisations and lost the loyal support of the working class. Indeed, a glance at the patterns of vote defection (Figure 7) might confirm such an interpretation because vote defection was particularly frequent in 2002 and 2005, that is, in the aftermath of the Harz IV reforms and two subsequent SPD campaigns focusing on society's 'new centre'. However, this political explanation can definitely not account for the steep increase in non-voting at the Federal Election in 2009. What then was the particularity of the 2009 election campaign? The 2009 election campaign was characterised by two aspects: first, after the narrow defeat of the red–green coalition in 2005, the SPD and the CDU/CSU formed a grand coalition. Due to the pollsters it was unclear whether the upcoming election in 2009 would not lead to the continuation of a grand coalition government. Hence, both parties were very hesitant to attack each other. Second, the severe economic crisis forced both parties to work together and formulate policies almost up to Election Day – hence, rather bad pre-conditions for a polarising and mobilising election campaign. As a result, journalists and political scientists were united in describing the 2009 campaign as particularly boring, unengaging and dull.[47] Our evidence indicates that the SPD's core clientele was particularly affected by this de-mobilising sleeping-car campaign.[48]

But how do matters look for the religious cleavage? Looking at non-voting among religious groups there is also evidence in favour of period effects related to the two most recent election campaigns. Hence, non-voting among core religious groups also increased but to a much more modest extent compared to the socio-economic cleavage. Moreover, there is also some evidence that among core religious groups it was particularly those from working class backgrounds which decided not to turn out. This piece of evidence squares well with non-voter research which clearly shows that non-voting is particularly, and increasingly, frequent among lower classes and low educational groups. Although levels of abstention among non-church affiliated workers are much higher, similar trends are thus visible with regard to the religious cleavage. That said, the dominant impression is still one of stability. This is also true if we consider vote defection among religious groups. As was the case with the socio-economic cleavage, vote defection has been rather declining and shown a very low level on occasion of the Federal Election 2013. In contrast, it was highest in 1998 when the first red–green government was elected into office and when apparently also many Christians felt weary of long-term Chancellor Helmut Kohl and opted instead for change. There is, however, clear evidence that middle-aged and younger birth cohorts are more inclined to defect than older birth cohorts. Looking at the socio-economic cleavage we found that non-voting has a very pronounced temporal dynamic while younger cohorts defect less than older cohorts. This is reversed in case of the religious cleavage: no cohort effect concerning non-voting, but clear evidence of increasing levels of party defection for later birth cohorts compared to early birth cohorts. Otherwise, the basic mechanisms of religious voting are still intact. Those who seldom attend church have a much higher defection probability than those who regularly visit church; Catholics are much more loyal than Protestants.

IN CONCLUSION

Integrating non-voting into the analyses clearly changes the picture. The classic strategy of analyses, that is, a treatment of non-voters as missing cases, would have come up with simply misleading results. The socio-economic cleavage dissolves not because workers turn to other parties, in fact, the contrary is the case: they increasingly tend to stay at home. In short, one could speak of *alignment without mobilisation*. Hence, in times of dramatically decreasing turnout, electoral abstention is an option that must be taken into account. To a far more moderate extent something similar is visible with regard to the religious cleavage, where Christian workers are most inclined to abstain. It was beyond the scope of this article to examine the causal mechanisms which render (younger) workers particularly susceptible to electoral abstention. Rather, we wanted to explore whether the religious cleavage is as stable as it looked at first sight and, more importantly, whether the collapse of the socio-economic cleavage is simply driven by cohort exchange and thus by irreversible social processes of milieu dissolution, or whether there is a political dimension inherent in this process. Our cohort–period analyses reveal that both processes are simultaneously in operation: there is a clear and strong increase in non-voting across cohorts, but there are also sudden fluctuations induced by the nature of specific campaigns or chancellor candidates. In recent years and with regard to non-voting, both mechanisms conjointly produced increasing abstention rates among workers. However, based on our analyses it is quite conceivable that the cohort trend can be halted, if not selectively reversed by particular mobilising campaigns.

For the time being, however, the Social Democrats suffer from a lack of cleavage mobilisation while the Christian Democrats, although the first fissures in the texture of religious voting are visible, are backed by a relatively intact cleavage-based alignment. Even more, non-voting is particular frequent among segments of society – the working class, the non-religious, Protestants – who are not among Christian Democracy's core clientele. By contrast, among the CDU/CSU's most loyal voters – Catholics, regular church attendants, the middle classes – turnout has hardly deteriorated. Hence, in contemporary German society Christian Democracy profits twice from low turnout rates. Vote abstention reduces the vote share of the Social Democrats while at the same time electoral participation among Christian voters is almost as high as ever.

DISCLOSURE STATEMENT

No potential conflict of interest was reported by the authors.

NOTES

1. M. Steinbrecher and H. Rattinger, 'Die Wahlbeteiligung', in H. Rattinger, S. Roßteutscher, R. Schmitt-Beck, B. Weßels et al., *Zwischen Langeweile und Extremen: Die Bundestagswahl 2009* (Baden-Baden: Nomos, 2011), p.77.
2. P. Lamers and S. Roßteutscher, 'Die Wahlbeteiligung', in R. Schmitt-Beck et al., *Zwischen Fragmentierung und Konzentration: Die Bundestagswahl 2013* (Baden-Baden: Nomos, 2014), pp.120–1.
3. A. Schäfer and W. Streeck, 'Introduction: Politics in the Age of Austerity', in A. Schäfer and W. Streeck (eds), *Politics in the Age of Austerity* (Cambridge: Polity Press, 2013), pp.1–25; A. Schäfer, S. Abendschön and S. Roßteutscher, 'Are Turnout Differences Small? A Closer Look at Western Europe', Paper Presented at the 8th ECPR General Conference, University of Glasgow, 3–6 Sept. 2014.
4. A. Schäfer and S. Roßteutscher, 'Die soziale Topografie der Nichtwahl', in K.-R. Korte (ed.), *Die Bundestagswahl 2013: Analysen der Wahl-, Parteien-, Kommunikations- und Regierungsforschung* (Wiesbaden: Springer VS, 2015), pp.99–118; A. Schäfer et al., 'Are Turnout Differences Small?'; A. Schäfer, 'Der Nichtwähler als Durchschnittsbürger: Ist die sinkende Wahlbeteiligung eine Gefahr für die Demokratie?', in E. Bytzek and S. Roßteutscher (eds), *Der unbekannte Wähler? Mythen und Fakten über das Wahlverhalten der Deutschen* (Frankfurt am Main: Campus, 2011), pp.133–54; S. Abendschön and S. Roßteutscher, 'Wahlbeteiligung junger Erwachsener – Steigt die soziale und Politische Ungleichheit', in S. Roßteutscher, T. Faas and U. Rosar (eds), *Bürger und Wähler im Wandel der Zeit. 25 Jahre Wahl- und Einstellungsforschung in Deutschland* (Wiesbaden: Springer VS, 2016), pp.67–91.
5. S.M. Lipset and S. Rokkan, 'Cleavage Structures, Party Systems, and Voter Alignments: An Introduction', in S.M. Lipset and S. Rokkan (eds), *Party Systems and Voter Alignments* (New York: The Free Press, 1967), pp.1–64; D.W. Rae and M. Taylor, *The Analysis of Political Cleavages* (New Haven, CT/London: Yale University Press, 1970); S. Bartolini and P. Mair, *Identity, Competition and Electoral Availability: The Stabilisation of European Electorates 1885–1985* (Cambridge: Cambridge University Press, 1990).
6. R. Inglehart, *Culture Shift in Advanced Industrial Society* (Princeton, NJ: Princeton University Press, 1990); R. Dalton, S. Flanagan and P.A. Beck, *Electoral Change in Advanced Industrial Democracies: Realignment or Dealignment?* (Princeton, NJ: Princeton University Press, 1984); S. Roßteutscher and

P. Scherer, 'Ideologie und Wertorientierungen', in Rattinger et al., *Zwischen Langeweile und Extremen*, pp.131–46; S. Roßteutscher and P. Scherer, 'Links und Rechts im politischen Raum: Eine vergleichende Analyse der ideologischen Entwicklung in Ost- und Westdeutschland', in B. Weßels, H. Schoen and O.W. Gabriel (eds), *Wahlen und Wähler. Analysen aus Anlass der Bundestagswahl 2009* (Wiesbaden: Springer VS, 2013), pp.380–406.

7. T.N. Clark and S.M. Lipset, 'Are Social Classes Dying?', *International Sociology* 6/4 (1991), pp.397–410; T.N. Clark, S.M. Lipset and M. Rempel, 'The Declining Political Significance of Class', *International Sociology* 8/3 (1993), pp.293–316; R. Dahrendorf, *The Modern Social Conflict: An Essay on the Politics of Liberty* (London: Weidenfeld & Nicholson, 1988).

8. J.H. Goldthorpe, D. Lockwood, F. Bechhofer and J. Platt, *The Affluent Worker in the Class Structure* (Cambridge: Cambridge University Press, 1968) and J. Myles, 'States, Labour Markets and Life Cycles', in R. Friedland and A.F. Robertson (eds), *Beyond the Marketplace: Rethinking Economy and Society* (New York: De Gruyter, 1990), pp.271–98.

9. S. Bartolini and P. Mair, *Identity, Competition and Electoral Availability: The Stabilisation of European Electorates 1885–1985* (Cambridge: Cambridge University Press, 1990), p.221.

10. See S. Roßteutscher, 'Die konfessionell-religiöse Konfliktlinie zwischen Säkularisierung und Mobilisierung', *Politische Vierteljahresschrift*, Sonderband 45 (2012), pp.114–16.

11. Ibid., p.116.

12. Although the SPD increasingly competes with the Left Party for the votes of workers, see M. Elff and S. Roßteutscher, 'Stability or Realignment? Class, Religion and the Vote in Germany', *German Politics* 20/1 (2011), pp.111–31. See also M. Debus, 'Sozialstrukturelle und einstellungsbasierte Determinanten des Wahlverhaltens und ihr Einfluss bei Bundestagswahlen im Zeitverlauf: Westdeutschland 1976 bis 2009', *Politische Vierteljahresschrift*, Special Issue 45 (2012), p.57.

13. M. Elff, 'Disenchanted Workers, Selective Abstention and the Electoral Defeat of Social Democracy in Germany', APSA 2010 Annual Meeting Paper, available from http://papers.ssrn.com/sol3/papers.cfm?abstract_id=1644676 (accessed 31 May 2015); A. Schäfer, *Der Verlust politischer Gleichheit. Warum die sinkende Wahlbeteiligung der Demokratie schadet* (Frankfurt am Main: Campus, 2015), pp.135–7; W. Müller and M. Klein, 'Die Klassenbasis in der Parteipräferenz des deutschen Wählers. Erosion oder Wandel?', *Politische Vierteljahresschrift*, Special Issue 45 (2012), pp.106–7, report a clear erosion of class voting among the youngest generations.

14. M. Elff and S. Roßteutscher, 'Parteiwahl und Nichtwahl: Zur Rolle sozialer Konfliktlinien', in H. Schoen and B. Wessels (eds), *Wahlen und Wähler. Analysen aus Anlass der Bundestagswahl 2013* (Wiesbaden: Springer VS, 2016), pp.45–69.

15. For a similar argument, see R. Rohrschneider, R. Schmitt-Beck and F. Jung, 'Short-Term Factors versus Long-Term Values: Explaining the 2009 Election Result', *Electoral Studies* 31/1 (2012), pp.20–34.

16. J.E. Lane and S. Ersson, *Politics and Society in Western Europe* (London: Sage, 1994); Rae and Taylor, *Analysis of Political Cleavages*; Z. Enyedi, 'The Role of Agency in Cleavage Formation', *European Journal of Political Research* 44/5 (2005), pp.697–720.

17. R. Schmitt-Beck, 'New Modes of Campaigning', in R.J. Dalton and H.-D. Klingemann (eds), *Oxford Handbook on Political Behavior* (Oxford: Oxford University Press, 2007), p.745.

18. See, for example, ibid., p.747; R. Rohrschneider, 'Mobilizing versus Chasing: How Do Parties Target Voters in Election Campaigns?', *Electoral Studies* 21/3 (2002), p.367.

19. J.E. Lane and S. Ersson, 'Parties and Voters: What Creates the Ties?', *Scandinavian Political Studies* 20/2 (1997), p.179.

20. Lane and Ersson, *Politics and Society*; Rae and Taylor, *Analysis of Political Cleavages*; Enyedi, 'The Role of Agency in Cleavage Formation'.

21. A. Przeworski and J. Sprague, *Paper Stones: A History of Electoral Socialism* (Chicago, IL: University of Chicago Press, 1986).

22. F.U. Pappi, 'Die konfessionell-religiöse Konfliktlinie in der deutschen Wählerschaft. Entstehung, Stabilität und Wandel?', in D. Oberndörfer, H. Rattinger and K. Schmitt (eds), *Wirtschaftlicher Wandel, Religiöser Wandel und Wertwandel* (Berlin: Duncker & Humblot, 1985), pp.263–90.

23. Ibid., p.264.

24. S. Roßteutscher, *Religion, Zivilgesellschaft, Demokratie. Eine international vergleichende Studie zur Natur religiöser Märkte und der demokratischen Rolle religiöser Zivilgesellschaften* (Baden-Baden: Nomos, 2009), pp.177–216.

25. See, for example, H. Wiesenthal, 'Gewerkschaften in Politik und Gesellschaft: Niedergang und Wiederkehr des "Modells Deutschland"', in W. Schröder (ed.), *Handbuch Gewerkschaften in Deutschland* (Wiesbaden: Springer VS, 2014), pp.400–1.

26. F.U. Pappi, 'Die politisierte Sozialstruktur heute', in F. Brettschneider, J.V. Deth and E. Roller (eds), *Das Ende der politisierten Sozialstruktur* (Opladen: Leske & Budrich, 2002), pp.25–64.

27. Ibid.; Roßteutscher, 'Die konfessionell-religiöse Konfliktlinie'.

28. For evidence on Germany, see K. Arzheimer and H. Schoen, 'Mehr als eine Erinnerung an das 19. Jahrhundert? Das sozioökonomische und das religiös-konfessionelle Cleavage und Wahlverhalten 1994–2005', in H. Rattinger, O.W. Gabriel and J.W. Falter (eds), *Der gesamtdeutsche Wähler: Stabilität und Wandel des Wählerverhaltens im wiedervereinigten Deutschland* (Baden-Baden: Nomos, 2007), pp.89–112; M. Debus, 'Soziale Konfliktlinien und Wahlverhalten: Eine Analyse der Determinanten der Wahlabsicht bei Bundestagswahlen von 1969 bis 2009', *Kölner Zeitschrift für Soziologie und Sozialpsychologie* 62/4 (2010), pp.731–49; M. Elff and S. Roßteutscher, 'Die Entwicklung sozialer Konfliktlinien in den Wahlen von 1994 bis 2005', in J.W. Falter, O.W. Gabriel and B. Wessels (eds), *Wahlen und Wähler. Analysen aus Anlass der Bundestagswahl 2005* (Wiesbaden: VS Verlag, 2009), pp.307–27; Elff and Roßteutscher, 'Stability or Realignment?', p.125. From a comparative perspective, see C. Raymond, 'The Continued Salience of Religious Voting in the United States, Germany, and Great Britain', *Electoral Studies* 30/1 (2011), pp.125–35; M. Elff, 'Social Structure and Electoral Behavior in Comparative Perspective: The Decline of Social Cleavages in Western Europe Revisited', *Perspectives on Politics* 5/2 (2007), pp.277–94; M. Elff, 'Social Divisions, Party Positions, and Electoral Behaviour', *Electoral Studies* 28/2 (2009), pp.297–308; G. Evans (ed.), *The End of Class Politics? Class Voting in Comparative Context* (Oxford: Oxford University Press, 1999).
29. Elff and Roßteutscher, 'Parteiwahl und Nichtwahl'.
30. C. Wolf and S. Roßteutscher, 'Religiosität und politische Orientierung – Radikalisierung, Traditionalisierung oder Entkopplung?', *Kölner Zeitschrift für Soziologie und Sozialpsychologie* 65/1 (2013), pp.149–81.
31. Ibid., p.171; Elff and Roßteutscher, 'Parteiwahl und Nichtwahl'.
32. Elff, 'Disenchanted Workers'; Schäfer et al., 'Are Turnout Differences Small?'; Schäfer and Roßteutscher, 'Die soziale Topografie der Nichtwahl'; Abendschön and Roßteutscher, 'Wahlbeteiligung junger Erwachsener'; A. Schäfer, *Der Verlust politischer Gleichheit: Warum die sinkende Wahlbeteiligung der Demokratie schadet* (Frankfurt am Main: Campus, 2015); Müller and Klein, 'Die Klassenbasis in der Parteipräferenz'.
33. Elff and Roßteutscher, 'Parteiwahl und Nichtwahl'.
34. H. Rattinger, S. Roßteutscher, R. Schmitt-Beck, B. Weßels and C. Wolf, *Vor- und Nachwahl-Querschnitt (Kumulation) (GLES2013)* (Köln: GESIS Datenarchiv, 2014, ZA5702 Datenfile Version 1.0.0, doi:10.4232/1.11891).
35. H.B.G. Ganzeboom and D.J. Treiman, 'International Stratification and Mobility File: Conversion Tools' (2001), available from http://www.harryganzeboom.nl/ISMF/index.htm (accessed 31. May 2015).
36. Elff and Roßteutscher, 'Stability or Realignment'.
37. Although there is no theoretical account why the free churches should be related to the German cleavage structure, we decided not to exclude this category from the analysis to avoid losses of cases.
38. J.W. Falter, O.W. Gabriel and H. Rattinger, *Politische Einstellungen, politische Partizipation und Wählerverhalten im vereinigten Deutschland: Repräsentativbefragungen 1994/1998/2002. ZA3065, ZA3066, ZA3861* (Köln: Zentralarchiv für Empirische Sozialforschung, 2004); B. Weßels, *Nachwahlstudie zur Bundestagswahl 2005: Testmodul der 3. Welle der 'Comparative Study of Electoral Systems' (CSES)* (Berlin: Wissenschaftszentrum Berlin (WZB), 2006), available from https://www.wzb.eu/en/research/dynamics-of-political-systems/democracy-and-democratization/downloads/cses-2005 (accessed 31 May 2015) H. Rattinger, S. Roßteutscher, R. Schmitt-Beck and B. Weßels, *Vor- und Nachwahl-Querschnitt (Kumulation) (GLES 2009)* (Köln: GESIS Datenarchiv, 2012, ZA5302 Datenfile Version 6.0.0, doi:10.4232/1.11373); H. Rattinger, S. Roßteutscher, R. Schmitt-Beck, B. Weßels and C. Wolf, *Vor- und Nachwahl-Querschnitt (Kumulation) (GLES 2013)* (Köln: GESIS Datenarchiv, 2014, ZA5702 Datenfile Version 1.0.0, doi:10.4232/1.11891). Where these election studies consist of a pre- and a post-election wave, we pool these waves and look at vote intentions and recalled vote decisions in combination.
39. Our attempts at tracking these changes with available panel data suffered from massive panel attrition between 2005 and 2009.
40. Przeworski and Sprague, *Paper Stones*.
41. See, for example, M.N. Franklin, *Voter Turnout and the Dynamics of Electoral Competition in Established Democracies since 1945* (Cambridge: Cambridge University Press, 2004).
42. As results concerning denomination and church attendance are almost identical, we restrict the following analyses to one of the two aspects of religious voting.
43. To be more precise, the tables in the Appendix show the complete models, whereas the following discussion rests on models where statistically insignificant factors were dropped.
44. B.J. Graubard and E.L. Korn, 'Predictive Margins with Survey Data', *Biometrics* 55/2 (1999), pp.652–9; M.J. Hanmer and K. Ozan Kalkan, 'Behind the Curve: Clarifying the Best Approach to Calculating Predicted Probabilities and Marginal Effects from Limited Dependent Variable Models', *American Journal of Political Science* 57/1 (2013), pp.263–77.
45. G. King, M. Tomz and J. Wittenberg, 'Making the Most of Statistical Analyses: Improving Interpretation and Presentation', *American Journal of Political Science* 44/2 (2000), pp.347–61.

46. It should also be noted that in the election study of 2009, respondents who did not state being a member of a church or religion were not asked about their church attendance under the assumption that they would not go to church. To make the data consistent over the election studies, we recoded all those who stated not being a member of a church or religion as never going to church.
47. For details, see, for example, I. Bieber and S. Roßteutscher, 'Große Koalition und Wirtschaftskrise: Zur Ausgangslage der Bundestagswahl 2009', in Rattinger et al., *Zwischen Langeweile und Extremen*, pp.17–31; M. Krewel, R. Schmitt-Beck and A. Wolsing, 'Geringe Polarisierung, unklare Mehrheiten und starke Personalisierung: Parteien und Wähler im Wahlkampf', in Rattinger et al., *Zwischen Lange-weile und Extremen*, pp.33–57.
48. The fact that in 2005 there was no decrease in turnout among the working class might be explained by the particularly polarising and mobilising election campaign. See, for example, R. Schmitt-Beck, 'Kampagnen-dynamik im Bundestagswahlkampf 2005', in O.W. Gabriel, B. Weßels and Jürgen W. Falter (eds), *Wahlen und Wähler. Analysen aus Anlass der Bundestagswahl 2005* (Wiesbaden: VS Verlag, 2009), pp.146–76. For the effects of electoral competition and mobilisation, see also Franklin, *Voter Turnout*.

APPENDIX

TABLE A
FACTORS OF CHANGE IN ELECTORAL BEHAVIOUR WITHIN THE WORKING CLASS –
MULTINOMIAL LOGIT MODEL ESTIMATES

	West			East		
	SPD	**PDS/ Linke**	**Abstain**	**SPD**	**PDS/ Linke**	**Abstain**
(Intercept)	−0.04	−1.96***	−0.93***	−0.25***	−0.51***	−0.92***
	(0.14)	(0.25)	(0.16)	(0.07)	(0.08)	(0.09)
1998–94	0.33*	−1.10	0.31	0.53***	0.52**	−0.19
	(0.15)	(0.83)	(0.29)	(0.15)	(0.20)	(0.27)
2002–1998	−0.48***	1.32	−0.01	−0.14	−0.35	0.66*
	(0.15)	(0.79)	(0.26)	(0.18)	(0.24)	(0.29)
2005–02	0.13	0.99*	−0.56	−0.45*	0.76**	−0.04
	(0.19)	(0.46)	(0.36)	(0.22)	(0.26)	(0.29)
2009–05	−0.37	0.64	1.58***	−0.70**	−0.33	0.92***
	(0.19)	(0.35)	(0.33)	(0.23)	(0.22)	(0.24)
2013–09	0.11	−0.62*	−0.12	0.72***	0.02	−0.37*
	(0.15)	(0.26)	(0.16)	(0.20)	(0.19)	(0.17)
Birth cohort	−0.12***	0.18**	0.19***	0.00	0.03	0.13**
	(0.03)	(0.07)	(0.04)	(0.03)	(0.04)	(0.04)
Voted first 2009/Voted before	0.74	0.71	1.14*	−1.41	−0.86	0.19
	(0.60)	(0.70)	(0.49)	(1.08)	(0.82)	(0.52)
Church: Seldom/Never	0.15	−0.45	−0.72***	−0.70**	−1.06**	−0.52
	(0.14)	(0.30)	(0.20)	(0.24)	(0.35)	(0.33)
Church: Several times/ Never	−0.10	−1.07**	−0.99***	−0.94***	−0.92**	−0.89**
	(0.14)	(0.33)	(0.19)	(0.24)	(0.31)	(0.32)
Church: Monthly/Never	−0.85***	−1.68**	−0.97***	−0.82**	−2.72***	−1.05*
	(0.18)	(0.63)	(0.25)	(0.31)	(0.76)	(0.44)
Church: Weekly/Never	−1.55***	−1.05	−1.34***	−1.90***	−2.22**	−1.01
	(0.22)	(0.57)	(0.31)	(0.53)	(0.79)	(0.56)
Other/None	0.81**	−0.65	0.18	0.19	0.46	0.74
	(0.31)	(0.67)	(0.36)	(0.66)	(0.87)	(0.75)
Protestant/None	0.31	−0.24	−0.15	0.38	−0.32	−0.17
	(0.18)	(0.29)	(0.21)	(0.20)	(0.25)	(0.26)
Catholic/None	−0.16	−1.05**	−0.16	−0.71*	−0.35	−0.47
	(0.18)	(0.33)	(0.21)	(0.34)	(0.39)	(0.39)
Log-likelihood	−2712.7			−3087.0		
N	2648			2538		

Note: Maximum likelihood estimates with standard errors in parentheses. $^*p < .05$; $^{**}p < .01$; $^{***}p < .001$.

TABLE B
FACTORS OF CHANGE IN ELECTORAL BEHAVIOUR AMONG CHURCHGOERS –
MULTINOMIAL LOGIT MODEL ESTIMATES

	West		East	
	Abstain	**CDU/CSU**	**Abstain**	**CDU/CSU**
(Intercept)	−2.37***	−0.65***	−1.96***	−0.08
	(0.16)	(0.08)	(0.27)	(0.12)
1998–94	−0.31	−0.22	−1.81	−0.27
	(0.33)	(0.12)	(1.08)	(0.22)
2002–1998	0.07	0.26*	2.09	0.05
	(0.33)	(0.11)	(1.11)	(0.26)
2005–02	−0.14	−0.15	0.65	−0.42
	(0.39)	(0.13)	(0.54)	(0.25)
2009–05	1.50***	0.17	0.97*	1.22***
	(0.33)	(0.13)	(0.40)	(0.23)
2013–09	−0.03	0.24*	−0.11	−0.08
	(0.17)	(0.10)	(0.35)	(0.23)
Birth cohort	0.07	−0.19***	−0.30***	−0.20***
	(0.04)	(0.02)	(0.09)	(0.04)
Voted first 2009/Voted before	1.00	1.04*	2.14	1.23
	(0.53)	(0.49)	(1.49)	(1.19)
Routine non-man/Manual	−0.62***	−0.08	−0.71*	−0.09
	(0.15)	(0.08)	(0.31)	(0.16)
Lower salariat/Manual	−1.82***	0.03	−1.02*	−0.01
	(0.30)	(0.10)	(0.45)	(0.19)
Upper salariat/Manual	−2.27**	0.31*	−1.64	0.17
	(0.72)	(0.14)	(1.06)	(0.32)
Self-employed/Manual	−0.87**	0.40**	−0.43	0.08
	(0.33)	(0.13)	(0.47)	(0.25)
Church: Monthly/Several times	0.32	0.37***	−0.11	0.32
	(0.17)	(0.08)	(0.34)	(0.16)
Church: Weekly/Several times	0.43	0.83***	0.41	0.50*
	(0.23)	(0.10)	(0.42)	(0.21)
Other/Protestant	0.56	−0.65**	1.52*	0.16
	(0.32)	(0.23)	(0.64)	(0.41)
Catholic/Protestant	0.52***	0.66***	0.48	0.87***
	(0.15)	(0.07)	(0.35)	(0.18)
Log-likelihood	−3533.5		−930.0	
N	4418		1146	

Note: Maximum likelihood estimates with standard errors in parentheses. $^*p < .05$; $^{**}p < .01$; $^{***}p < .001$.

An 'Angela Merkel Effect'? The Impact of Gender on CDU/CSU Voting Intention between 1998 and 2013

MARC DEBUS

By referring to the theoretical and empirical literature on 'same gender voting' and the 'modern gender gap', this contribution aims to analyse whether gender played a role in party choice in Bundestag elections. We concentrate on the time period between 1998 and 2013, enabling us to cover three elections while Angela Merkel was the chancellor candidate of CDU and CSU (2005, 2009 and 2013), while she was CDU party chair (2002) and while no women served as chancellor candidate or party chair of CDU and CSU. The results of a dataset compiled from five German national election studies show that women were not more likely to opt for the CDU/CSU since the nomination of Angela Merkel as chancellor candidate, nor were they less likely to vote for the Christian Democrats due to their rather conservative programmatic profile on the order of society.

INTRODUCTION AND RESEARCH QUESTION

Socio-structural and demographic characteristics of citizens and their interests are key factors in explaining political participation in general and voter decision making in particular.[1] While in many modern democracies, for instance in the United States, the gender of a voter plays a decisive role in his/her preference for a political party or a candidate, research on voting behaviour in Germany conversely does not emphasise the role of this demographic factor.[2] This is surprising, given that recent analyses based on aggregate election statistics show significant differences in the voting decisions between men and women.[3] Nevertheless, experimental research designs suggest that gender bears no influence on individual voting behaviour in Germany at all.[4] However, international comparative research provides evidence that voting behaviour of women has significantly changed over time: whereas female voters long preferred parties and candidates from the right wing of the ideological spectrum, women tend to vote for parties belonging to the left ideological camp since the 1970s.[5]

This article aims to answer the question of whether the gender of the voters exerts a significant effect on the CDU/CSU vote intention at the German Federal Elections in the recent past. We will concentrate on the period from 1998 to 2013 at which time a woman, Angela Merkel, played an increasingly important role in the respective election campaigns: she was the candidate of the Christian Democrats (CDU/CSU) for the chancellorship in 2005 and ran again as the incumbent chancellor in 2009 and 2013. The 1998 and 2002 Bundestag elections, in which Angela Merkel had not been the chancellor candidate, serve as reference elections, although Angela Merkel already served as CDU party chair since 2000. This reference further assists us in detecting the effect of the voters' gender on CDU/CSU voting behaviour.

With regard to the theoretical and empirical literature on interest-based voting, on the one hand, and the research on effects of descriptive and substantive representation as well as on 'same gender voting', on the other, this contribution argues that women should see a growing benefit in voting for the CDU/CSU since 2005 because Angela Merkel won control over an outstanding position in the Federal Government that allows her to shape the political agenda and policies. However, the analysis of pro-grammatic documents of German political parties reveals that – in contrast to CDU and CSU – particularly Social Democrats (SPD), Greens, Free Democrats (FDP) and the socialist Left adopt socially progressive positions and claim further emancipa-tion efforts, for example towards a better reconciliation of work and family life or the introduction of a quota of women on boards of listed companies. Based on the literature on the 'modern gender gap',[6] we thereby formulate a second, competing hypothesis that female voters exhibit lower chances of voting for parties located to the right of the ideological centre, that is, for the CDU or the CSU, even despite their nomination of a woman as chancellor candidate in 2005, 2009 and 2013.

To test these two competing hypotheses, we present a brief overview on the state of research on 'same gender voting' and the 'modern gender gap' in the following section. The third section provides an overview on the methodological and statistical proceed-ing and the operationalisation of the variables. Section four evaluates the hypotheses on the basis of a dataset compiled of the five German federal election studies from 1998 to 2013. Finally, we summarise the findings and discuss incentives for further research.

THEORETICAL ARGUMENT AND HYPOTHESES

To derive the hypotheses that will structure the empirical analysis, a theoretical argu-ment is needed that can explain why gender should have a decisive impact on individ-ual voting behaviour. The fact that the share of female votes in favour of the CDU/CSU was considerably higher than that of male votes at Federal Election 2013 on the aggre-gate level[7] does not necessarily point to a theoretically founded connection between gender and voting for the Christian Democrats. Based on research emphasising the influence of socio-structural factors on voting behaviour, literature regarding the effects of social group representation in political offices, and studies highlighting utility-maximising interest voting, we will develop two hypotheses in the following sub-sections concerning why and in which direction the voter's gender should influ-ence individual voting behaviour at Bundestag elections in the interval between 1998 until 2013.

Socio-Structural and Demographic Determinants of Voting Behaviour

Theoretical approaches, explaining individual voting behaviour by referring to socio-structural and socio-demographic characteristics of citizens, argue that interests result-ing from social status lead voters both to prefer a certain political party and to vote for the corresponding candidate.[8] These approaches adopt either a micro- or a macrosociological perspective. While Lazarsfeld et al.[9] argue that a long-term stable party identification of a voter can be traced back to his/her socio-structural characteristics, as well as to the homogeneity of his/her daily contacts with persons having the same or similar social background, Lipset and Rokkan[10] focus on the macro-level and identify a set of cleavages dividing social groups, whose interests are represented by the emerging political parties in European countries. The class cleavage differentiating capital owners from (industrial) workers should, for instance, help members of these social groups to define themselves by their socio-economic and professional status. In order to maximise their utility and get their interests implemented in the political process, members of these social groups will tend to vote for the party, which has formed an alliance with the respective social group and thereby represents their interests in all stages of political decision making.

While Lipset and Rokkan[11] distinguished four central cleavages that considerably shape party competition and voting behaviour in Western European countries, gender is largely neglected in this theoretical model and its empirical applications. This is also true for the micro-sociological approach although Lipset[12] mentioned explicitly that gender belongs to the socio-structural factors that have – according to empirical studies – a significant impact on voting behaviour. Historical election research, for instance, provides evidence that women supported Christian conservative parties considerably more often than men in Weimar Germany and in the two decades after World War II.[13] In addition, women in the United States voted more frequently for candidates of the Republican Party until the end of the 1960s; this pattern has changed since the beginning of the 1970s in the USA and in many other modern democracies[14] so that the 'modern gender gap' became noticeable. In the context of the USA since the 1970s, women have opted significantly more often for candidates of the Democratic Party than men; a similar pattern can be observed among Western European countries in which women have supported parties or candidates from the left wing of the ideological spectrum significantly more frequently since the last quarter of the twentieth century.

This change can be theoretically explained by the fact that women were formerly more often restricted to professional positions with lower wages, and thereby subject to discrimination in the workplace. Increasing professional activity among women since the 1970s, as well as a growing feminist awareness should directly increase the chances that women vote for left-wing parties representing the interests of professional groups with low wages.[15] Moreover, the impact of religion and the church on individual behaviour and attitudes has decreased considerably over time, causing the decrease of traditional values and attitudes to impinge on women even where they tended to be more committed to the church than men.[16] Finally, recent research has shown that – because of the growing legitimation of divorces over time – women are aware that a marriage can be a short-term arrangement and that, in case of a divorce, they can benefit from welfare state institutions and a progressive social policy.[17]

Based on these theoretical considerations, we expect an effect of gender on individual voting behaviour: women should have lower chances to vote for Christian conservative parties, whereas the chances should be higher that female voters cast their ballot for parties with socially progressive positions that contradict traditional concepts regarding the role of women in the society. In order to develop a hypothesis for the

German case on which we concentrate in this contribution, we perform a simple descriptive analysis of the parties' manifestos drafted in the run-up to the German Federal Elections between 1998 and 2013.[18] Figure 1 shows that the CDU/CSU integrated traditional conservative ideas regarding societal policy into their platform to a greater extent than parties located to the left of the ideological centre, that is, the SPD, Greens, Socialists (PDS/the Left) or the Free Democrats, all of which traditionally adopt progressive positions on the order of society.[19] Even if the CDU/CSU showed a slight tendency to turn away from explicitly conservative positions,[20] a gap between the societal policy positions of CDU/CSU and the remaining parties can still be clearly observed. On that basis, we derive the following hypothesis:

> H1: Female voters should be less likely to vote for the Christian Democrats at elections for the German Bundestag.

Descriptive and Substantive Representation and Voting Behaviour

The research on descriptive representation has empirically shown that the participation of members in specific social groups and in elections increases when members of these groups, possibly defined according to ethnic-linguistic factors or by gender, are represented in parliaments or governments proportionally according to their share among the total population.[21] Furthermore, the literature on substantive representation suggests that elected representatives are better equipped to represent the interests of specific social groups if they also belong to these particular groups.[22] For example, Phillips[23] shows that female members of governments and/or parliaments are more inclined to represent and enforce interests of women than their male colleagues when formulating policy proposals.[24] Male representatives do not only set other priorities than women on the political agenda,[25] but also act and decide – even under control of numerous theoretical factors influencing legislative behaviour and activity – on the

FIGURE 1
SOCIETAL POLICY POSITIONS OF THE PARTIES REPRESENTED IN THE GERMAN
BUNDESTAG FROM 1990 TO 2013

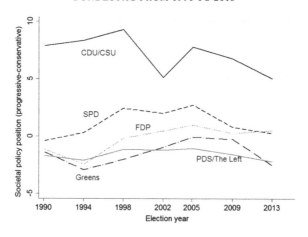

Note: Evaluation on the basis of the dataset of the Comparative Manifesto Project.

basis of other factors when initiating a bill, participating in a parliamentary debate, or voting on a law.[26]

Based on the specific behaviour of female representatives, several studies give empirical evidence that women have an incentive to support and/or to vote for particularly female candidates. Plutzer and Zipp show that – for the case of the elections for the US Senate in 1992 – female candidates that emphasised the gender issue during the election campaign and, therefore, exhibited both a stronger representation of women in the American Congress, as well as a better implementation of female interests in the policy outcomes could benefit from an above-average support by the female electorate.[27] More recent studies focusing on other modern democracies like Finland[28] also provide evidence that, in electoral systems with open lists, the gender of the candidates plays a decisive role: female voters cast their ballot more often for female candidates, thereby increasing the chances of female candidates to win a seat in the Finnish parliament. Although in Germany the partisan composition of the government or the party affiliation of the chancellorship is not determined directly in a Bundestag election, the findings of the literature on 'same gender voting' suggest that the nomination of Angela Merkel as chancellor candidate should represent an incentive for women to vote for the CDU/CSU in the Federal Elections in 2005, 2009 and 2013. Because the German chancellor has a strong agenda-setting power,[29] women should be more likely to see their specific interests implemented in the political process if a woman controls the office of the chancellor in the cabinet. Following these considerations and the findings of the studies on descriptive and substantive representation, we derive the following hypothesis:

> H2: Women are more likely to have voted for the Christian Democrats in the Federal Elections of 2005, 2009 and 2013 because of the nomination of Angela Merkel as their chancellor candidate compared to the elections of 1998 and 2002.

Before empirically testing the hypotheses, the next section presents the data used in this article, the operationalisation of the explanatory and dependent variables and the applied statistical methodology.

DATA AND METHODS

The evaluation of the two hypotheses derived in the previous section is based on the German election studies 1998, 2002, 2005, 2009 and 2013.[30] These studies do not only cover information about the voting intentions of the respondents and their gender, but also other explanatory variables that reflect common theories on voting behaviour in modern democracies and can be integrated into the statistical models. Among these variables, the following ones are particularly relevant: the party identification as the central concept of the 'Michigan School';[31] the evaluation of the candidates as expressed in the preference for a chancellor candidate; the problem-solving competence as attributed to parties by the survey respondents; the ideological distance between the position of the respondents and the perceived positions of the parties on a left–right scale;[32] and socio-structural characteristics like professional status, religious denomination and closeness to a church, which should exert, according to the cleavage theory of Lipset and Rokkan,[33] a positive influence on the vote for parties that have created a long-term and organisationally anchored coalition with the correspondent social groups.

The voting intention in favour of the CDU or the CSU serves as the dependent variable in the empirical analysis.[34] According to the first hypothesis, women should exhibit a lower chance of voting for the CDU/CSU because they cannot expect the Christian Democrats to implement a progressive social policy that would strengthen the role and position of women in economy and society. However, if the second expectation, which is based on the literature on 'same gender voting' and the research on the representation of social groups in parliaments and governments, as well as their effects on participation and voting behaviour, is to be true, then women should be more likely to vote for the CDU or CSU at the Federal Elections 2005, 2009 and 2013 because of the nomination of Angela Merkel as the chancellor candidate of the Christian Democrats.

Party identification is measured by a dummy variable: if a respondent feels close to the CDU or the CSU, the variable is coded code '1', if not '0'. We identify respondents that attend the church at least once per month as a social group that favours voting for the Christian Democrats.[35] The ideological distance between a respondent and the CDU/CSU is measured by the squared difference between the left–right self-placement of the respondent and the position of the Christian Democrats, as perceived by the respective respondent on the ideological left–right dimension. The impact of issue-orientated voting is measured by whether the respondents have indicated that the CDU/CSU is the party able to solve the problem considered the most important. The variable 'chancellor preference' covers information on whether the respondents want the chancellor candidate of the Christian Democrats to become the next head of the German government.

We apply simple logit models to estimate the effect of the independent variables on vote intention for the CDU and the CSU. In doing so, we created a pooled dataset consisting of the five election studies for the Bundestag elections held between 1998 and 2013.[36] Applying a logit model to a pooled dataset allows for testing whether the effect of the gender variable – and also of the other theoretically derived independent variables – varies across time. The regression models include interaction terms between the respective explanatory variables and dummy variables that identify the election years 2002, 2005, 2009 and 2013. The estimated baseline effects of all independent variables provide information on the impact of the respective variables on the CDU/CSU vote intention in 1998, which means that the 1998 Bundestag election serves as the reference category. Since the interpretation of interaction terms and their substantive effects on the basis of the respective regression coefficients and their levels of statistical significance can be misleading,[37] we additionally present the interactions between the gender variable and election year variables also with the support of graphical illustrations.[38]

ANALYSIS

This section presents the results of the regression models and evaluates the two hypotheses. The statistical models are estimated on the basis of a pooled dataset, covering the 1998, 2002, 2005, 2009 and 2013 election studies. In order to take the still-existing different patterns in the voting behaviour between the West and East German states into account, we estimate separate regression models for respondents living in

Western and Eastern Germany, respectively.[39] If the hypothesis about 'same gender voting' is true, women should be less likely to vote for the CDU and the CSU in 1998 and 2002, because the Christian Democrats did not nominate a woman as their chancellor candidate. The effect should change in 2005, 2009 and 2013 when Angela Merkel became the chancellor candidate of the CDU and the CSU. If the first hypothesis, which states that women should rather intend to vote for societally progressive parties because they are supposed to better implement their interests in economic and welfare policy, is confirmed, women should exhibit a significantly lower chance of voting for the Christian Democrats during the whole time period covered in the analysis.

Table 1 presents the results of the logit model for respondents that lived in West German states and Berlin at the point at which the respective election survey was conducted. The effect of the independent variables provides information on their impact on CDU/CSU voting intention at the 1998 Bundestag election. The interaction terms indicate whether the effect for 2002, 2005, 2009 or 2013 is significantly different from the 1998 baseline effect. To begin with the control variables, we find significant effects for the standard explanatory variables: respondents are significantly more likely to have a vote intention in favour of the Christian Democrats if they frequently attend church services; if they prefer the CDU/CSU candidate for chancellorship; if they consider the Christian Democrats to be able to solve the most important problems; if they have a CDU/CSU party identification and the closer their ideological position is located to the perceived position of the Christian Democrats. These effects do – according to the interaction terms – not significantly change in one way or another in 2002, 2005, 2009 and 2013 compared to the 1998 baseline effect.

Is there evidence that gender mattered for the CDU/CSU vote intention in the time period in question, and can we possibly identify changes over time? As Table 1 reveals, there was no statistically significant effect of the gender variable in 1998: female respondents were neither more nor less likely to show a vote intention in favour of the Christian Democrats in that particular Bundestag election. This changed in 2002. The interaction term indicates that female respondents were significantly less likely to vote for the CDU or the CSU in 2002 compared to 1998. The effect of the remaining interaction terms shows also a negative direction, but fails to reach statistical significance. According to Figure 2, which presents the predicted probabilities that male and female respondents from West Germany have a CDU/CSU voting intention, the 2002 election is the only one in the covered time period where gender was significant in explaining the CDU/CSU vote intention: men were more likely to vote for the Christian Democrats than women. There is no empirical evidence suggesting that female respondents were more likely to vote for the Christian Democrats when Angela Merkel ran as the CDU/CSU chancellor candidate. There is, therefore, no support for our second hypothesis on 'same gender voting', at least not in the case of West Germany. There is also no support for the first hypothesis, stating that a 'modern gender gap' should be observable also in Germany: only in 2002 did the gender of a respondent constitute a decisive element for explaining CDU/CSU vote choice. Women were less likely to vote for the Christian Democrats with their chancellor candidate Edmund Stoiber compared to 1998.

Do we find similar results when shifting the perspective to East Germany? Our findings suggest the affirmative. First, there are statistically significant effects of the

TABLE 1

DETERMINANTS OF CDU/CSU VOTING INTENTION BETWEEN 1998 AND 2013
(RESPONDENTS FROM WEST GERMANY)

	Estimated coefficient	Standard error
Main explanatory variable		
Female	0.37	(0.24)
Female (2002)	−0.86*	(0.38)
Female (2005)	−0.30	(0.30)
Female (2009)	−0.33	(0.33)
Female (2013)	−0.03	(0.32)
Control variables		
Frequent church attendance	0.95**	(0.36)
Frequent church attendance (2002)	0.34	(0.55)
Frequent church attendance (2005)	−0.63	(0.47)
Frequent church attendance (2009)	−0.71	(0.58)
Frequent church attendance (2013)	−0.14	(0.44)
Ideological distance	−0.04**	(0.01)
Ideological distance (2002)	−0.01	(0.02)
Ideological distance (2005)	0.01	(0.02)
Ideological distance (2009)	−0.03	(0.02)
Ideological distance (2013)	−0.01	(0.02)
Chancellor preference H. Kohl	1.78**	(0.26)
Chancellor preference E. Stoiber (2002)	−0.17	(0.41)
Chancellor preference A. Merkel (2005)	−0.35	(0.32)
Chancellor preference A. Merkel (2009)	−0.13	(0.37)
Chancellor preference A. Merkel (2013)	−0.11	(0.39)
Problem-solving competence	1.03**	(0.29)
Problem-solving competence (2002)	0.29	(0.43)
Problem-solving competence (2005)	0.00	(0.35)
Problem-solving competence (2009)	0.31	(0.37)
Problem-solving competence (2013)	0.09	(0.37)
CDU/CSU party identification	2.33**	(0.27)
CDU/CSU party identification (2002)	−0.18	(0.40)
CDU/CSU party identification (2005)	−0.24	(0.33)
CDU/CSU party identification (2009)	0.20	(0.36)
CDU/CSU party identification (2013)	−0.36	(0.37)
Dummy variables for election years		
2002	0.05	(0.38)
2005	0.05	(0.31)
2009	−0.77*	(0.38)
2013	−0.71+	(0.38)
Constant	−2.86**	(0.25)
N	5470	
pseudo R^2	0.524	
AIC	3123.38	

Note: The 1998 Bundestag election serves as the reference category. Robust and non-standardised coefficients with standard errors in parentheses. Significance levels: $+p < .10$; $*p < .05$; $**p < .01$.

'usual suspects' that explain voting behaviour (see Table 2). Respondents living in Eastern Germany were more likely to vote for the CDU[40] if they were frequent church-goers; if their ideological position is close to the one of the Christian Democrats; if they prefer the CDU/CSU chancellor candidate to become the next head of the government; and if they consider the Christian Democrats to be able to solve the most important problems. Not surprisingly, a CDU party identification has a positive impact on CDU/CSU vote intention also in Eastern Germany. However, the gender of a

FIGURE 2
PREDICTED PROBABILITY THAT RESPONDENTS HAVE A CDU/CSU VOTING INTENTION, BY
GENDER (WEST GERMANY)

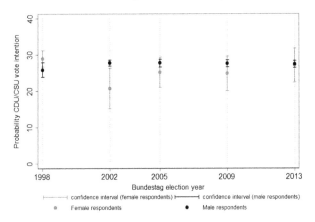

FIGURE 2
PREDICTED PROBABILITY THAT RESPONDENTS HAVE A CDU/CSU VOTING INTENTION, BY
GENDER (WEST GERMANY)

Note: Calculations are based on the logit model presented in Table 1. The range is based on a 95 per cent confidence interval.

respondent does not matter at all. There was no significant impact of that variable on CDU/CSU vote intention in 1998, and this did not change in the following four Bundestag elections (see also Figure 3). However, we find some changes over time in the effects of the standard factors explaining voting behaviour. For instance, the impact of frequent church attendance on the vote intention for the Christian Democrats seems to decrease over time, whereas the influence of the ideological distance on CDU/CSU vote intention gets stronger. With regard to the two hypotheses derived from the literature review in section two of this contribution, we find no evidence that the voters' gender matters for explaining CDU/CSU vote intention when investigating standard factors that reflect important theories of voting behaviour.

In summation, there is – on the basis of the pooled dataset of German election studies from 1998 until 2013 – almost no empirical evidence that provides support for the hypothesis that the interests of a voter mediated by gender have an impact on voting behaviour in Germany. The only exception is West Germany in 2002. Moreover, the nomination of Angela Merkel as chancellor candidate has not resulted in an increased likelihood that women vote for the Christian Democrats. Therefore, there is no robust empirical evidence for a 'modern gender gap' in Germany during the time period in question.

The same is true for 'same gender voting': on the basis of the findings presented here, we can conclude that gender has not gained importance for voting behaviour because of the nomination of Angela Merkel as chancellor candidate in 2005. The considerable differences in the voting behaviour between men and women shown by Jesse,[41] on the basis of the 2013 representative election statistics, are not caused by incentives that emerge from the gender of the voters and corresponding interests. In fact, the variables derived from the Michigan model such as party identification, candidate preference and policy issue orientation, as well as the perceived ideological distance between voters and parties, are the dominant factors determining voting behaviour in Germany.

TABLE 2
DETERMINANTS OF CDU/CSU VOTING INTENTION BETWEEN 1998 AND 2013
(RESPONDENTS FROM EAST GERMANY)

	Estimated coefficient	Standard error
Main explanatory variable		
Female	0.00	(0.38)
Female (2002)	0.01	(0.50)
Female (2005)	0.23	(0.47)
Female (2009)	0.64	(0.49)
Female (2013)	−0.41	(0.47)
Control variables		
Frequent church attendance	0.98*	(0.46)
Frequent church attendance (2002)	−1.63	(1.17)
Frequent church attendance (2005)	−1.94*	(0.80)
Frequent church attendance (2009)	−1.09	(0.72)
Frequent church attendance (2013)	−1.40[+]	(0.78)
Ideological distance	−0.02[+]	(0.01)
Ideological distance (2002)	−0.01	(0.02)
Ideological distance (2005)	−0.05*	(0.03)
Ideological distance (2009)	−0.05[+]	(0.03)
Ideological distance (2013)	−0.03	(0.03)
Chancellor preference H. Kohl	1.98**	(0.39)
Chancellor preference E. Stoiber (2002)	−0.06	(0.56)
Chancellor preference A. Merkel (2005)	−0.98[+]	(0.51)
Chancellor preference A. Merkel (2009)	−0.17	(0.57)
Chancellor preference A. Merkel (2013)	0.86	(0.63)
Problem-solving competence	1.93**	(0.50)
Problem-solving competence (2002)	0.05	(0.60)
Problem-solving competence (2005)	−0.77	(0.58)
Problem-solving competence (2009)	−0.27	(0.58)
Problem-solving competence (2013)	−1.03[+]	(0.59)
CDU/CSU party identification	2.41**	(0.43)
CDU/CSU party identification (2002)	−0.87	(0.58)
CDU/CSU party identification (2005)	0.11	(0.54)
CDU/CSU party identification (2009)	−0.15	(0.53)
CDU/CSU party identification (2013)	−0.17	(0.55)
Dummy variables for election years		
2002	0.77	(0.50)
2005	0.71	(0.51)
2009	−0.39	(0.60)
2013	−0.05	(0.64)
Constant	−3.25**	(0.41)
N	3017	
pseudo R^2	0.554	
AIC	1554.14	

Note: The 1998 Bundestag election serves as the reference category. Robust and non-standardised coefficients with standard errors in parentheses. Significance levels: $+p < .10$, $*p < .05$; $**p < .01$.

CONCLUSION

The aim of this article was to study the impact of gender on voting behaviour in elections for the German Bundestag between 1998 and 2013. On the basis of the theoretical arguments and findings of the literature on the 'modern gender gap' and on 'same gender voting', we derived two competing hypotheses. We argued that, first, women should have lower incentives to vote for Christian democratic parties and that, second, the chances for women to vote for the CDU or the CSU should increase since Angela

FIGURE 3

PREDICTED PROBABILITY THAT RESPONDENTS HAVE A CDU/CSU VOTING INTENTION, BY GENDER (EAST GERMANY)

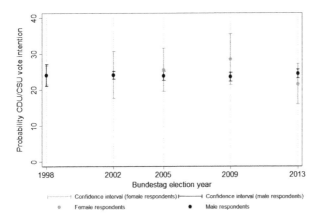

Note: Calculations are based on the logit model presented in Table 2. The range is based on a 95 per cent confidence interval.

Merkel was nominated as chancellor candidate in 2005, 2009 and 2013. By pooling the German election studies of 1998, 2002, 2005, 2009 and 2013 into one dataset, we tested whether there is empirical evidence for these two expectations. The analyses have shown that there is – with the exception of the 2002 election – no evidence for interest-based voting among women that would have caused a 'modern gender gap', implying that female voters are more likely to vote for a party to the left of the centre. There was also no evidence that women have been more likely to support the Christian Democrats since 2005 because of Angela Merkel being the chancellor candidate of the CDU and the CSU. Therefore, the gender of a voter hardly plays a decisive role in voting intention in Germany, at least in the case of the Christian Democrats.

Nevertheless, the findings suggest that it would be worthwhile to examine the role of gender on the voting behaviour in Germany in greater depth. The present analysis suffers from the fact that the chancellor candidate, his or her personal characteristics and policy positions play a central role in the election campaign and that the chancellor has a high competence in agenda-setting anchored in the constitution while the names of the chancellor candidates – for instance, Angela Merkel und Peer Steinbrück at the Federal Election 2013 – do not appear on the ballot in this specific role. Therefore, further studies should examine the impact of gender in elections for specific political offices like mayoral elections.[42] In doing so, the theoretical approach of 'same gender voting' can be put directly to the test. Experimental designs were already successfully applied in this context.[43] In addition, the argument made here could be theoretically refined by taking the respondent's age or birth cohort into account, both of these possibly having a decisive impact in combination with the gender of a respondent.[44] Younger women in particular, who should be influenced to a lower extent by traditional role concepts during their socialisation,[45] should favour policies that strengthen the position of women in economy and society, so that younger women should less prefer conservative and/or Christian democratic parties at the polls compared to older female voters. The investigation of this hypothesis could be the starting point for a new analysis, which could also refer to additional datasets in order to increase the number of covered elections.[46] For instance, focusing on the election studies conducted at the German state level would not only increase the number of covered elections significantly, but would also help to enlarge the number of cases in which women stood as the candidates of a major party – the CDU, the CSU and the SPD – for the prime ministerial office.

DISCLOSURE STATEMENT

No potential conflict of interest was reported by the author.

FUNDING

This work was supported by the German Research Foundation (DFG) [grant number DE 1667/4-1].

NOTES

1. This contribution is a shortened and methodologically revised version of the following book chapter: Marc Debus, 'Weder ein "modern gender gap" noch "same gender voting" in Deutschland? Zum Einfluss des Geschlechts auf das individuelle Wahlverhalten bei den Bundestagswahlen zwischen 1998 und 2013', in Harald Schoen and Bernhard Weßels (eds), *Wahlen und Wähler. Analysen aus Anlass der Bundestagswahl 2013* (Wiesbaden: Springer VS, 2016), pp.271–93.
2. For exceptions see Markus Klein and Ulrich Rosar, 'Ist Deutschland reif für eine Kanzlerin? Eine experimentelle Untersuchung aus Anlass der Bundestagswahl 2005', in Frank Brettschneider, Oskar Niedermayer and Bernhard Weßels (eds), *Die Bundestagswahl 2005. Analysen des Wahlkampfes und der Wahlergebnisse* (Wiesbaden: VS Verlag für Sozialwissenschaften, 2007), pp.271–92; Bettina Westle and Steffen Kühnel, 'Geschlecht als Determinante des Wahlverhaltens? Analysen mit der Repräsentativen Wahlstatistik 2005', in Brettschneider et al. (eds), *Die Bundestagswahl 2005*, pp.293–320; Ina Bieber, 'Der weibliche Blick: Verhalten sich Frauen in der Politik anders?', in Evelyn Bytzek and Sigrid Roßteutscher (eds), *Der unbekannte Wähler? Mythen und Fakten über das Wahlverhalten in Deutschland* (Frankfurt: Campus, 2011), pp.253–72.
3. See Eckhard Jesse, 'Die Bundestagswahl 2013 im Spiegel der repräsentativen Wahlstatistik', *Zeitschrift für Parlamentsfragen* 45/1 (2014), pp.113–27.
4. See, for example, Katharina Rohrbach and Ulrich Rosar, 'Merkel reloaded. Eine experimentelle Untersuchung aus Anlass der Bundestagswahl 2009', in Thorsten Faas, Kai Arzheimer, Sigrid Rossteutscher and Bernhard Weßels (eds), *Koalitionen, Kandidaten, Kommunikation. Analysen zur Bundestagswahl 2009* (Wiesbaden: Springer VS Verlag für Sozialwissenschaften, 2013), pp.79–105.
5. See Ronald Inglehart and Pippa Norris, 'The Developmental Theory of the Gender Gap: Women's and Men's Voting Behavior in Global Perspective', *International Political Science Review* 21/4 (2000), pp.441–63; Nathalie Giger, 'Towards a Modern Gender Gap in Europe? A Comparative Analysis of Voting Behavior in 12 Countries', *Social Science Journal* 46/3 (2009), pp.474–92.
6. Inglehart and Norris, 'Developmental Theory of the Gender Gap'; Ronald Inglehart and Pippa Norris, *Rising Tide: Gender Equality and Cultural Change* (Oxford: Cambridge University Press, 2003).

7. Jesse, 'Die Bundestagswahl 2013'.
8. For an overview see Schoen, 'Soziologische Ansätze in der empirischen Wahlforschung'.
9. Paul Lazarsfeld, Bernhard Berelson and Hazel Gaudet, *The People's Choice: How the Voter Makes Up His Mind in a Presidential Campaign* (New York: Columbia University Press, 1944).
10. Seymour M. Lipset and Stein Rokkan, 'Cleavage Structures, Party Systems and Voter Alignments', in Seymour M. Lipset and Stein Rokkan (eds), *Party Systems and Voter Alignments: Cross-National Perspectives* (New York: The Free Press, 1967), pp.1–64.
11. Ibid.
12. Seymour M. Lipset, *Political Man: The Social Bases of Politics* (New York: Doubleday, 1960), p.220.
13. See Jürgen W. Falter, *Hitlers Wähler* (München: Beck, 1991); Karl Rohe, *Wahlen und Wählertraditionen* (Frankfurt am Main: Suhrkamp, 1992).
14. Inglehart and Norris, 'Developmental Theory of the Gender Gap'; Giger, 'Towards a Modern Gender Gap'.
15. Jeff Manza and Clem Brooks, 'The Gender Gap in US Presidential Elections: When? Why? Implications?', *American Journal of Sociology* 103/5 (1998), pp.1235–66; Giger, 'Towards a Modern Gender Gap', p.481; see also Julian Bernauer, Nathalie Giger and Jan Rosset, 'Mind the Gap: Do Proportional Electoral Systems Foster a More Equal Representation of Women and Men, Poor and Rich?', *International Political Science Review* 36/1 (2015), pp.78–98.
16. See Mattei Dogan, 'Political Cleavage and Social Stratification in France and Italy', in Seymour M. Lipset and Stein Rokkan (eds), *Party Systems and Voter Alignments: Cross-National Perspectives* (New York and London: Free Press, 1967), pp.129–95; Wilma Rule, 'Electoral Systems, Contextual Factors and Women's Opportunity for Election to Parliament in Twenty-Three Democracies', *Western Political Quarterly* 40/3 (1987), pp.477–98; Patrick Emmenegger and Philip Manow, 'Religion and the Gender Vote Gap: Women's Changed Political Preferences from the 1970s to 2010', *Politics and Society* 42/2 (2014), pp.166–93.
17. Manza and Brooks, 'Gender Gap in US Presidential Elections'.
18. See Andrea Volkens, Judith Bara, Ian Budge, Michael McDonald and Hans-Dieter Klingemann (eds), *Mapping Policy Preferences from Texts: Statistical Solutions for Manifesto Analysts* (Oxford: Oxford University Press, 2014).
19. See also Eric Linhart and Susumu Shikano, *Die Generierung von Parteipositionen aus vorverschlüsselten Wahlprogrammen für die Bundesrepublik Deutschland (1949–2002)* (Mannheim: MZES Working Paper No. 98, 2007); Eric Linhart and Susumu Shikano, 'Ideological Signals of German Parties in a Multi-Dimensional Space: An Estimation of Party Preferences Using the CMP Data', *German Politics* 18/3 (2009), pp.301–22; Thomas Bräuninger and Marc Debus, *Parteienwettbewerb in den deutschen Bundesländern* (Wiesbaden: VS Verlag für Sozialwissenschaften, 2012). The societal policy position is calculated by using the Comparative Manifesto Project (CMP) coding scheme and by subtracting the category per604 ('Traditional morality: negative') of progressive societal statements from the category per603 ('Traditional morality: positive') of conservative societal positions. Values below a score of zero indicate that a party has more progressive positions than conservative ones while values above zero suggest a stronger accent on conservative attitudes than on progressive, libertarian attitudes.
20. See Marc Debus and Jochen Müller, 'The Programmatic Development of CDU and CSU since Reunification: Incentives and Constraints for Changing Policy Positions in the German Multi-Level System', *German Politics* 22/1–2 (2013), pp.151–71.
21. See, for example, Carole J. Uhlaner, 'Turnout in Recent American Presidential Elections', *Political Behavior* 11/1 (1989), pp.57–79; Louis DeSipio and Carole J. Uhlaner, 'Immigrant and Native Mexican American Presidential Vote Choice across Immigrant Generations', *American Politics Research* 35/2 (2007), pp.176–201; Lena Wängnerud, 'Women in Parliaments: Descriptive and Substantive Representation', *Annual Review of Political Science* 12/1 (2009), pp.51–69; Joshua N. Zingher and Benjamin Farrer, 'The Electoral Effects of the Descriptive Representation of Ethnic Minority Groups in Australia and the UK', *Party Politics* (2014), online first 30 October 2014, doi: 10.1177/1354068814556895.
22. Iris M. Young, *Inclusion and Democracy* (Oxford: Oxford University Press, 2000).
23. Anne Phillips, *The Politics of Presence* (Oxford: Oxford University Press, 1995).
24. See Sue Thomas, *How Women Legislate* (Oxford: Oxford University Press, 1994); for an empirical analysis see, for example, Li-Ju Chen, 'Do Gender Quotas Influence Women's Representation and Policies?', *The European Journal of Comparative Economics* 7/1 (2010), pp.13–60.
25. See Thomas, *How Women Legislate*; Jason A. MacDonald and Erin E. O'Brien, 'Quasi-Experimental Design, Constituency, and Advancing Women's Interest: Reexamining the Influence of Gender on Substantive Representation', *Political Research Quarterly* 64/2 (2011), pp.472–86.

26. See Markus Baumann, Marc Debus and Jochen Müller, 'Personal Characteristics of MPs and Legislative Behavior in Moral Policy Making', *Legislative Studies Quarterly* 40/2 (2015), pp.179–210; Hanna Bäck, Marc Debus and Jochen Müller, 'Who Takes the Parliamentary Floor? The Role of Gender in Speech-Making in the Swedish Riksdag', *Political Research Quarterly* 67/3 (2014), pp.504–18; Marc Debus and Martin E. Hansen, 'Representation of Women in the Parliament of the Weimar Republic: Evidence from Roll Call Votes', *Politics & Gender* 10/3 (2014), pp.341–64. Hanna Bäck and Marc Debus, *Parties, Parliaments and Legislative Speechmaking* (Basingstoke, London, New York: Palgrave Macmillan, 2016).
27. Eric Plutzer and John F. Zipp, 'Identity Politics, Partisanship, and Voting for Women Candidates', *Public Opinion Quarterly* 60/1 (1996), pp.30–57.
28. Anne M. Holli and Holli Wass, 'Gender-Based Voting in the Parliamentary Elections of 2007 in Finland', *European Journal of Political Research* 49/5 (2010), pp.598–630.
29. Karlheinz Niclauß, *Kanzlerdemokratie* (Paderborn: Schönigh, 2004).
30. ZA-No.4301 (for the Federal Elections 1998 and 2002), ZA-No.4332 (for the Federal Election 2005), ZA-No.5300 (for the Federal Election 2009) and ZA-No.5700 (for the Federal Election 2013).
31. Angus Campbell, Philip E. Converse, Warren E. Miller and Donald E. Stokes, *The American Voter* (New York: Wiley, 1960); for an overview Harald Schoen and Cornelia Weins, 'Der sozialpsychologische Ansatz zur Erklärung von Wahlverhalten', in Jürgen W. Falter and Harald Schoen (eds), *Handbuch Wahlforschung* (Wiesbaden: Springer VS, 2014), pp.241–329.
32. Anthony Downs, *An Economic Theory of Democracy* (New York: Harper, 1957).
33. Lipset and Rokkan, 'Cleavage Structures, Party Systems'.
34. For the Federal Election Studies 1998, 2002, 2009 and 2013, we use the pre-election waves; the election study 2005 was executed only after the parliamentary election on 18 September 2005.
35. See Sigrid Roßteutscher, 'Die konfessionell-religiöse Konfliktlinie zwischen Säkularisierung und Mobilisierung', in Rüdiger Schmitt-Beck (ed.), *Wählen in Deutschland*, PVS Sonderheft 45 (Baden-Baden: Nomos, 2012), pp.111–33.
36. Performing logit models separately for each election study provides very similar results, see Debus, 'Weder ein "modern gender gap"', pp.281–9.
37. See Thomas Brambor, William Clark and Matt Golder, 'Understanding Interaction Models: Improving Empirical Analyses', *Political Analysis* 14/1 (2006), pp.63–82; Michael N. Mitchell, *Interpreting and Visualizing Regression Models Using Stata* (College Station, TX: Stata Press, 2012).
38. There could be a causal relationship between the theoretical concepts discussed here and the dependent variable. With regard to the theoretical discussion about the connection between gender, ideological orientation, candidate preference and voting behaviour, one could expect – on the basis of the 'funnel of causality' concept – that the gender factor does not (only) impact directly on voting intention, but also on moderating variables like ideological distance and chancellor candidate preference. If this would be the case, women should have a greater ideological distance to the CDU/CSU than men and prefer Angela Merkel as chancellor candidate to a greater extent in accordance with the hypotheses derived in this article. We tested whether such a causal relationship exists, but did not find empirical evidence, see Debus, 'Weder ein "modern gender gap"', pp. 281–9.
39. In this context, respondents residing in Berlin are attributed to the West German states.
40. Because the CSU is not competing for votes in any of the East German states, we just refer to the CDU when interpreting the model estimates for respondents living in East Germany.
41. Jesse, 'Die Bundestagswahl 2013'.
42. See Maciej A. Górecki and Paula Kukołowicz, 'Gender Quotas, Candidate Background and the Election of Women: A Paradox of Gender Quotas in Open-List Proportional Representation Systems', *Electoral Studies* 36/1 (2014), pp.65–80; Mary Stegmaier, Jale Tosun and Klara Vlachova, 'Women's Parliamentary Representation in the Czech Republic: Does Preference Voting Matter?', *East European Politics and Societies* 28/1 (2014), pp.187–204.
43. See Bernhard Kittel, Wolfgang Luhan and Rebecca Morton (eds), *Experimental Political Science: Principles and Practices* (Houndsmills: Palgrave-Macmillan, 2012).
44. See Debus, 'Weder ein "modern gender gap"'.
45. See George H. Mead, *Mind, Self and Society: From the Standpoint of a Social Behaviorist* (Chicago, IL: University of Chicago Press, 1934); Donald D. Searing, 'Roles, Rules, and Rationality in the New Institutionalism', *The American Political Science Review* 85/4 (1991), pp.1239–60; Donald D. Searing, *Westminster's World: Understanding Political Roles* (Cambridge, MA: Harvard University Press, 1994).
46. See Kerstin Völkl, Kai-Uwe Schnapp, Everhard Holtmann and Oscar W. Gabriel (eds), *Wähler und Landtagswahlen in der Bundesrepublik Deutschland* (Baden-Baden: Nomos, 2008); Marc Debus and Jochen Müller, 'Expected Utility or Learned Familiarity? The Formation of Voters' Coalition Preferences', *Electoral Studies* 34/1 (2014), pp.54–67.

Another Dog that didn't Bark? Less Dealignment and more Partisanship in the 2013 Bundestag Election

KAI ARZHEIMER

Using new data for the 1977–2012 period, this article shows that dealignment has halted during the last decade amongst older and better educated West German voters, and that party identification is now more widespread than it was in the 1990s in the east. For voters who identified with one of the relevant parties at the time of the 2013 election, their vote choice was more or less a foregone conclusion, as candidates and issues played only a minor role for this group. A detailed analysis of leftist voters shows that supporters of the Greens, the Left, and the SPD have broadly similar preferences but diverging partisan identities. Even amongst western voters of the Left, most respondents claim to be identifiers. This suggests that the fragmentation of the left is entrenched, and that 'agenda' policies have triggered a realignment.

INTRODUCTION

For the last 25 years or so, party identification has been said to be in decline in Germany. And yet those two parties which are most closely associated with traditional concepts of partisanship, i.e. the Christian Democrats (CDU/CSU) on the right and the Social Democrats (SPD) on the left, are once more jointly governing Germany, with the CDU/CSU coming tantalisingly close to an outright majority in parliament.

This article tries to shed some light on this apparent puzzle by first revisiting the major stations of the debate on partisanship in Germany before considering new longitudinal data, which demonstrate that the rate and pattern of dealignment in Germany have changed in an unexpected way: various political shocks of the last decade notwithstanding, dealignment has come to a virtual halt amongst older and better educated West German voters and slowed down considerably in other western groups. In East Germany, party identification is now more widespread than it was in the 1990s.

The article then turns to the 2013 Bundestag election to show that persistent party identifications are not a mere curiosity but retain the power to shape voting decisions. For voters who identify with one of the relevant parties, their vote choice is more or less a foregone conclusion, as candidates and issues play only a minor role. Finally, the paper turns to the left end of the political spectrum. The SPD's unexpected pursuit of welfare reforms in the early 2000s has left many party members and supporters baffled and helped bring about the Wahlalternative Arbeit und Soziale Gerechtigkeit (WASG)/PDS merger that resulted in the rise of a third relevant party on the left. These radical policy changes as well as the complicated lineage of the new party clearly had the potential to reduce the role of party identification, but even here, party identification trumps policy considerations, while differences in policy preferences amongst leftist voters are small.

IS PARTISANSHIP IN GERMANY IN DECLINE?

The question whether Michigan-style party identifications do exist in West Europe, where politics was shaped along the lines of ideologies and cleavages, was hotly debated in the 1970s.[1] However, towards the end of the decade a consensus emerged that the concept could indeed be transplanted to the polities on the old continent including Germany, conditional on an operationalisation that caters for multi-party systems.[2] Such an operationalisation – developed by Frank Dishaw in the early 1970s[3] – has been employed since the first Politbarometer surveys (dating back to the late 1970s) and has been replicated in Germany's general social survey (Allgemeine Bevölkerungsumfrage der Sozialwissenschaften or ALLBUS), in the national election studies, and in countless other opinion surveys.

Yet the late 1970s may very well have marked the height of partisanship in Germany. Mutually reinforcing processes of socio-economic modernisation, secularisation, and value change began to undermine the cleavage base of the German party system,[4] which in turn facilitated the rise of the Green party in the 1980s. Moreover, according to Dalton's very influential account,[5] the expansion of higher education and the increase in the availability of political information reduced the heuristic value of party identification as a device that reduces cognitive costs.

The political crises of the 1980s and early 1990s, on the other hand, had very little effect on levels of party identification in Germany. Neither the various party funding scandals nor the end of the Cold War nor the post-unification economic slump of the early 1990s resulted in a sudden drop of partisanship. Rather, partisan decline was glacial and concentrated in those social groups whose loyalties have shaped the modern German party system: working class voters, Catholics, and churchgoers more generally.[6]

These findings are complemented by the results presented by Neundorf and colleagues.[7] Using a very sophisticated model for panel data, the authors show that partisanship in Germany is 'bounded': Even those Social/Christian Democrats who change their allegiance usually move back and forth between their original party and independence. Crossing over to the other major party is a rare exception.

More recently, Dassonneville and colleagues have revisited Dalton's cognitive mobilisation hypothesis.[8] Based on their analysis of the Sozio-oekonomisches Panel (SOEP), a long-running, large-scale panel survey, they claim that dealignment is now most prevalent amongst voters with *low levels of formal education*. Such a positive correlation between formal education on the one hand and party identification on the other would seem to go against the grain of Dalton's original argument (but see Dalton's rejoinder for a different interpretation[9]). Similar findings have also been presented by Albright,[10] who uses comparative cross-sectional data to demonstrate that cognitive skills and access to mass media have a positive effect on partisanship in a number of European countries including Germany, and by Arzheimer and Schoen,[11] who also make use of the SOEP to show that higher levels of political interest are associated with higher levels and greater stability of party identifications.

While the SOEP is a valuable tool for studying attitude stability at the micro level, it is not ideally suited for plotting the long-term levels of partisanship in the electorate or its importance in any given election. Therefore, the remainder of this section will use the monthly Politbarometer survey series to chart the decline of partisanship, while the next section will make use of the German Longitudinal Election Study (GLES) to assess the relevance of party identification for voters in the 2013 Bundestag election.

Forschungsgruppe Wahlen (FGW) has been tracking German political attitudes with its monthly Politbarometer surveys since the golden age of party identification in the late 1970s. The Politbarometer follows a classic repeated cross-sectional survey design, where each group of interviewees is sampled independently and thought to be representative of the German population in the respective year and month.

Although FGW is a commercial operation, its raw data are made available for secondary analysis after an embargo of two to three years. Previous analyses of these data for the 1977–2002 period have shown that in line with theories of secular dealignment, party identification in Western Germany declines fairly slowly and steadily at a rate of less than 1 percentage point per year.[12]

Since then, FGW has released new data which cover ten years that have been nothing but turbulent for the German party system: following a narrow victory in the 2002 election, the red–green government quite unexpectedly embarked on an ambitious 'Agenda 2010' of welfare state retrenchment, much of which was enacted with the support of the centre-right parties. Mirroring the SPD's move to the right, the CDU then committed itself to an even more market-liberal manifesto at its 2003 party conference, while the new government policies created unrest within the SPD that in turn led to the formation of the breakaway WASG group.

Following a string of electoral defeats for the SPD at the Land level and the early Bundestag election of 2005, the SPD and the Christian Democrats eventually formed the second grand coalition in 2005, which softened some of the 'Agenda' reforms but raised the retirement age. Arguably, the existence of a grand coalition also facilitated the merger between the eastern PDS and the western WASG that formed the Left in 2007, and the short but meteoric rise of the FDP just before the 2009 election, which resulted in the largest ever FDP delegation in the Bundestag.

Finally, the series also covers the brief period in 2011/12 when the new Pirate party won between 7.4 and 8.9 per cent of the vote in Land elections in Berlin, North Rhine-Westphalia, Saarland, and Schleswig-Holstein, only to disappear from the political radar just before the 2013 election. Clearly, these tumultuous events make the 2002–2012 period an interesting one for studying dealignment in Germany.

The Politbarometer series is quite noisy, with a standard deviation of 5.4 percentage points. This is to be expected, as sampling error alone should result in a standard deviation of roughly 1.5 percentage points, disregarding any additional error due to multistage sampling. Even after applying a moving average smoother using a five-month (2-1-2) window, the series is rather jittery (see Figure 1), with some of the peaks probably being the result of campaign effects (the diamond-shaped symbols mark the dates of federal elections). However, it also seems clear that the downward trend of the 1980s and 1990s has slowed down considerably in the new millennium, with the average yearly attrition rate falling well below 0.5 percentage points.

FIGURE 1
PARTISANSHIP IN WEST GERMANY, 1977–2012

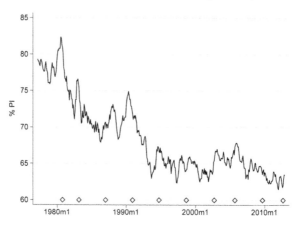

As the micro data are readily available, it is possible to model the decline in partisanship directly without resorting to the aggregated time series.[13] A simple descriptive model would start with a logistic regression of holding a party identification (a dichotomous variable) on calendar time, controlling for campaign effects. For simplicity's sake, only federal elections and Land elections in Bavaria, Baden-Wurttemberg, and North Rhine-Westphalia – the three most populous states which are collectively home to more than half of the West German population – were considered, and campaigns were assumed to run uniformly for three months, including the month in which the election was held. Logistic regression enforces an S-shaped link between partisanship and its predictors, which, given the empirical distribution of party identifications in the sample (between 59 and 84 per cent) will result in a nearly linear relationship. To accommodate the apparent non-linear decline of partisanship, following Royston and Sauerbrei,[14] a number of fractional polynomial transformations of calendar time were included in a bivariate model (not shown), with an additional square root transformation providing the best fit.

Since the purpose of the model is descriptive, only two variables were included to account for changes in the composition of the population that occurred over the 35-year period: formal education (people who were educated beyond *Mittlere Reife* vs. everyone else) and age. As outlined above, formal education is interesting in itself, but it also serves as a useful proxy for not belonging to the working class and not attending church frequently, rendering a durable affiliation with either the SPD or the CDU/CSU much less likely.

Age, or rather the time at which a person was born, will affect partisanship in two ways. On the one hand, partisanship is partly a habit, which is reinforced over the course of one's life.[15] Therefore, older voters should be more likely to identify with a party. On the other hand, dealignment theory suggests that independent of individual age and across the span of their lives, members of younger *cohorts* are less likely to identify with a party compared to those who were socialised into the largely stable German party system of the 1960s and 1970s.

Lifecycle and cohort effects are notoriously difficult to separate.[16] Because age is only recorded in a categorised fashion in the Politbarometer surveys anyway, no such attempt was made. Instead, respondents were split into three broad categories (under 35, 35 to 60, and over 60) to control for the slow but momentous demographic changes Germany is undergoing. Finally, the effects of age and education were allowed to vary over time to account for generational replacement and the new relationship between education and partisanship postulated by Dassonneville and colleagues.[17]

Although the additional complexity introduced by the interaction terms is a disadvantage, model comparisons (not shown) based on the Bayesian Information Criterion (BIC) demonstrate that such a fully interactive model fits the data much better than either a non-interactive variant or a model that regresses partisanship on calendar time and campaign effects alone.

Table 1 shows the results. However, since the substantive meaning of logit coefficients is hard to grasp, particularly in the face of additional non-linearities and interactions, the interpretation will focus on a graphical representation. Figure 2 shows that the decline of partisanship has slowed down considerably. In theory, anything could have happened in the nine months between the current end of the time series and the 2013 election, but the graph makes it abundantly clear that dealignment has effectively halted during the last decade under study. The estimated attrition rate for the five-year period from December 2007 to December 2012 is a mere 0.8 percentage points, just over the estimated *yearly* average for the 1980s.

Including education, age, and their interaction with time in the model makes it possible to look into group-specific trends in dealignment. Figure 3 shows that partisanship has fallen much more rapidly amongst those with lower formal qualifications, leading to a gap that has become increasingly wider in recent years, as dealignment has essentially petered out amongst those with higher levels of educational attainment. Yet dealignment has slowed down for the lower attainment group, too: the change from, for

TABLE 1
MICRO MODEL OF PARTISANSHIP IN WEST GERMANY, 1977–2012

	Party ID
Sqrt(Time)	−0.481*** (0.0451)
Time	0.00912*** (0.00111)
Campaign (all)	0.0400* (0.0162)
Age: 35–59	−2.923*** (0.413)
Age: 60+	−3.117*** (0.490)
Educ: high	0.0941 (0.468)
Age: 35–59 × Sqrt(Time)	0.317*** (0.0417)
Age: 60+ × Sqrt(Time)	0.299*** (0.0498)
Age: 35–59 × Time	−0.00747*** (0.00103)
Age: 60+ × Time	−0.00579*** (0.00124)
Educ: high × Sqrt(Time)	−0.0210 (0.0457)
Educ: high × Time	0.00134 (0.00110)
Constant	6.340*** (0.00110)
Observations	439120

Source: own calculation based on Politbarometer series, ZA2391.

FIGURE 2
ESTIMATED OVERALL LEVELS OF PARTISANSHIP IN WEST GERMANY, 1977–2012
(ADJUSTED PREDICTIONS AT REPRESENTATIVE VALUES (APR))

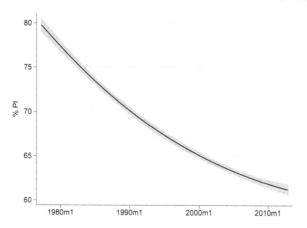

example, 2000 to 2010 is much less dramatic than the development for the 1990 to 2000 period, hinting once more at stabilisation on a lower level.

One intriguing aspect of this pattern is that average levels of formal education are higher for younger generations as a result of the ongoing expansion of education. Figure 4 offers a more direct look into the age-specific trajectories of dealignment. One first insight is that – at least according to the underlying model – age did not matter much in the late 1970s and early 1980s but quickly became a factor over the course of this decade as younger respondents were increasingly less likely than their older compatriots to report an identification with a party. This can mean two things: relevant segments of the new cohorts entering the political system either never acquired such an identification or did not retain it to the same degree as their

FIGURE 3
ESTIMATED LEVELS OF PARTISANSHIP IN WEST GERMANY BY FORMAL EDUCATION,
1977–2012 (ADJUSTED PREDICTIONS AT REPRESENTATIVE VALUES (APR))

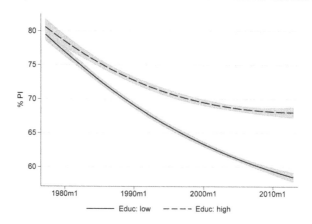

FIGURE 4
ESTIMATED LEVELS OF PARTISANSHIP IN WEST GERMANY BY AGE GROUP, 1977–2012
(ADJUSTED PREDICTIONS AT REPRESENTATIVE VALUES (APR))

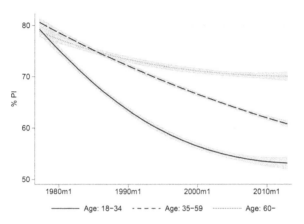

predecessors. As outlined above, it is not possible with the data at hand to separate age, cohort, and period effects. But given how steep the estimated decline of their partisanship is compared to the other groups, it seems safe to assume that the dealignment of the 1980s and mid-1990s that reduced the number of partisans by nearly a quarter must have been driven largely by this group.

However, once more the estimated attrition rate in this youngest age group began to fall appreciably around the turn of the century. Moreover, nearly everyone who belonged to this group in the 1980s had now moved on to the next age band, which exhibits a nearly linear pattern of decline that is currently steeper than that of the youngest group, although levels of partisanship are still noticeably higher. While it is tempting to speculate about what could have caused change in these cohorts, there is simply not enough information in the data to support such an investigation.

Finally, the over-60s, who began at roughly the same level as the middle age group, did outstrip them in terms of partisans by the mid-1990s. Levels of partisanship have been essentially stable in this group for more than a decade now. Once more one must keep in mind that by the early 2000s everyone who was in the middle group in the 1980s had moved on to this upper age band.

Demographic changes imply that the mean age of people belonging to an age group will fluctuate somewhat over time: from the 1940s until the mid-1960s almost every birth cohort was bigger than the one before, but since then this pattern has been reversed.[18] Yet, even accounting for this effect and for the rising life expectancy, the changes in the impact of age on party identification are too big to be the result of stable lifecycle effects. They point to either a massive shift in what it means for partisanship to be young, middle-aged, or old, or, equivalently, substantial cohort effects.

One final aspect that must be considered is the relative size of the three age groups. During the first five years of polling, 29 per cent of all respondents were under 35, while 26 per cent of those interviewed were older than 60. For the 2008–2012 period, this balance has been reversed. The share of older citizens has risen to just under 30 per cent, and only 18 per cent of all respondents are younger than 35. Voters aged 35 to 59 currently make up 52 per cent of the sample, but their share is now peaking, while the oldest group is rapidly growing and already stands at 33 per cent in the 2012 data. In essence, this means that dealignment in Germany is slowed down by demographic change, because the combined shares of middle-aged and older voters, who are more likely to be partisans, is growing. Either way, party identification has neither collapsed nor withered away in West Germany.

Assessing the state and trajectory of party identification in the former East Germany is less straightforward. First, theories of dealignment do not apply because there should not have been any alignment in the first place. After all, easterners had not been exposed to the West German party system before 1990 and, more generally, had had no experience with free elections since the (partially free) Land elections of 1946. While it has been argued that many easterners had access to West German TV and hence could form 'quasi-attachments' to West German parties,[19] these attachments can hardly have been comparable to Michigan-type identifications. After all, the latter are the result of socialisation effects in the family and intermediary associations, exposure to fellow partisans, party members and party communication, first-hand experience of policies and policy outcomes, and last but not least the habit-forming experience of repeatedly voting for one's party. Accordingly, the number of self-reported partisans in the east was lower than in the west all through the 1990s, while attachments were weaker and less stable.

Second, the East German subsamples of the Politbarometer poll are often relatively small. Until 1995, East Germans were massively overrepresented in the polls: Essentially, easterners were sampled separately and in numbers approaching those for West Germany (about 1000 per month and region) to account for the idiosyncratic and very fluent nature of public opinion in the post-unification east. From 1996 to 1998, FGW used a single sampling frame, interviewing about 1000 respondents per month in total. In 1999, FGW reinstated separate regional subsamples of roughly equal size, but from the early 2000s on they considerably reduced eastern sample sizes for most *months*, boosting them occasionally to cover election campaigns. As a result, the eastern time series is very noisy even after applying the moving average smoother (Figure 5).

Despite these fluctuations, it is clear that the massive decline of self-reported identifications in the early 1990s was a temporary phenomenon. From the mid-1990s on, the number of identifiers moved up, although in fits and starts. This pattern is at least compatible with a process of socio-political learning, during which East Germans became familiar with the party system and the wider liberal-democratic political system. Then, for the last decade or so, levels of partisanship in East Germany have been by and large stable in the 55–65 per cent range, roughly just five percentage points below West German levels.

Because the East German sample sizes are so small (particularly for younger and highly educated voters), because the time series is comparatively short, and because of the absence of any clear trends, I refrain from modelling developments in subgroups. At this stage, the more important point to note is that partisanship was clearly still a relevant political factor at the time of the 2013 election. While the group of non-partisans is large, in both regions more than half of the voters report a party identification, and there is no sign of a sudden and imminent decline.

FIGURE 5
PARTISANSHIP IN EAST GERMANY, 1991–2012

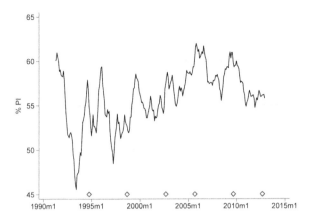

THE ROLE OF PARTY IDENTIFICATION IN THE 2013 ELECTION

Party Identification and Party Choice

Just because respondents report identifications, they need not necessarily be politically meaningful. In this section, a simple model of voting in the 2013 election is presented in order to assess the political relevance of party identification.

The most commonly employed statistical model for multi-party elections is the multinomial logit (MNL), but the MNL becomes unwieldy very quickly, because each possible outcome (minus a reference category) is given its own set of coefficients. Fortunately, there is another option: The Conditional Logit Model (CLM)[20] has only a single parameter for the effect of each variable that varies across alternatives within voters. This includes many variables which are deemed to affect electoral behaviour: evaluations of candidates, policies, and parties including party identification. The CLM resembles the MNL in that it can be extended to also incorporate variables that are constant across alternatives,[21] like more general attitudes, or socio-demographic variables, but for these, the number of parameters is once more proportional to the number of choices minus one.

Table 2 shows the estimates for the parameters of a conditional logistic model of electoral choice in the 2013 election. Party choice has been simplified to just five outcomes: SPD (the reference category), CDU/CSU, FDP, Greens, and the Left. Non-voters and voters of 'other' parties, including the new AfD, which was founded only months before the election,[22] are disregarded.

Data come from the pre-election cross-sectional survey component of the German Longitudinal Election Study. The model itself is built around the Michigan triad of party identification, candidate evaluations, and issue considerations. The measurement of party identification is self-explanatory. To operationalise candidate evaluations, standard thermometer scores for Angela Merkel, Peer Steinbrück, Rainer Brüderle, Jürgen Trittin, and Gregor Gysi were used.[23] Issue considerations were operationalised in multiple ways. For the 'ideological distance' measure, respondents were asked to

TABLE 2
MICRO-MODEL OF ELECTORAL CHOICE IN THE 2013 BUNDESTAG ELECTION (EAST VS. WEST)

	West	East
choice		
PI	1.885*** (0.177)	2.906*** (0.366)
Evaluation: Candidate	0.555*** (0.0600)	0.625*** (0.155)
Ideolocal Distance	−0.374*** (0.0679)	−0.423*** (0.101)
Union	0.0797 (0.620)	0.621 (0.908)
FDP	−1.190 (0.914)	−1.066 (1.655)
B90Gruene	0.733 (0.761)	−0.0441 (1.267)
Left	0.528 (0.787)	2.077* (0.872)
Union × Tax vs Welfare	−0.00368 (0.103)	−0.121 (0.165)
FDP × Tax vs Welfare	0.259 (0.110)	0.220 (0.213)
B90Gruene × Tax vs Welfare	−0.0118 (0.111)	0.224 (0.277)
Left × Tax vs Welfare	−0.0122 (0.115)	−0.0614 (0.155)
Union × Immigration	−0.0750 (0.0731)	−0.0729 (0.117)
FDP × Immigration	−0.0658 (0.0812)	−0.176 (0.290)
B90Gruene × Immigration	−0.124 (0.0807)	−0.260 (0.152)
Left × Immigration	−0.151 (0.0791)	−0.379** (0.131)
Observations	3887	1711

Source: own calculation based on GLES 2013 pre-election cross-section, ZA5700. 'Observations' are observed choices. The number of cases is 888 for the Wwest and 206 for the east. Standard errors take into account the nesting of choices within electors and the complex survey design, including the weights supplied by the GLES team.

place themselves and the main parties on a standard left–right scale to gauge the general agreement between voters' preferences and the parties' policy proposals. To get a more rounded impression of the impact of policy considerations, preferences on two more specific positional issues that were deemed to be important in the 2013 election were included as well: lower taxes vs. more welfare spending, and immigration.[24]

While respondents were asked for their perceptions of party positions on these issues so that alternative-specific measures of distance could be calculated, the number of missing values for these items is quite high. Hence, only voters' personal preferences regarding immigration and tax/welfare enter the model. Including such case-specific variables in a CLM of electoral choice requires one to include a series of party-specific constants and interaction terms,[25] which pick up the effect of a change in the case-specific variables on the chance of choosing the respective party vs. the baseline alternative (here: the SPD).

Extant research has shown that voters in both regions still apply diverging mechanisms when making electoral choices.[26] To account for any differences between East and West Germany, parameters were estimated separately for both regions.[27] While the interpretation is slightly complicated by the presence of multiple interaction terms, it is clear from Table 2 that such differences played a role in the 2013 election. To see why this is the case, consider a voter who is in favour of both raising welfare spending (0) and facilitating immigration (0). For these persons, all interaction terms drop out of the equation so that the constant reflects the odds of voting for the respective party vs. voting for the SPD. In the west, the odds seem to favour the Left (e0.528

≈ 1.7), but the coefficient is not statistically different from zero. In the east, however, the Left's advantage is significant, and massive (e2.077 ≈ 8). Even for eastern voters who hold a more centrist position (5) on the immigration scale, the Left will be slightly more attractive, ceteris paribus, whereas in the west, the balance is tilting towards the SPD.

While these differences are certainly interesting, the main concern of this section is the role of party identification. From the first line of Table 2, it can be gleaned that in both regions, identifying with a party has a very strong effect on the odds of actually voting for this party even after controlling for specific issue positions, general ideological distance, and candidate evaluations.

The latter two do certainly also matter. Because of the range of the underlying scales (0–10 and 1–11, respectively), their potential effect is even bigger than that of party identification. But in practice, the perceived ideological distances between voters and parties are relatively small, with a median of 2 points and a mean of 2.3. Candidate evaluations display more variation with a mean of 6.2 and a median of 6, implying that a plausible candidate could possibly compensate for a lack of attachment to the party. Yet one should bear in mind that for candidate evaluations (and ideological distances), only the differential is relevant, because all candidates will appeal to some degree. If a voter likes or dislikes all candidates in equal measure, their joint effect on that individual's voting behaviour is nil. For the average voter, the standard deviation of candidate evaluations is just 1.9 points, suggesting that in many cases the differential and hence the candidate effect will be considerably smaller than the potential effect. Having a party identification, on the other hand, will by definition benefit only a single party, to which the maximal potential effect will apply.

One intuitive (though potentially problematic) approach towards assessing the relevance of party identifications is to compare actual electoral choices to those expected, given the data and the parameter estimates.[28] In both regions, about 85 per cent of voters are classified correctly.[29] However, simply assuming that those who hold an identification will vote in accordance with it works just as well, with 85 per cent of the subgroup correctly classified in the west and 92 per cent in the east. Accordingly, the match between party identification and model-derived predictions is almost perfect (98 per cent) for identifiers.

This shows that at least in this election, candidate evaluations and policy concerns were rarely able to offset the effect of longstanding loyalties amongst those who have an identification and turned out to vote. Nonetheless, they will shape voting decisions amongst the slowly growing group of those who do not identify with a party.

The Importance of being Left: Ideology, Party Identification and Choice Amongst Left Parties

In German politics, one of the most interesting developments in recent years has been the breakaway of the WASG from the SPD following the enactment of the 'Agenda 2010' reforms (see section 2), and the ensuing PDS/WASG merger.[30] Pursuing this set of ambitious welfare reforms has not just put considerable strain on the relationships between the trade unions and the SPD. Given the high-profile defection of Oskar Lafontaine, one of the most prominent Social Democrats of his generation and former party leader of the SPD, as well as the involvement of the trade unions, this chain of events can be construed as the first major split of the SPD since 1917. As a result, the left camp is now more fragmented than the right, at least for the time being. Moreover, the (ongoing) conflict over the 'Agenda' and its legacy has reasserted the importance of distributional issues (which were overshadowed by moral questions, at least in many academic analyses) for party competition.

The question of whether this new divide within the left camp has already become entrenched in the guise of (new) party identifications has rarely been addressed. After all, it is not implausible that the vote for the Left (particularly in the west) could be driven by policy concerns alone that could be alleviated by another shift of the SPD's position on welfare, or even by more generalised 'protest'.

Yet the short answer to the question is that this does not seem to be the case. Admittedly, voters of the Left party position themselves significantly closer to the left end of the political spectrum than voters of the SPD or the Greens. This even holds when the analysis is restricted to the subsample of voters who self-identify as leftists by reporting a position on the continuum that is clearly left of the centre (4 or less). Moreover, voters of the Greens are slightly more in favour of immigration than voters of the other two parties. Again, this holds for both regions, and for both the general population and the leftist subsample (not shown as a table).

But on the crucial tax/welfare spending issue, there are hardly any policy preference differences between the supporters of the three parties. Here, the real difference is that between easterners and westerners, and this gap is particularly pronounced amongst those who consider themselves to be left-wing. TABLE 4 lists the adjusted predictions derived from a simple linear model (TABLE 3) that regresses tax/welfare spending preferences amongst leftist (self-placement on scale points 1–4) voters on region and electoral choice. Lines 1–4 show *national* estimates by party choice. Clearly, the differences between the respective supporters of the SPD, the Greens, and the Left are small and statistically insignificant, whereas any other voters position themselves more than two points closer to the 'lower taxes' pole of the scale on average.

TABLE 3
LEFTIST VOTERS' POSITIONS ON TAXES/WELFARE SPENDING AS
A FUNCTION OF PARTY CHOICE AND REGION

	Tax/spend
SPD	−2.529*** (0.482)
B90Gruene	−2.866*** (0.535)
Left	−2.415*** (0.592)
East	−2.439*** (0.592)
SPD × East	1.606* (0.708)
B90Gruene × East	1.987* (0.848)
Left × East	1.296 (0.794)
Constant	7.003*** (0.400)
Observations	1839

Source: own calculation based on GLES 2013 pre-election cross-section, ZA5700. The size of the subpopulation is 333. Standard errors take into account the complex survey design, including the weights supplied by the GLES team.

TABLE 4
LEFTIST VOTERS' POSITIONS ON TAXES/WELFARE SPENDING (ADJUSTED PREDICTIONS
AT REPRESENTATIVE VALUES)

	Tax/spend	
No/other	6.561	(0.337)
SPD	4.323	(0.276)
B90Gruene	4.055	(0.275)
Left	4.381	(0.446)
West	5.589	(0.243)
East	4.051	(0.236)
No/other × West	7.003	(0.400)
No/other × East	4.564	(0.436)
SPD × West	4.474	(0.332)
SPD × East	3.641	(0.280)
B90Gruene × West	4.137	(0.315)
B90Gruene × East	3.685	(0.525)
Left × West	4.588	(0.540)
Left × East	3.444	(0.349)
Observations	1339	

Source: own calculation based on GLES 2013 pre-election cross-section, ZA5700. Adjusted predictions derived from model presented in TABLE 3. The size of the subpopulation is 333. Standard errors take into account the complex survey design, including the weights supplied by the GLES team.

Perhaps even more striking are the estimates for the overall difference between East Germans and West Germans given in the next two lines. Although all respondents in this subsample consider themselves to be on the left, western respondents lean slightly towards the 'lower taxes/fewer benefits' pole of the continuum. Eastern respondents, on the other hand, position themselves 1.6 points closer to the 'higher taxes/more benefits' pole. The rest of the table breaks down the preferences of leftists along party lines and region. Because of the small sample sizes, the regional differences within electorates are not statistically significant, but they clearly show that within each region, the voters of the three parties hold broadly similar views on taxation and welfare.

While policies seem hence to matter less than one would have expected for party choice within the leftist camp, party identification once more plays a prominent role. Table 5 shows the party affiliation of western leftist voters by electoral choice. From the main diagonal, it can be seen that between 72 and 85 per cent report a party identification that is congruent with their electoral choice. Crucially, this also holds for the Left party, which is still relatively new by West German standards, although its predecessor PDS certainly had enough time to develop ties to its primarily eastern supporters. Here, 73 per cent of the voters claim to be longstanding supporters. Although the sampling error is relatively large for this small group, one can be confident that more than half of the Left's western voters are identifiers.

In the east, the results are virtually identical (not shown as a table). Flipping the perspective demonstrates that similarly high numbers of identifiers vote for the 'correct' party, and again, this holds for both regions (not shown as a table). Taken together, these findings suggest that the fragmentation of the left-wing electorate has indeed become entrenched. The result of the 'Agenda' policies is realignment, not

	Vote			
	No/other	SPD	B90Gruene	Left
No/other	0.844 (0.0958)	0.0812 (0.0327)	0.0552 (0.0286)	0.0846 (0.0402)
SPD	0.156 (0.0958)	0.847 (0.0511)	0.193 (0.0553)	0.0735 (0.0450)
B90Gruene	0 (0)	0.0717 (0.0427)	0.723 (0.0643)	0.110 (0.0815)
Left	0 (0)	0 (0)	0.0291 (0.0177)	0.731 (0.0891)
N	1282			

Source: own calculation based on GLES 2013 pre-election cross-section, ZA5700. The size of the subpopulation is 254. Standard errors take into account the complex survey design, including the weights supplied by the GLES team.

dealignment. Obviously, this does not bode well for any attempts by the SPD to win (back) voters from the Left.

CONCLUSION: PARTY IDENTIFICATION IN GERMANY – NOT DEAD YET

The notion of party decline in western countries is as old as the post-war political order.[31] But at least for the old Federal Republic, and then for the western states during the first decade after unification, there is no evidence of any sudden collapse of party loyalties. Instead, the available data from the Politbarometer series point to an almost glacial process of dealignment that is driven by social and generational change.[32]

This article expands on earlier contributions by first extending the study of the Politbarometer series by a full decade to the whole 1977–2012 period. The most important finding from this analysis is that dealignment in Western Germany has slowed down even further. On average, partisanship declined by about one percentage point per year in the 1980s, by half a percentage point per year in the 1990s, and by one-third of a percentage point or less per year in the new millennium. Data for East Germany are sparser but suggest that levels of partisanship have actually *risen* and are now higher than they were in the 1990s.

One reason for this unforeseen development is the emerging positive relationship between formal education and partisanship, coupled with the ongoing expansion of the German education system. This positive effect of education (which confirms some of Dassonneville and colleagues' findings using a different database) is both unexpected and remarkable, because it contradicts classic cleavage theory as well as the original argument about cognitive mobilisation. Whether it hails a new age of 'cognitive partisans' remains to be seen,[33] although the results are certainly suggestive. Demographic changes play an important part, too. While it is not quite clear whether this is primarily a result of lifecycle or of cohort effects, late-middle-aged voters and younger pensioners are more likely to be partisan than younger voters, whose share of the electorate is rapidly shrinking.

Turning from the longitudinal to a cross-sectional perspective, it could further be demonstrated that in both East and West Germany, party identifications are a very strong predictor of voting intentions, even if the other core elements of the Ann Arbor model – candidate evaluations and issues orientations – are controlled for in various ways. Those voters who identify with a party rarely report diverging voting intentions so that issues and candidates matter almost exclusively for the apartisans.

Although the analysis was restricted to the pre-election survey to avoid any post-hoc rationalisations on behalf of the respondents, the spectre of endogeneity obviously looms large in any such model. After all, it is reasonable to assume that at least some respondents cannot distinguish between their current voting intentions and any long-term loyalties they may or may not harbour. However, measures of candidate evaluations and issue orientations are equally or even more prone to contamination by voting intentions. Therefore, the estimate for the *relative* importance of party identification should be unaffected even if the absolute size of its effect may be overstated.

Finally, a detailed analysis of leftist voters interviewed for the GLES showed that even in the (small) subgroup of western voters of the Left party, most respondents said they were identifiers. Again, this is a significant and largely unexpected finding. The formation of the WASG and ultimately the WASG/PDS merger were triggered by the SPD's shift to the right on social and economic policy, yet the leftists amongst the voters of the SPD and of the Left take broadly similar positions on these issues while claiming to identify with their respective parties. This suggests that the fragmentation of the left camp has become entrenched and cannot be easily overcome by another programmatic shift of the SPD.

DISCLOSURE STATEMENT

No potential conflict of interest was reported by the author.

NOTES

1. See Russell J. Dalton, Scott C. Flanagan, and Paul Allen Beck (eds), *Electoral Change in Advanced Industrial Democracies: Realignment or Dealignment* (Princeton, NJ: Princeton University Press, 1984) for a useful summary.
2. Jürgen W. Falter, 'Zur Validierung theoretischer Konstrukte – Wissenschaftstheoretische Aspekte des Validierungskonzepts', *Zeitschrift für Soziologie* 6 (1977), pp.349–69.
3. Dieter Roth, *Empirische Wahlforschung. Ursprung, Theorien, Instrumente und Methoden*, 2nd ed. (Wiesbaden: VS Verlag für Sozialwissenschaften, 2008), p.156.
4. Colin Crouch, *Social Change in Western Europe* (Oxford: Oxford University Press, 1999).
5. Russell J. Dalton, 'Cognitive Mobilization and Partisan Dealignment in Advanced Industrial Democracies', *Journal of Politics* 46 (1984), pp.264–84.
6. Kai Arzheimer, '"Dead Men Walking?" Party Identification in Germany, 1977–2002', *Electoral Studies* 25 (2006), pp.791–807.
7. Anja Neundorf, Daniel Stegmueller, and Thomas J. Scotto, 'The Individual-Level Dynamics of Bounded Partisanship', *Public Opinion Quarterly* 75/3 (2011), pp.458–82. doi: 10.1093/poq/nfr018.

8. Ruth Dassonneville, Marc Hooghe, and Bram Vanhoutte, 'Age, Period and Cohort Effects in the Decline of Party Identification in Germany: An Analysis of a Two Decade Panel Study in Germany (1992–2009)', *German Politics* 2 (2012), pp.209–27.
9. Russell J. Dalton, 'Interpreting Partisan Dealignment in Germany', *German Politics* 23/1–2 (2014), pp.134–44.
10. Jeremy J. Albright, 'Does Political Knowledge Erode Party Attachments? A Review of the Cognitive Mobilization Thesis', *Electoral Studies* 28/2 (2009), pp.248–260.
11. Kai Arzheimer and Harald Schoen, 'Erste Schritte auf kaum erschlossenem Terrain. Zur Stabilität der Parteiidentifikation in Deutschland', *Politische Vierteljahresschrift* 46 (2005), pp.629–54.
12. Arzheimer, '"Dead Men Walking?" Party Identification in Germany, 1977–2002'.
13. Ibid.
14. Patrick Royston and Willi Sauerbrei, *Multivariable Model-building: A Pragmatic Approach to Regression Analysis Based on Fractional Polynomials for Modelling Continuous Variables* (Chichester: Wiley, 2008).
15. Philip E. Converse, 'Of Time and Partisan Stability, *Comparative Political Studies* 2 (1969), pp.139–71.
16. Karen Oppenheim Mason et al., 'Some Methodological Issues in Cohort Analysis of Archival Data', *American Sociological Review* 38 (1973), pp.242–58.
17. Dassonneville et al., 'Age, Period and Cohort Effects in the Decline of Party Identification in Germany'.
18. Petra Buhr and Johannes Huinink, 'The German Low Fertility. How We Got There and What We Can Expect for the Future', *European Sociological Review* 31/2 (2015), pp.197–210.
19. Carsten Bluck and Henry Kreikenbom, 'Die Wähler in der DDR: Nur issue-orientiert oder auch parteigebunden?', *Zeitschrift für Parlamentsfragen* 22 (1991), pp.495–502.
20. R. Michael Alvarez and Jonathan Nagler, 'When Politics and Models Collide. Estimating Models of Multiparty Elections', *American Journal of Political Science* 42 (1998), pp.55–96.
21. J. Scott Long and Jeremy Freese, *Regression Models for Categorical Dependent Variables Using Stata*, 2nd ed. (College Station: Stata Press, 2006), p.307.
22. Kai Arzheimer, 'The AfD: Finally a Successful Right-Wing Populist Eurosceptic Party for Germany?', *West European Politics* 38 (2015), pp.535–56.
23. For the Greens, Trittin and Katrin Göring-Eckardt were joint frontrunners, but Trittin received many more votes in the internal ballot for the position and was much more prominent in the media, and the GLES did not even collect thermometer data for Göring-Eckardt. Similarly, Merkel as the sitting chancellor was treated as the only relevant candidate for the Christian Democrats, although technically Gerda Hasselfeldt, who topped the CSU's list, could also be deemed to have been a 'Spitzenkandidat'.
24. Taxes/welfare spending: 'And what is your own opinion regarding taxes and social welfare services? 0 – more benefits offered by the social state, even if this means an increase in taxation; 10 – lower taxes, even if this means a reduction in the benefits offered by the social state'. Immigration: 'And what is your opinion regarding immigration? 0 – immigration should be facilitated; 10 – immigration should be restricted'.
25. Long and Freese, *Regression Models for Categorical Dependent Variables Using Stata*, p.305.
26. Robert Rohrschneider, Rüdiger Schmitt-Beck, and Franziska Jung, 'Short-term Factors versus Long-term Values: Explaining the 2009 Election Results', *Electoral Studies* 31/1 (2012), pp.20–34.
27. Obviously, it would have been possible to estimate a single model for all of Germany by including appropriate interaction terms, but this would have introduced an additional layer of complexity.
28. Long and Freese, *Regression Models for Categorical Dependent Variables Using Stata*, p.111.
29. The correction suggested by Long and Freese yields a slightly lower rate of 72 per cent.
30. Dan Hough, Michael Koß, and Jonathan Olsen. *The Left Party in Contemporary German Politics* (Houndmills: Palgrave Macmillan, 2007).
31. Howard L. Reiter, 'Party Decline in the West. A Skeptic's View', *Journal of Theoretical Politics* 1 (1989), pp.325–48.
32. Arzheimer, '"Dead Men Walking?" Party Identification in Germany, 1977–2002'.
33. Dalton, 'Interpreting Partisan Dealignment in Germany', p.140.

Merkwürdig oder nicht? What Economic Voting Models and the 2013 Bundestag Elections Have to Say about Each Other

KATSUNORI SEKI and GUY D. WHITTEN

The 2013 Bundestag elections took place at a time when public opinion was strongly focused on a wide range of economic issues. But, given the coalition government and the complex array of policymakers whose hands were on the wheels of the German economy, some economic voting models would predict that the economy would play little role in deciding these elections. In this article, we use a mixture of aggregate and survey data to test what a range of different economic voting models predicted about the 2013 Bundestag elections and the extent to which these predictions were supported. The results from this exercise provide insights not only about the nature of the 2013 elections, but also about the applicability and adaptability of economic voting models to different political and economic circumstances.

INTRODUCTION

The vast literature on economic voting has demonstrated that the economy is a powerful force in national elections around the world.[1] But this literature has also demonstrated that there is substantial variation in terms of the strength of the basic economic voting relationship. In particular, economic voting has been shown to be strongest when responsibility for policymaking is most clear and weak to non-existent when responsibility for policymaking is not clear.[2]

In this article, we examine economic voting in the 2013 Bundestag elections. From a cross-national comparative perspective, this is an interesting case. On the one hand, responsibility for economic policymaking was not particularly clear in Germany in 2013. But, on the other hand, German voters have been demonstrated to be highly concerned with economic issues.[3] Between the sluggish performance of Germany's economy and the controversies over bailouts of other members of the Eurozone, the 2013 elections took place at a time when economic issues were clearly front and centre in the minds of the German public. Another key determinant in national elections, is the public's evaluation of political leaders and other valence voting considerations.[4] A study of the 2009 Bundestag elections showed that Angela Merkel and thus the Christian Democrats enjoyed a substantial advantage in terms of leadership evaluations.[5] In 2013, Merkel and the Christian Democrats enjoyed a similar advantage. Thus a key question is how did all of these different factors come together to shape the 2013 election outcome?

To answer this question, we use a mixture of aggregate and survey data to test what a range of different voting models predicted about the 2013 Bundestag elections and the extent to which these theoretical predictions were supported. The results from this exercise provide insights not only about the nature of the 2013 elections, but also about the applicability and adaptability of economic voting models to different political and economic circumstances. To put the election into a broader perspective, we start with a set of cross-national aggregate-level models and then focus on the micro-level forces that drive observed macro-level results through models of individual-level survey responses from German voters.

GERMAN ELECTIONS AND THE ECONOMY IN COMPARATIVE PERSPECTIVE

The first models of economic voting were estimated using measures of macro-economic performance to predict national vote percentages for incumbent politicians.[6] These early models, estimated mostly with data from either the United States or the United Kingdom, demonstrated support for the basic economic voting theory that the economy would exert an influence on the electoral fortunes of incumbent politicians. When such studies were expanded into more countries, however, the theory found only mixed empirical support.[7] Faced with the puzzle of why economic voting did not always occur in every nation and in every election year, scholars turned to institutional explanations and the theory of clarity of responsibility.[8] While scholars have differed in how they have measured clarity of responsibility, this theoretical proposition has found robust support across a multitude of different settings[9] – when responsibility for policymaking is clear, the economy is a powerful determinant of the vote, and, when responsibility for policymaking is less clear, the estimated impact of the economy has been weak to non-existent.

In order to assess the impact of the economy on the German elections in general and 2013 from a broad perspective, we turn to a set of models of economic voting across nations and over time. The general specification of these models is:

$$Vote_{it} = f(Vote_{it-1} + Economy_{it} \times Clarity_{it}).$$

Vote for the incumbents in election 'i' and time 't', $Vote_{it}$, is theorised to be a function of their vote in the previous election, $Vote_{it-1}$, plus recent economic performance, $Economy_{it}$, interacted with clarity of responsibility, $Clarity_{it}$. In order to test this model in the context of the German 2013 elections, we rely on data from another paper[10] which we have extended to include Germany in 2013.[11] These data include 280 elections from the 1960s up through 2012 in 21 established democracies with advanced economies plus data from the Germany 2013 elections.[12] Scholars have generally found that economic voting evidence is strongest for the party of the chief executive.[13] Thus we use two different measures of incumbent vote, one which is constructed by summing the percentage of the popular vote cast for each party in a governing coalition and a second in which we use only the percentage of votes cast for the party of the chief executive.[14]

For our measures of the economy, we use measures of what are known in economic voting as the 'big three' – growth, inflation and unemployment. For our measure of growth and inflation, we followed the example of Palmer and Whitten of creating both regular versions of these variables and unexpected versions.[15] The unexpected versions of each variable are calculated by subtracting the actual value of each indicator from the predicted value from an autoregressive nation-specific business cycle model of that indicator.[16] The theoretical logic behind these measures is that, depending on the economic circumstances in which voters find themselves, they will have expectations for both growth and inflation. Governments will then be rewarded for how the economy performs relative to these expectations. In our models, we consistently found that a regular measure of growth outperformed our unexpected growth measure while our unexpected inflation outperformed our regular inflation measure. We thus specified the economy in our models as growth, unexpected inflation and unemployment.

We have followed the lead of earlier articles to measure clarity of responsibility.[17] We first collected data on five key factors that obscure responsibility for policymaking: politically relevant bicameral opposition, politically relevant cohabitation, minority government, caretaker government and the number of governing parties. We then used these variables to divide cases into two categories – if a government was a caretaker or a minority, faced politically relevant bicameral opposition, or politically relevant cohabitation it was coded as being unclear. Otherwise, we coded cases as having clear responsibility. In order to account for the role of the number of government parties in obscuring clarity of responsibility, we added this variable to our model specifications when we modelled the vote for all parties in the government.[18] Ten of the 14 German elections that are covered by our data were classified as being 'not clear'. The main reason for this was opposition control of a majority of the seats in the Bundesrat.

In Table 1 we display the results from four different models of aggregate-level economic voting across nations and over time. Together Models 1 and 3, in which votes for all governing parties are lumped together, are essentially a replication of the basic models of cross-national economic voting that were estimated by Powell and Whitten and Palmer and Whitten.[19] In Models 2 and 4, we follow the same specification except that the dependent variable is the votes for only the party of the chief executive. Across all four models in Table 1, the unit of analysis is a single election in one nation. These results show robust support for the basic clarity of responsibility argument; when responsibility for policymaking is clear, there is strong evidence of economic voting, and, when responsibility is not clear there is little to no evidence of economic voting. We see this general pattern in both the models of vote for all government parties (Models 1 and 3) and the models of vote for only the party of the chief executive (Models 2 and 4). In the models with clear responsibility, the parameter estimates for all six economic indicators are statistically significantly in the expected direction.[20] In the models estimated on elections where responsibility was not clear, only the effect of growth on vote for all government parties is statistically significant. While some evidence of economic voting in less than clear cases is not a refutation of the clarity of responsibility theory, the strength of this particular estimate is somewhat surprising.

Having found strong support for the clarity of responsibility theory in this updated sample of data from established democracies, we now turn to an assessment of what is going on inside these models in terms of German cases in general and 2013 in particular. At the bottom of Table 1, we report the average absolute value of the model's error

TABLE 1
CROSS-NATIONAL MODELS OF ECONOMIC VOTING

Independent variable	Clear responsibility		Not clear	
	Model 1	Model 2	Model 3	Model 4
Lagged Vote	0.86**	0.81**	0.87**	0.92**
	(0.05)	(0.04)	(0.09)	(0.04)
Growth	0.23†	0.31*	0.58*	0.27
	(0.12)	(0.12)	(0.21)	(0.20)
Unexpected inflation	−1.63**	−1.54**	0.21	0.24
	(0.47)	(0.40)	(0.48)	(0.40)
Unemployment	−0.57**	−0.44**	−0.16	−0.21
	(0.16)	(0.13)	(0.15)	(0.15)
Number of govt parties	1.14†		−0.52	
	(0.34)		(0.47)	
Constant	2.89	4.92*	3.80	2.33
	(2.77)	(1.48)	(3.47)	(2.11)
Dependent variable	All parties	Chief party	All parties	Chief party
R^2	.81	.74	.64	.74
N	151	151	129	129
Absolute average error	4.36	3.86	4.24	3.91
Absolute average error Germany	4.89	2.58	3.53	3.07

Notes:
** $= p < .01,$; * $= p < .05,$; † $= p < .1$ (two-tailed, despite directional hypotheses).
Heteroscedasticity-robust standard errors are reported underneath OLS parameter estimates. Sample includes elections from the 1960s through 2012 in 21 established democracies, plus Germany in 2013. More details on this are provided in the online appendix. At the bottom of this table we report the average model error for all cases included in each model and for all of the German cases included in each model.

estimates for all observations and for the German cases.[21] We can see from these values that the German cases are fit pretty well by the model's estimates. To get a closer look at the accuracy of our models for the German elections, we plot the prediction errors in Figure 1 from the models of vote for all parties and Figure 2 from the models of vote for the party of the chief executive. The horizontal line across both Figures 1 and 2 identifies a value of zero for the difference between the actual vote measure and the corresponding model's predictions for a particular case. Thus in both figures, a point on the line indicates a perfect prediction, a point above the line indicates that the vote for the parties (in Figure 1) or party (in Figure 2) was higher than expected, and a point below the line indicates that vote for the parties or party was lower than expected. In both figures, the values for cases for which the predicted vote was estimated using the clear responsibility models are identified by open circles while the values for cases for which the predicted vote was estimated using the not clear responsibility models are identified by solid circles.

From Figures 1 and 2, we can confirm that these models generally fit German cases quite well and that there is a general pattern of German governing parties doing better than we would expect based on the models presented in Table 1. Turning to the specific case of 2013, we can see that the combined vote for the Christian Democrats and the FDP was 2.7 percentage points above what would be expected based on our model. Compared with other elections, this was not a particularly noteworthy result. However, when we examine the predictions versus expectations for the Chancellors'

FIGURE 1
GOVERNING PARTIES MODEL PREDICTIONS 1965–2013

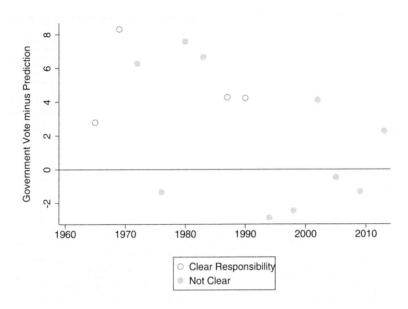

FIGURE 2
CHIEF MODEL PREDICTIONS 1965–2013

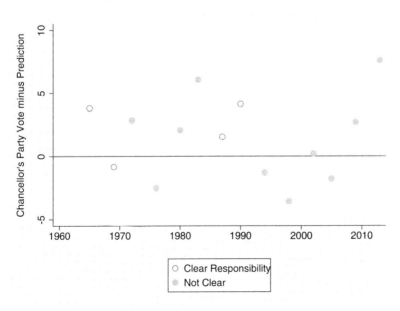

parties in Germany in Figure 2, we see that 2013 was a truly exceptional result with votes for the Christian Democrats being 7.6 percentage points above what would be expected based on our model. This is the largest error for our model of vote for the Chancellors' parties across the entire sample of German cases with the next closest case being the Christian Democrats' performance in 1983 under Helmut Kohl when their vote percentage beat model expectations by 6.1 percentage points.

To develop a deeper understanding of our models of the economy and German elections, in Figures 3 through 9 we provide a series of scatter plots with change in the value of one of our two dependent variables on the vertical axis and one of our economic independent variables on the horizontal axis.[22] Throughout these figures, we follow the convention of depicting the values from elections with clear responsibility with an open circle and depicting the values from elections with not clear responsibility models with a solid circle. We also display the linear fit lines for each set of cases.

At first glance, Figure 3 appears to provide strong evidence of economic voting in Germany regardless of whether or not there was clarity of responsibility. The pairwise correlation across all 15 elections depicted in Figure 3 is strong ($r = .57$) and statistically significant ($p = .03$), and the two linear fit lines are almost identical. This general trend is driven largely by the nearly linear relationship between growth and change in government vote in the four clear responsibility cases ($r = .97$, $p = .02$). The positive correlation between growth and change in government vote among not clear cases ($r = .44$, $p = .14$) actually becomes slightly negative ($r = -.02$) and is statistically insignificant ($p = .96$) when we remove 2009, as we depict in Figure 4. In Figure 5 we see

FIGURE 3
CHANGE IN GOVERNMENT VOTE AND GROWTH IN GERMAN ELECTIONS

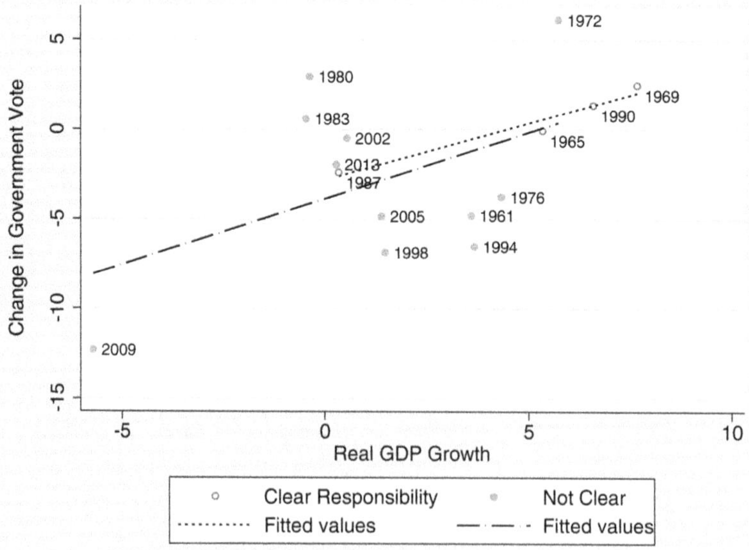

the same general patterns between changes in votes for the Chancellor's party and growth. For the four elections where responsibility for policymaking was clear, we continue to see a positive relationship (r = .64), but one which is not statistically significant (*p* = .35) with only four observations. In cases where responsibility is not clear, we see a slight negative relationship (r = −.16) which is also not statistically significant (*p* = .64).

In Figure 6 we see a somewhat puzzling relationship between unexpected inflation and government vote for the 11 cases where responsibility was not clear. Contrary to expectations, this relationship is positive (.57) and on the borderline in terms of statistical significance (*p* = .07). The relationship between unexpected inflation and government vote among the clear responsibility cases is in the expected negative direction (r = −.37) but is far from statistically significant (*p* = .63). In Figure 7 we see similarly puzzling results for the relationship between unexpected inflation and votes for the Chancellor's party. Both pairwise correlations are positive (r = .24 for not clear cases and r = .60 for clear cases) although neither relationship is statistically significant (*p* = .50 for not clear cases and *p* = .40 for clear cases).

The relationships between unemployment and vote depicted in Figures 8 and 9 are much more consistent with theoretical expectations. First, in Figure 8 we see a strong negative overall relationship (−.65) between unemployment and government vote that is statistically significant (*p* = .01). We see nearly identical relationships across cases when we divide them in terms of clarity of responsibility (*r* = −.63 for not clear cases and r = −.57 for clear cases), though there is the expected divergence in terms of statistical significance given the different sample sizes (*p* = .05 for not clear cases

FIGURE 4

CHANGE IN GOVERNMENT VOTE AND GROWTH IN GERMAN ELECTIONS OTHER THAN 2009

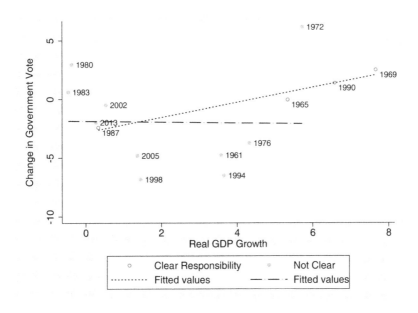

FIGURE 5
CHANGE IN CHANCELLOR'S PARTY VOTE AND GROWTH IN GERMAN ELECTIONS

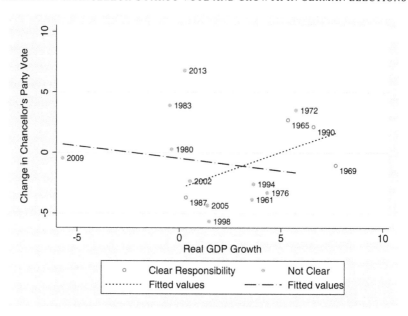

FIGURE 6
CHANGE IN GOVERNMENT VOTE AND UNEXPECTED INFLATION IN GERMAN ELECTIONS

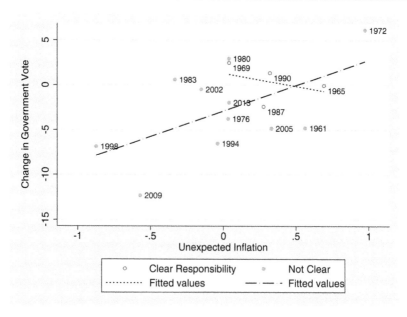

and $p = .48$ for clear cases). In Figure 9 we see a slightly less strong negative overall relationship $(-.49)$ between unemployment and government vote that is on the borderline of statistical significance $(p = .08)$. And again we see nearly identical relationships across cases when we divide them in terms of clarity of responsibility $(r = -.52$ for not clear cases and $r = -.54$ for clear cases), with the expected divergence in terms of statistical significance given the different sample sizes $(p = .12$ for not clear cases and $p = .46$ for clear cases).

Together Figures 1 through 9 indicate that Germany fits in pretty well with the cross-national models of economic voting presented in Table 1. Although we have only four German cases in our sample for which there was clear responsibility, those cases provide strong evidence of economic voting. This is especially the case for Model 1 in Table 1 where the dependent variable is the combined vote for all government parties. The economic voting results for the 11 cases with less clear responsibility are, as expected, less clear. But these cases also seem to conform more with economic voting expectations when the dependent variable is the combined vote for all government parties (Model 3 in Table 1).

Throughout Figures 1 to 9 we see an interesting pattern emerging in terms of what happened in the 2013 German elections. We consistently see that in visual depictions of change in the combined government vote (Figures 1, 3, 4, 6 and 8), 2013 is not a particularly noteworthy case. The same can certainly not be said about 2013 in our visual depictions of changes in the vote for the Chancellor's party (Figures 2, 5, 7 and 9). In 2013, the Christian Democrats under Angela Merkel managed to achieve

FIGURE 7

CHANGE IN CHANCELLOR'S PARTY VOTE AND UNEXPECTED INFLATION IN GERMAN ELECTIONS

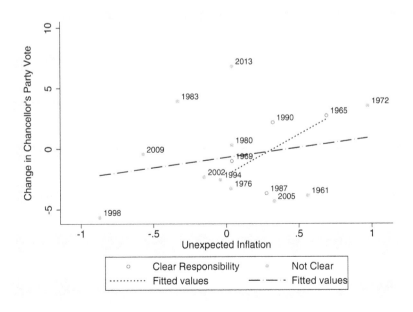

FIGURE 8
CHANGE IN GOVERNMENT VOTE AND UNEMPLOYMENT IN GERMAN ELECTIONS

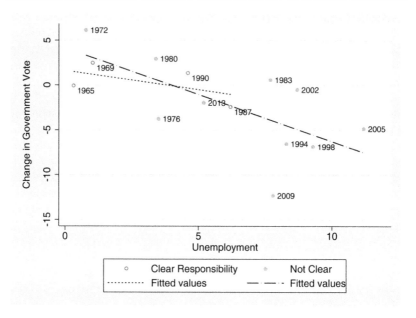

FIGURE 9
CHANGE IN CHANCELLOR'S PARTY VOTE AND UNEMPLOYMENT IN GERMAN ELECTIONS

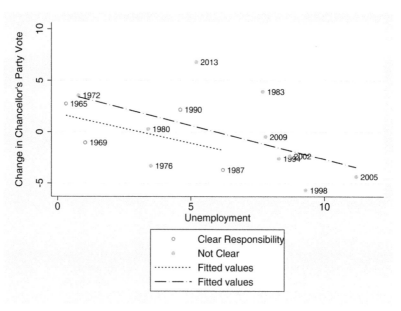

the greatest gains for a German Chancellor's party in our sample despite a relatively poor growth performance and poor to middling performances in terms of unexpected inflation and unemployment. So, what was the secret of the Christian Democrats' success in 2013? One possible answer is provided by Clarke and Whitten who found that in 2009 a major reason for the Christian Democrats' success was their substantial advantage in leadership evaluations despite the poor state of the German economy going into that election.[23] This finding was consistent with the findings of other researchers of growing effects of candidate evaluations in German voting behaviour.[24] Might the same factors have helped to create the Christian Democrats' substantial gains in 2013? To attempt to answer this question, we turn to an individual-level model of survey data collected around the 2013 elections.

THE MICRO-FOUNDATIONS OF ECONOMIC VOTING IN 2013

In this section we try to unravel the puzzle of why the Christian Democrats gained substantial support in 2013 despite a collection of macro-economic performance measures that were poor to middling. To do this, we replicate the analyses of Clarke and Whitten which were performed on survey data collected at the time of the 2009 election.[25] For our purposes, there are important similarities between and differences across these two cases. In terms of similarities, in both cases Angela Merkel was the incumbent Chancellor heading a coalition government which governed without a majority in the Bundesrat. Thus responsibility for policymaking was not clear. In both cases, the German economy was in poor shape, although it was clearly worse in 2009 than in 2013. One other major difference between 2009 and 2013 was the Christian Democrats' coalition partner going into the elections. In 2009, it was the second largest party, the SPD, and thus the major opponent for control of the chancellery while in 2013 it was the FDP.

For our analyses in this section, we use data from the German Longitudinal Election Study.[26] In Table 2 we present a cross-table of respondents' evaluations of how the national economy and their personal economic situation had changed in the last one to two years. The modal response to both questions was that things had stayed the same. Given the general weakness of the German economy, these sentiments are not favourable for the electoral prospects of incumbent politicians. Where was public opinion on the major valence issues? As we discussed above, one of the main findings of Clarke

TABLE 2
NATIONAL AND PERSONAL RETROSPECTIVE ECONOMIC EVALUATIONS IN 2013

	National			
Personal	**Better**	**Same**	**Worse**	**Row total**
Much better	0.5	0.8	0.1	1.4
Better	4.9	8.5	1.6	14.9
Same	11.6	43.6	6.2	61.4
Worse	3.1	10.4	5.4	18.9
Much worse	0.4	1.5	1.5	3.4
Column total	20.5	64.8	14.7	100.0

Note: Cell entries are percentages.

and Whitten was that in 2009 Angela Merkel enjoyed a substantial advantage in terms of her ratings relative to the SPD leader, Frank-Walter Steinmeier, and the leaders of all of the other major political parties, and that leadership effects were large in 2009.[27] In Figure 10 we see that Merkel enjoyed a similar advantage in 2013. In fact, the gap between Merkel and the second-highest rated leader in 2013, 1.1 points, is slightly larger than the gap that Merkel enjoyed over Steinmeier in 2009. In Figures 11 and 12, we can see that, as was the case in 2009, the Christian Democrats also enjoyed a substantial advantage over all other parties in terms of party identification and being the party most frequently identified as the best at dealing with the problems that respondents identified as the most important. How did these factors affect individual-level voting decisions?

To answer this question, we replicated the analyses of Clarke and Whitten.[28] We first estimated a series of logistic regression models of rival specifications with the dependent variable being individual vote choice.[29] As we can see from Table 3, we find a pattern identical to Clarke and Whitten in terms of the progression of model fit.[30] That is, we find that a valence politics model, comprised of partisan identification, evaluations of which party would best handle the most important issues facing the nation and leadership evaluations, outperforms rival models in terms of fit. We also find that the best model fit for vote on both sides of the German ballot comes from a composite model that contains independent variables reflecting all four rival models: socio-demographics; economic evaluations; left–right proximity scores; and valence politics.[31]

Our findings from composite models are consistent with the findings of Clarke and Whitten.[32] In order to get a better handle on the substantive implications of these

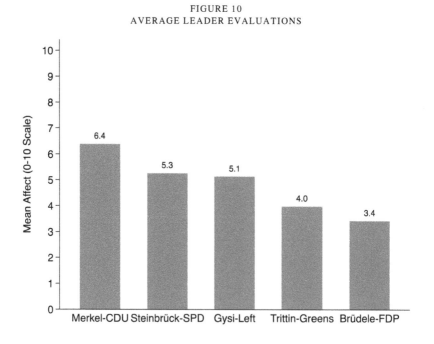

FIGURE 10
AVERAGE LEADER EVALUATIONS

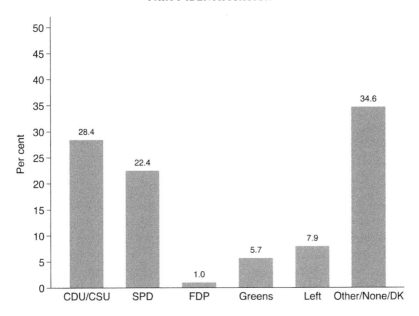

FIGURE 11
PARTY IDENTIFICATION

complicated models, we now turn to graphical presentations of the average marginal effects in Figure 13.[33] Not too surprisingly, we see in this figure that identifying with a political party is a very strong predictor of voting for that party. The next

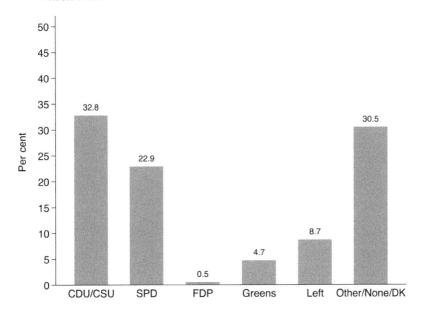

FIGURE 12
WHICH PARTY IS BEST AT HANDLING THE MOST IMPORTANT ISSUE?

TABLE 3
FIT OF RIVAL MODELS

Model	List vote McFadden R^2	AIC	Methods
Socio-demographics	.07	3001.7626	ML
Economic evaluations	.01	3508.6475	ML
Left–Right proximity	.26	1884.1413	CL
Valence politics	.63	983.8672	MXL
Composite	.67	934.6324	MXL

Notes: ML: Multinomial Logit; CL: Conditional Logit; MXL: Mixed Logit
Composite model includes socio-demographics (age, gender, income, region), economic evaluations (retrospective egotropic and sociotropic evaluation), left–right self-party proximities and valence politics variables (leader image, party best able to handle most important issue, party identification).

strongest marginal effects are the leadership evaluations, with the effects for the only two parties that have controlled the Chancellorship in recent years being the strongest. When we combine this evidence with the lead that we see Chancellor Merkel enjoyed over Peer Steinbrück, displayed in Figure 10, we can see that leadership effects played a major role. Similarly, we can see in this figure that being the party rated best on the most important issue had strong effects, particularly for the two largest parties. In summary, the Christian Democrats were ahead of their opponents on every valence issue in 2013 and these variables appear to have had major effects on individual-

FIGURE 13
MARGINAL EFFECTS – PARTY LIST VOTE

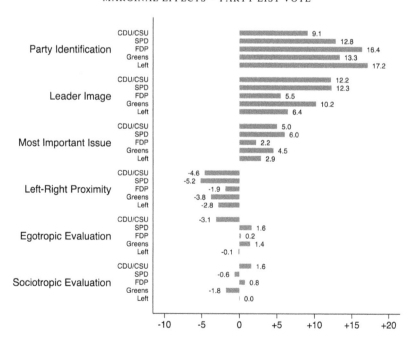

level voting choices. The effects for our proximity measures are substantial in the expected direction – the further a respondent placed a party from their own ideological position, the less likely they were to support that party. When controlling for all of these factors and socio-demographic characteristics, we find that the effects of economic evaluations were quite modest in 2013.

As a final check for the influence of economic factors, and consistent with the analyses by Clarke and Whitten, we also estimated a model of evaluations of Angela Merkel.[34] Both measures of retrospective economic evaluations have statistically significant and substantively strong effects, with the effects of the national/sociotropic measure being substantially larger than the effects for the personal/egotropic measure. Given that this dependent variable is an 11-point scale, the coefficients of .46 for sociotropic evaluations and .27 for egotropic evaluations are quite large. Respondents with better evaluations of the economy also have better evaluations of Angela Merkel.[35]

In summary, our individual-level analyses indicate that, despite the poor to middling state of the German economy in 2013, the Christian Democrats were able to increase their vote because they had strong leads over their opponents on all three valence politics measures. To the extent that individual economic evaluations mattered, they appear to have worked their way through these valence measures.

CONCLUSION

Although the clarity of responsibility theory of economic voting has been demonstrated to be quite robust, there is still a fair amount of work to be done in the study of economic voting. Cases like the German election of 2013 help to underscore this point. Essentially, what this cross-national theory of political behaviour gives us for cases like Germany in 2013, where responsibility for policymaking is not clear, is a prediction about what is not going to happen, or what is likely to not matter very much. Our evidence at both the aggregate and individual levels confirms this expectation, but this is clearly suboptimal. We want to be in the business of explaining what *does* happen in elections.

Our individual-level analyses of survey data point to one possible way forward. We have demonstrated, consistent with Clarke and Whitten,[36] that valence variables were the main drivers of individual-level vote choice in 2013 and that, to the extent economic evaluations mattered, it was indirectly through their influence on these valence evaluations. But as a lively debate has demonstrated, cross-sectional survey-based models like these are subject to questions about the direction of the causal arrow.[37] Although instrumental variables strategies might be a way to refute such claims,[38] a more satisfying path is through aggregate-level time series studies in which we can model the evolution of valence evaluations over time. While studies along these lines have been carried out in a number of clear responsibility cases,[39] they have not yet been carried out in settings like Germany where responsibility is usually not clear. Ultimately, in order to engage the broader literature on cross-national economic voting, these studies need to be carried out in a mixture of clarity settings.

In conclusion, the answer to the question posed in the title of our article, is both 'nein' and 'ja'. On the one hand, the German elections in 2013 were not remarkable because responsibility for policymaking was not clear and there was scant evidence of economic voting. On the other hand, though, the advantage that Angela Merkel and the Christian Democrats built up on all dimensions of valence politics in 2013 was quite remarkable and is worthy of further scholarly attention.

ACKNOWLEDGEMENTS

The authors thank Robert Rohrschneider and Rüdiger Schmitt-Beck for organising this special edition and for their helpful suggestions for our article. Despite their help, we take full responsibility for any remaining errors.

DISCLOSURE STATEMENT

No potential conflict of interest was reported by the authors.

SUPPLEMENTAL DATA AND RESEARCH MATERIALS

Supplementary documents and replication files associated with this article can be found on the authors' own websites: http://sites.google.com/site/katsunoriseki/home; and http://pols.tamu.edu/about-us/faculty-directory/guy-d-whitten-professor/, respectively.

NOTES

1. For reviews of this vast literature, see Michael S. Lewis-Beck and Mary Stegmaier, 'Economic Models of Voting', in Russell Dalton and Hans-Dieter Klingemann (eds), *The Oxford Handbook of Political Behavior* (Oxford: Oxford University Press, 2007), pp.518–37 and Timothy Hellwig, 'Elections and the Economy', in Lawrence LeDuc, Richard G. Niemi and Pippa Norris (eds), *Comparing Democracies: Elections and Voting in the 21st Century* (London: Sage, 2010), pp.184–202.
2. G. Bingham Powell, Jr and Guy D. Whitten, 'A Cross-National Analysis of Economic Voting: Taking Account of the Political Context', *American Journal of Political Science* 37/2 (1993), pp.391–414; Christopher J. Anderson, *Blaming the Government: Citizens and the Economy in Five European Democracies* (New York: M.E. Sharpe, 1995); Raymond Duch and Randolph T. Stevenson, *The Economic Vote: How Political and Economic Institutions Condition Election Results* (Cambridge: Cambridge University Press, 2008).
3. E.g. Christopher J. Anderson and Jason D. Hecht, 'Voting When the Economy Goes Bad, Everyone is in Charge, and No One Is to Blame: The Case of the 2009 German Election', *Electoral Studies* 31/1 (2012), pp.5–19.

4. Donald E. Stokes, 'Spatial Models of Party Competition', *American Political Science Review* 57/2 (1963), pp.368–77; Harold D. Clarke and Marianne C. Stewart, 'Economic Evaluations, Prime Ministerial Approval and Governing Party Support: Rival Models Reconsidered', *British Journal of Political Science* 25/2 (1995), pp.145–70; Harold D. Clarke, Allan Kornberg and Thomas J. Scotto, *Making Political Choices: Canada and the United States* (Toronto: University of Toronto Press, 2009).
5. Harold D. Clarke and Guy D. Whitten, 'Hard Choices in Hard Times: Valence Voting in Germany (2009)', *Electoral Studies* 32/3 (2013), pp.445–51.
6. E.g. C.A.E. Goodhart and R.J. Bhansali, 'Political Economy', *Political Studies* 18/1 (1970), pp.43–106; Gerald H. Kramer, 'Short-Term Fluctuations in U.S. Voting Behavior,1896–1964', *American Political Science Review* 65/1 (1971), pp.131–43; Ray C. Fair, 'The Effects of Economic Events on Votes for Presidents', *Review of Economics and Statistics* 60/2 (1978), pp.159–72.
7. Martin Paldam, 'How Robust Is the Vote Function? A Study of Seventeen Nations over Four Decades', in Helmut Norpoth, Michael S. Lewis-Beck and Jean-Dominique Lafay (eds), *Economics and Politics: The Calculus of Support* (Ann Arbor, MI: University of Michigan Press, 1991), pp.9–31; Michael S. Lewis-Beck, 'Comparative Economic Voting: Britain, France, Germany, Italy', *American Journal of Political Science* 30/2 (1986), pp.315–46.
8. Powell and Whitten, 'A Cross-National Analysis'.
9. Anderson, *Blaming the Government*; Timothy Hellwig and David Samuels, 'Electoral Accountability and the Variety of Democratic Regimes', *British Journal of Political Science* 38/1 (2008), pp.65–90; Duch and Stevenson, *The Economic Vote*.
10. Katsunori Seki and Guy D. Whitten, 'Clarity in Chaos? Economic Voting in Transitional Polities', unpublished manuscript (2015).
11. Our data set was constructed by incorporating measures of clarity of responsibility as well as election results in a data set on governments that was collected by Katsunori Seki and Laron K. Williams, 'Updating the *Party Government* Data Set', *Electoral Studies* 34 (2014), pp.270–9.
12. The countries included in these data are Australia, Austria, Belgium, Canada, Denmark, Finland, France, Germany, Greece, Ireland, Italy, Japan, Netherlands, New Zealand, Norway, Portugal, Spain, Sweden, Switzerland, United Kingdom and United States. Further details on all measurement and sample decisions are discussed in Seki and Whitten, 'Clarity in Chaos?'.
13. See, for instance, Duch and Stevenson, *The Economic Vote* and Laron K. Williams and Guy D. Whitten, 'Don't Stand So Close to Me: Spatial Contagion Effects and Party Competition', *American Journal of Political Science* 59/2 (2015), pp.309–25.
14. For cases of single party government, these measures are identical. For our popular vote measure in German elections, we use party votes.
15. Harvey D. Palmer and Guy D. Whitten, 'The Electoral Impact of Unexpected Inflation and Economic Growth', *British Journal of Political Science* 29/4 (1999), pp.623–39.
16. As we discuss in Seki and Whitten, 'Clarity in Chaos?', this is a form of benchmarking. For each indicator, we developed country-specific quarterly models specified as $Y_t = \gamma_1 + \gamma_2 Y_t + \gamma_3(Y_{t-1} - Y_{t-5}) + \delta_1 Q2_t + \delta_2 Q3_t + \delta_3 Q4_t + \varepsilon_t$ where Y is the economic indicator, and Q2, Q3 and Q4 are dummy variables identifying quarters. For more details on benchmarking, see Mark Andreas Kayser and Michael Peress, 'Benchmarking across Borders: Electoral Accountability and the Necessity of Comparison', *American Political Science Review* 106/3 (2012), pp.661–84.
17. E.g. Powell and Whitten, 'A Cross-National Analysis'.
18. In our online appendix, we include a table in which we display the component measures for clarity and the clarity classification for each German national election that is included in our sample of cases. We do not display cohabitation because Germany is widely classified as having a parliamentary system of government in which the President's role is politically minor. For the purpose of counting the number of coalition parties, we make an adjustment for cases where ideological blocks of parties do not compete against each other in agreed-upon geographic areas. Thus, for the purpose of measuring this indicator of clarity of responsibility, the CDU and the CSU count as a single party.
19. Ibid.; Palmer and Whitten, 'The Electoral Impact'.
20. Some readers might quibble with the designation of the estimated effect of growth in Model 1 as statistically significant since the two-tailed p-value is between .05 and .10. However, given that we have a strong directional hypothesis for the effect of growth, a one-tailed t-test is in order and the p-value for that test is less than .05.
21. This is different from the root mean squared error (RMSE) calculations that are commonly reported as regression model output. RMSE calculations include degree of freedom adjustments which would be large given the small number of cases involved in the Germany-specific calculations. Our measure is more appropriate since we want to get only a rough indication of how the model fits the German calculations and are not making any assessments about statistical significance.

22. For each of these plots, we subtract the percentage of votes for that group of parties or single party from the percentage of votes that they obtained in the previous election.
23. Clarke and Whitten, 'Hard Choices in Hard Times', pp.447–8.
24. E.g. Robert Rohrschneider, Rüdiger Schmitt-Beck and Franziska Jung, 'Short-Term Factors versus Long-Term Values: Explaining the 2009 Election Results', *Electoral Studies* 31/1 (2012), pp.20–34.
25. Clarke and Whitten, 'Hard Choices in Hard Times'.
26. Hans Rattinger, Sigrid Roßteutscher, Rüdiger Schmitt-Beck, Bernhard Weßels and Christof Wolf, *Post-Election Cross-Section (GLES 2013)* (GESIS Data Archive, Cologne, 2014. ZA5701 Data File Version 2.0.0).
27. Clarke and Whitten, 'Hard Choices in Hard Times', pp.447–8.
28. Ibid., pp.449–50.
29. The full results from these analyses are available from the authors upon request.
30. Ibid., p.449.
31. Estimation results that use constituency-level votes as the dependent variable are available in the online appendix.
32. Ibid., p.449. We present numerical results from models with both the list vote and constituency vote as the dependent variable in our online appendix. Valence voting model specifications such as these are frequently critiqued over the possibility of some of the indicators being endogenous. This is difficult to test for or rule out in the context of a model estimated with survey data collected at a single time period. Evidence from time series data are better suited for testing for the endogeneity of such models and there is substantial evidence from time series analyses that these same valence variables are weakly exogenous. See, for instance, Harold D. Clarke, David Sanders, Marianne C. Stewart and Paul F. Whiteley, *Performance Politics and the British Voter* (Cambridge: Cambridge University Press, 2009).
33. The bars in each of these figures were produced by first calculating for each respondent the change in their probability of voting for the relevant party when we shift the relevant independent variable. We then calculate the average of these changes across all respondents. The shifts in independent variables were as follows: 0 to 1 for the dummy variables (party identification and party best on the most important issue), one standard deviation shifts for the continuous variables (leader ratings and left-right proximity) and one-unit shifts in the ordinal variables (egotropic and sociotropic retrospective evaluations).
34. Clarke and Whitten, 'Hard Choices in Hard Times'. These full results from this model are presented in our online appendix.
35. But, as we discuss in the conclusion, results along these lines have come under attack for the possibility that they are endogenous.
36. Ibid., pp.449–50.
37. Geoffrey Evans and Robert Andersen, 'The Political Conditioning of Economic Perceptions', *Journal of Politics* 68/1 (2006), pp.194–207; Geoffrey Evans and Mark Pickup, 'Reversing the Causal Arrow: The Political Conditioning of Economic Perceptions in the 2000–2004 US Presidential Election Cycle', *Journal of Politics* 72/4 (2010), pp.1236–51.
38. Michael S. Lewis-Beck, Nicholas F. Martini and D. Roderick Kiewiet, 'The Nature of Economic Perceptions in Mass Publics', *Electoral Studies* 32/3 (2013), pp.524–8.
39. Clarke et al., *Making Political Choices*; Clarke et al., *Performance Politics and the British Voter*.

Party Positions about European Integration in Germany: An Electoral Quandary?

ROBERT ROHRSCHNEIDER and
STEPHEN WHITEFIELD

Given the rise of EU-scepticism in Germany and elsewhere, spatial models suggest that the SPD and the CDU/CSU have incentives to move towards a more critical position about integration. However, mainstream parties have developed a pro-integration reputation over several decades so it is difficult for them to adopt a stance reflecting outright opposition to Europe's integration. A comparison of party positions in 2008 and 2013 shows that the SPD hardly changed its policy stances on EU issues, whereas the CDU/CSU moved noticeably to a more EU-critical stance. However, situating German parties within the West European universe of party families shows that both remain quite positive about integration. The upshot of this is to illustrate the 'blind corner' of party representation on integration issues in the German party system which created electoral opportunities for the Euro-sceptic AfD.

INTRODUCTION

Does the EU's economic crisis prompt mainstream parties in Germany to appeal to EU-sceptical voters? It would appear that Europe's crisis provides especially the SPD and the CDU/CSU with incentives to become more critical about the EU. Public opinion in Germany (and elsewhere) has clearly shifted towards a more critical view about Europe's integration as financial rescue policies may substantially drain Germany's resources if a troubled country defaults on her debt, the EU's effectiveness as a competent actor is being undermined and national resentment against the perceived profligacy of governments in crisis countries generated a backlash against further financial support Therefore, we ask: to what extend have mainstream parties modified their programmes about European integration? Have they moved with the German public towards a more EU-critical stance? Or is the articulation of an EU-sceptical position in the German party system left to Die Linke and the newly formed Alternative for Germany (AfD)? A first goal is to describe the programmatic stances of Germany's party system on European integration between 2008 and 2013 on the basis of two expert surveys.

Theoretically, we are motivated to examine parties' programmatic behaviour about European integration on the basis of two conflicting perspectives. First, spatial models suggest that political parties have incentives to move where voters position themselves programmatically. If this is the case, then mainstream parties in Germany (and elsewhere) have clear incentives to become more EU-sceptical.[1] The near-entry of the

AfD into the Bundestag in 2013 highlights the resentment many voters harbour against the way that the EU structured financial bailout packages. Moreover, its rise means that criticisms of the EU at the party level are articulated in public debates not just by individual party members within the established parties (as occurred within the CDU and the FDP) but now it is possible to vote for a party that is devoted to achieve an exit from the Euro.

Another set of incentives, however, follows from the historically grown reputation of mainstream parties as unwavering promoters of Europe's integration, as well as their issue ownership on domestic cleavages. Reputationally, parties face clear incentives to remain supportive of the EU given that they were instrumental in creating the 'permissive consensus' – a ubiquitous agreement that integration is desirable – which provided the support required to develop Europe's integrated market up to the 1970s and, more recently and precariously, to advance Europe's ambitious attempt to unify the continent politically.[2] Since the SPD or the CDU/CSU have been part of every government since 1949, it is difficult for them to run away from their historically grown pro-EU stance. [3] As a consequence, major parties have good reasons to stay programmatically on a pro-integration position because they promoted the 'ever closer union' of Europe during much of the post-war era. In addition, mainstream parties have incentives to compete on familiar divisions (primarily economic) and eschew conflicts where they may be internally divided, like integration. Thus, in contrast to the spatial mechanisms, reputational imperatives predict that the SPD and the CDU/CSU maintain their support for Europe's integration several years into the crisis.

On the basis of the German case – and using two expert surveys conducted in Germany (and elsewhere) in the spring of 2008 and 2013[4] – we will shed light on which of these conflicting mechanisms more aptly describes the programmatic position of Germany's parties on European integration. The results show that the SPD continues to support integration as does the CDU/CSU, though we will also see show that the CDU/CSU has moved a bit more towards a more muted support for integration over time, presumably in response to the rise of the AfD. Still, in comparison to other Christian Democrats in Western Europe, our analyses show that the Union remains steadfastly supportive of the EU. We recognise that a two-wave panel survey of party positions generates limited evidence of how much party positions change over time and we therefore do not wish to overstate our results. We would argue, however, that two reasons support our argument that the findings are of theoretical significance. First, the substantial drop in support for Europe's integration among the German public (see Table 1) provides parties with clear incentives to respond to these opinion movements. The permissive consensus that undergirded Europe's integration has clearly given way to a 'restrained dissent'[5] which means that political integration is considerably more controversial than economic integration has ever been. If parties choose not to address the shift in public opinion, it does point to the potential for underrepresentation of voters' preferences on this salient political issue. Second, as our analyses will show, one party – the CSU – has begun to cautiously respond to these pressures and, moreover, other parties of the Christian Democratic party family in Europe are also moving noticeably towards an EU-sceptical position. There is therefore nothing 'natural' about the lack of response among Germany's mainstream parties we find in our study – parties have a choice and, in most cases, they opted for stasis.

TABLE 1
PUBLIC SUPPORT FOR EUROPEAN INTEGRATION IN GERMANY, 2009–14 (%)

Germany's membership in the EU is:			Integration has gone:		
	2009	*2014*		*2009*	*2014*
Good	77.7	68.5	Too far	34.2	42.5
Neither	15.8	23.8	Neutral	22	21.3
Bad	6.5	7.8	Push further	43.8	35.2
N	999	1624		999	1559

Membership: 'Generally speaking, do you think that (OUR COUNTRY)'s membership of the EU is ... ?'
Integration pace: 'Some say European unification should be pushed further. Others say it already has gone too far. What is your opinion? Please indicate your views using a scale from 0 to 10, where "0" means unification "has already gone too far" and "10" means it "should be pushed further". What number on this scale best describes your position?' Too far (0–4); neutral (5), push further (6–10).
Sources: European Election Studies 2009, 2014.

To explain how we arrived at these conclusions, we will first discuss the potential pressures parties face over integration, and how spatial and reputational considerations capture the cross-pressures that parties face. We will then use two expert surveys conducted at the beginning of the crisis in 2007/08 and again in 2013 to study party positions on integration over time. A third section will assess the degree to which parties in Germany follow the general European patterns across party families.

HOW DO THE SPD AND THE CDU/CSU RESPOND TO EUROPE'S CRISIS? SPATIAL AND REPUTATIONAL CONSIDERATIONS

Since the onset of the greatest economic crisis around 2007, German governments have faced a series of challenges. Initially, governing parties (up to 2009 a Grand Coalition of the SPD and the CDU/CSU) had to support German banks and some companies (e.g. GM's subsidiary Opel) which experienced serious financial problems in the wake of the Lehman flop, the fallout from the near-collapse of the US banking system and questionable investments made by German banks. Germany's economy weathered these events comparatively well, in part because of its booming export sector, in part because of the labour market reforms undertaken a decade earlier, whereas other national sovereigns which had become deeply entwined with their financial sectors, suffered dearly, especially in Greece, Ireland, Portugal and Spain. In short, the economic crisis never fully arrived in Germany, certainly not at the level of citizens who continued to experience a booming economy, low inflation and unemployment rates (see the introduction to this special issue).

However, despite the positive economic conditions in Germany – conditions which typically generate support for European integration among mass publics[6] – scepticism began to form among the German public. It developed because growing debates over the soundness of financial rescue packages for troubled economies raised the salience of economic issues among voters. While the crises did not require the German taxpayer to transfer significant resources right away, the German treasury committed substantial sums to the European Stability Mechanism (ESM for short) which was designed as a 'firewall' to secure the financial liquidity of European governments from fiscal upheavals.[7] Controversies also arose because of the perceived profligacy of especially the Greek government to live beyond its means (e.g. early retirement options), its presumed inefficiency (e.g. does not collect taxes effectively) and a perception of significant corruption. As a result, public opinion in Germany lowered its support for the EU in the wake of these debates which were not only covered extensively in the mass media but also obtained a focal point through the newly founded AfD which advocates Germany's withdrawal from the Euro.

Table 1 suggests that there is indeed a decline in support for variously phrased integration measures. Although the drop does not reach the levels in Southern Europe – in Greece, for example, public evaluations of whether Greece's membership was a good thing declined from 76 per cent in 2009 to 43 per cent in 2014 – it is also noticeable in Germany. What is more, it emerges with different indicators. The membership indicator continues to show clear support for the EU when roughly two-thirds of the German public respond that Germany's EU membership has been good – but this indicator focuses more on the past than the current events. The second indicator – on the pace of reform – shows a bit more ambivalence when only one-third indicate that integration should go further, down from nearly 44 per cent in 2009. Note that the 2009 baseline already reflects some of the decline that took place before then[8] – so these estimates in weaker public support are conservative. In a word, national interests – above all economic and fiscal ones – became more salient and began to undermine Germany's traditionally strong support for Europe's integration.[9]

Given this backdrop, spatial models suggest that parties have incentives to become more EU-sceptical. If voters become more critical about integration, then parties which have historically supported the integration project – especially the SPD and the CDU/ CSU – have incentives to mute their support for European integration in order to attract voters who are dissatisfied with the current EU policies.[10] What is more, Social Democrats may increasingly be unhappy with the content of financial rescue packages which often require austerity measures that lower the standard of living of many ordinary citizens in crisis-plagued nations which conflicts with a 'social vision' of Europe that Social Democrats subscribe to.[11] In turn, the CDU and, especially the CSU may well be dissatisfied with the way that national sovereignty is lowered as a result of the way that top-level meetings in Brussels (and elsewhere) determine the fate not only of countries-in-need but also reduce Germany's sovereign ability to spend its resources as it sees fit. Thus, on the basis of spatial incentives the way the economic crisis unfolded leads to the following hypothesis:

> Hypothesis 1: By 2013, the SPD and the CDU/CSU moved to a (moderate) criticism of Europe's market and political integration.

Reputationally, however, the historical commitment of German mainstream parties conflicts with the incentives to become more EU-sceptical. From Germany's vantage point, Europe's integration was historically seen as a way to resuscitate Germany from the ashes of World War II; a memory that motivated Union and SPD-led governments to push the development of the single European market from Adenauer and Kiesinger (CDU) up to the 1960s, Brandt and Schmidt (SPD) throughout the 1970s, to Kohl (CDU) up to the 1990s.[12] All mainstream parties, in short, helped to develop the European project and thus have developed a reputation as staunch supporters of integration. Given this policy reputation, and the fact that both the SPD and the CDU/CSU designed the financial rescue packages over the past five years, German voters typically view mainstream parties as supporters of the EU. Because a reputation cannot be easily changed without running the serious risk of appearing implausible to voters, it is difficult now for the mainstream parties to 'run away' from their historic support for Europe's integration.[13] In short, the reputational argument suggests that the SPD and the CDU/CSU remain largely supportive of Europe's integration.

In contrast, the main critics of the EU should be found at both the right and left extreme of Germany's party system. The left has historically sided with the underdog and continues to be the champion of economically weak citizens both at home and internationally.[14] This strategy works well for Die Linke because extreme parties have incentives to use a wedge issue like integration, which does not fit well with domestic party positions, to unsettle established party–voter alliances.[15] In turn, the AfD is a newly founded party with the explicit aim to withdraw from the Euro.[16] Both mainstream parties thus face a credible threat on the integration dimension on their left and right flanks. Any attempt to usurp an EU-sceptical position by the SPD and the CDU/CSU thus runs the risk of being viewed as the 'copy' which may just serve to raise the salience of EU-scepticism and in the end might prompt voters to support Die Linke or the AfD as the 'original' provider of an EU-sceptical stance. Therefore, the reputational perspective hypothesises:

> Hypothesis 2: Mainstream parties have remained positive about integration; EU-scepticism is mainly found among Die Linke and the AfD.

The following analyses will test the two hypotheses.

PARTY POSITIONS ON EUROPEAN INTEGRATION DURING THE 2013 FEDERAL ELECTION CAMPAIGN

How have the parties responded to the crisis since 2008? To begin with, we examine the importance of integration issues during the 2013 election campaign. Generally, the political divisions in Germany follow the well-known narrative that the CDU/CSU, the FDP and the SPD constituted the bulwark of Germany's party democracy until about the mid-1970s.[17] The Social Democrats have typically attracted working and lower middle class voters, along with secular voters, whereas the CDU/CSU appealed mostly to the middle and upper class voters, in addition to religiously motivated voters.[18] The FDP, meanwhile, restricts its appeal to higher income voters. From the mid-1970s onwards, changes in the party system led to the rise of the Green Party and, after Germany's unification, the current version of Die Linke. While unification temporarily unsettled historically grown party–voter alliances, the German party system nowadays approximates the partisan patterns one observes historically.[19] At the centre–left, three parties vie for left-leaning voters – Die Linke, Die Grünen and the SPD; at the centre–right, we see mainly the CDU/CSU and the presently almost-defunct liberals (FDP). Historically, the main divisions have been over domestic issues and, increasingly, cultural issues such as environmentalism, gender equality and migration, whereas integration played second fiddle, if that at all and, moreover, does not neatly align with party positions on domestic stances.[20]

Given this backdrop, and the economic malaise, how important is Europe's integration as a basis for party competition in Germany during 2013? As part of a comprehensive assessment of party stances in Europe, we conducted an expert survey in Germany in the spring of 2008 and again in the spring and summer of 2013, about five years after the economic crisis began to unfold – and a few months before the 2013 election campaign took place.[21]

To begin with, we asked our experts to identify the most salient political divisions that divide parties:

> We would like to begin by asking about the party system as a whole. Some countries may have multiple issue dimensions structuring party competition, others only one, and some of course may have none at all. Could you please indicate how important each issue dimension is in the party system of [country]? If two issue dimensions are about equally important, please still rank order them for the purpose of the next question.

We showed experts a card that contained several potential divisions (see the Appendix for a complete list). There is a clear consensus that domestic, re-distributional issues top the list (Table 2). This is the case in 2008 and, again, in 2013. A bit surprising in light of the economic malaise is that the second most important issue continues to be cultural issues – over gay rights, gender equality, migration and environmentalism – which end up near the top in in 2008 *and* in 2013. Even though the economic crisis gripped Europe during this time, and much of the party elites in Germany debated financial bailout packages, domestic cultural issues still trump international ones according to our experts. Clearly, one reason is that Germany's unemployment rate remains at low levels, hovering around 6–7 per cent at the time of the surveys; growth is noticeable, inflation rates remain acceptably low and the federal budget is balanced. Only when we look at the third place, do we see international issues surface in 2013. While this slight increase in importance no doubt is due to the enormous difficulties the economic crisis produced in Europe, we interpret the overall ranking as a sign of Germany's economic strength. In the end, EU issues do not trump the two domestic conflict dimensions that shaped much of post-war Germany – a situation which reflects the resilience of the German economy.

TABLE 2
THE MOST IMPORTANT DIVISIONS IN GERMANY'S PARTY SYSTEM, 2008–13

	Spring 2008	Spring 2013
Redistribution (welfare state)	1	1
Cultural issues (gay rights; environmentalism)	2	2
Markets vs state control of economy	3	3
Nationalism vs internationalism (European integration)	4	3

Entries indicate the importance of political divisions in Germany's party system.
Source: All party-level data in this table and Figures 2–6 are taken from two expert surveys conducted in Germany in 2008 and 2013 (see the Appendix for a description). A '1' indicates that a division is the most important; '2' second most important, etc.

What are the positions of Germany's parties on European integration five years into the economic crisis? We asked four questions in our expert survey, beginning with a general indicator of their orientation towards integration:

> How about the EU? Regardless of the specific form that integration may take, where do parties stand on creating a politically unified Europe? Do they strongly support a politically unified Europe (in which case they would score 7) or do they strongly oppose a politically unified Europe (in which case they would score 1) or something in between?

We also asked them to indicate where parties stand on market integration: 'Where do the parties in [country] stand on creating a Europe-wide, integrated market for the European Union?'

Finally, a nearly identical question taps whether parties support Europe's political integration (see the Appendix). We created an additive indicator based on these three questions given its high correlations where '3' expresses complete opposition to the EU and '21' expresses complete support.[22]

We also asked how parties evaluate the current performance of the EU: 'And what about the party's view of how well democracy works in the EU?' A '1' denotes 'Does not work at all' and '7' denotes 'Works very well.'

We kept the performance indicator separate from the principles indicator because it measures the actual operating procedures of the EU which is conceptually distinct. It is conceivable that parties support the idea of integration while being dissatisfied with its current performance.

The top part of Figure 1 displays the left–right ideology score of parties on the x-axis and a summary score ranging from '3' (opposition) to '21' (support) on the y-axis; the bottom part of Figure 1 displays the way that parties evaluate the performance of the 'EU Democracy'. We included both the 2008 and 2013 scores in order to convey their position as well as any changes that may have taken place within individual parties. We note, first, that in 2008 there is only one party that is clearly EU-sceptical – Die Linke. It has traditionally viewed the market structures of the EU's integrated market with some suspicion. Although the left generally has become a bit more supportive over time of the EU as the supra-national institutions increasingly adopt a regulatory framework for the integrated economy, Die Linke at the extreme ideological left end of the party system is clearly seen as EU-critical in 2013 (along with the Pirate Party). Moreover, it hardly changed its position since the onset of the economic crisis (and our surveys) in 2008. Thus, the left-polar end of the German party system has supplied EU-critical voters with an established and distinct choice since at least 2008. In contrast, since we did not include the Alliance for Germany in our expert survey, there is no party in Figure 1 that can be seen to articulate the critical EU orientations of conservative voters. This clearly illustrates why the AfD nearly succeeded in entering the Bundestag in the 2013 election on the basis of EU-critical stances (Schmitt-Beck, this volume): it covers the 'blind spot' of EU-sceptical representation.[23]

Among mainstream parties, we see that the SPD was pro-EU principles in 2008 and by and large adopts the same position in 2013. This is consistent with the 'reputational' perspective arguing that the SPD cannot move towards a more EU-sceptical position

FIGURE 1
PARTY POSITION ON EUROPEAN INTEGRATION IN 2008 AND 2013

EU principles:

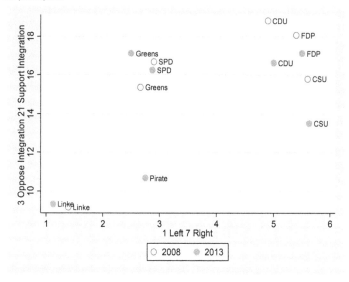

EU democracy:

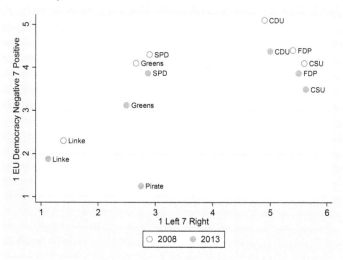

Note: Entries are mean ideology scores of parties on the x-axis (1–7); mean scores on the EU-principles indicator (3–21); and mean scores on the EU democracy indicator (1–7) in the bottom figure.

on the left without raising the salience of the issue and thereby increasing the relevance of Die Linke which has positioned itself as the owner of EU-scepticism among Germany's left. We see a bit more movement among the Union, though this amounts to muting its previously strong support for the EU rather than expressing opposition to integration. To illustrate, the CDU decreased its support from an unequivocal support score of 18.2 (where 21 expresses maximum support) in 2008 to 16.6 in 2013. Thus, despite the changes, the 2013 score still falls squarely into the support category (see also below). Similarly, the CSU – which elevated the outspoken EU-critic Peter Gauweiler to a prominent position in recent years – is seen by experts as moving from moderate support to a more ambiguous position (mean = 15.8 in 2008 and mean = 13.5 in 2013). Despite these dynamics, we again note that these scores still mean that the CDU and to a lesser extent the CSU support Europe's integration. To illustrate, British Conservatives who are clearly among the most vocal EU-sceptic party in the conservative, mainstream party camp, adopt a distinctly EU-sceptical position (mean = 8.4 and mean = 8.5 in 2008 and 2013, respectively).

We see virtually identical patterns for expert perceptions of how parties evaluate the performance of the EU. Most parties have become more negative about the performance of the EU between 2008 and 2013. However, we observe one noticeable outlier. The Greens have become significantly more supportive of EU principles reflecting their vocal support for the idea of a more integrated Europe in principle in order to sustain the EU. At the same time, however, the Greens have become significantly more negative about the performance of the EU, presumably because they are highly critical of the way the EU has structured financial rescue packages. Thus, the Greens remain a steadfast bearer of Europe's integration as an idea – but clearly lament its current performance and, indirectly, that of the German government's during the crisis.

All told, Germany's party system reflects two familiar camps even five years into the crisis. Mainstream parties in the ideological centre support integration, and are fairly positive about the EU's performance – the latter, possibly because certainly governing parties evaluate themselves. And we find the familiar opposition to the EU at the left and, now with the AfD, conservative polar end of Germany's party system.

PARTY STANCES IN COMPARISON

To what extent are the positions of Germany's parties comparable to those in other countries? Was the response of German parties especially modest considering that economic fundamentals in Germany continued to look strong during our expert surveys (January 2013 through February 2014)? Given the relative economic tranquillity in Germany in the year leading up to the election, we would like to know whether the fact that German parties were partly isolated from the economic shocks led to a uniquely positive or at least stable outlook on the EU. This is important not only to assess the political implications of the Germany-based patterns but also their theoretical relevance. For example, parties in Germany may not have changed their integration stances by much because there was no perceived economic and fiscal urgency to do so. Consequently, we would not want to conclude that the historically grown pro-EU reputation of German mainstream parties supports the reputational perspective when in fact the response among German parties is uniquely stable compared to other European parties, especially those in the same programmatic camp. If most other mainstream parties in Western Europe changed more substantially, then we would conclude that the German case provides only a restricted base to generalise from, though it is still relevant politically. For these reasons, we wish to examine the position of parties' integration stances in Western Europe, paying particular attention to where Germany's stances fall within this broader universe.

Figure 2 presents the scores for all 139 parties we have information for in Western Europe. The figure's layout is identical to that in Figure 1 and conveys a simple but

FIGURE 2
INTEGRATION STANCES OF GERMAN PARTIES IN COMPARISON, 2013

EU principles:

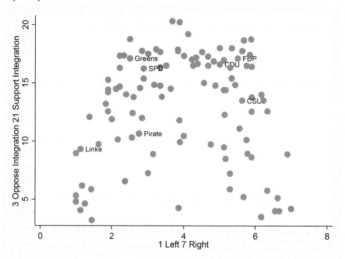

EU democracy

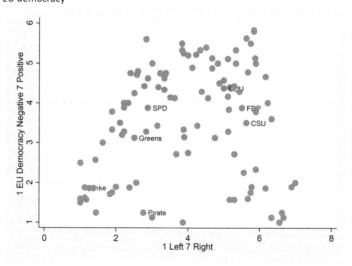

Note: Entries are mean ideology scores of parties on the x-axis (1–7); mean scores on the EU-principles indicator (3–21); and mean scores on the EU democracy indicator (1–7) in the bottom figure.

powerful conclusion: the major and minor parties fall squarely into the middle of their respective party camp. The Greens and the SPD at the centre–left fall squarely into the pro-EU camp, continuing to advocate a 'social vision' of Europe.[24] Similarly, the support of the CDU and the FDP is comparable to that of other centre–right parties, though we note again that the CSU is moving towards a somewhat unusually strongly voiced EU-scepticism amid this camp, likely reflecting its unique position as a regional, Bavarian party. In turn, Die Linke and the Pirate Party cover the left EU-sceptical spectrum in Germany. Their opposition is comparable to that of other left EU-sceptical parties, such as the Dutch and French Socialists. Finally, the placement of a range of EU-sceptical parties at the right spectrum outside of Germany shows that the AfD (not included in our surveys) appeals to the kind of voter that, for example, the Dutch PVV or the British UKIP attract.

In addition to the absolute position of parties, we would also like to examine the degree to which changes in the German party system are comparable to those of other countries. To begin to describe the comparative dynamics, we first created two change scores of parties' EU position – one for each dependent variable, EU principles and the EU's performance. We subtracted the 2013 score from the 2008 scores. A positive score means that parties have increased their support for EU principles and the EU's democracy by 2013; a negative score means that parties have become more EU-sceptical over time. Figure 3 displays the scatterplot with the labels of German parties to convey the amount of change relative to other European parties (N = 90). The y-axis displays the change scores; the x-axis shows parties' left–right placement scores. Given that this comparison requires that parties were politically relevant as defined earlier, this analysis does not include new anti-EU-sceptic parties that evolved since our first survey (e.g. the Italian M5S).

Figure 3 indicates, first, that most parties are located within one plus/minus unit change of the 0 line which denotes identical positions in 2008 and 2013. This suggests that most parties did not change their position by much over time. However, to say that change is completely absent would be inaccurate. For example, the most dramatic turn against the EU between 2008 and 2013 is found in Hungary where FIDESZ under Victor Orban's stewardship has become very EU-sceptical (a five-point drop in support for EU principles). In Western Europe, the most negative turn is found in Denmark where the conservative Liberal Alliance (NA) moved nearly four points towards EU-scepticism by 2013 (mean = −3.8) followed by the Duch PVV (mean = −3.6). Visually, being located in the lower right quadrant, we see that the CDU and CSU are also among the parties that turned noticeably away by about two points from their previously strong support when compared to the West European universe. The comparatively significant change in the Union is particularly noticeable when we focus on governing parties only (Figure 4) where we observe the strongest turn against Europe within the West among incumbents. However, these developments should not lead us to overlook that both parties still fall into the 'support' territory (as Figures 1 and 2 indicate).

All told, the change among German parties is comparatively non-trivial and suggests that the electoral campaign of the AfD has left its imprint on the position of these parties. But we also note that the governing CDU/CSU continues to support EU principles, though clearly in a more muted form. In contrast, the SPD is nearly

FIGURE 3
COMPARING CHANGING INTEGRATION STANCES OF GERMAN PARTIES TO OTHER
WESTERN EUROPEAN PARTIES

EU democracy:

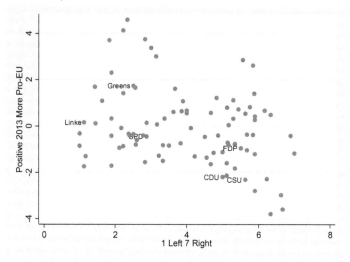

EU performance:

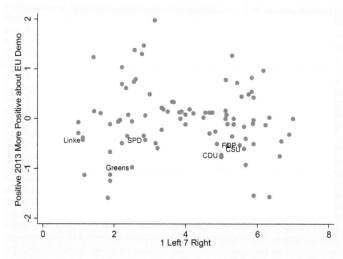

Note: Entries are mean ideology scores of parties on the x-axis (1–7); on the y-axis, mean change scores about EU-principles (top figure) and EU performance evaluations (bottom figure), with negative scores indicating a shift towards a critical
view about the EU between 2008 and 2013.

exactly at the same location where it was positioned in 2008 which is quite astounding
given that it had one of the worst election results in the 2009 Federal Election.[25]

In a final step, we systematically examine the degree to which the German parties
are different from their programmatic families in 2008 and 2013. We do so in order to

FIGURE 4
COMPARING CHANGING INTEGRATION STANCES OF GOVERNING PARTIES IN WESTERN
EUROPE

EU principles:

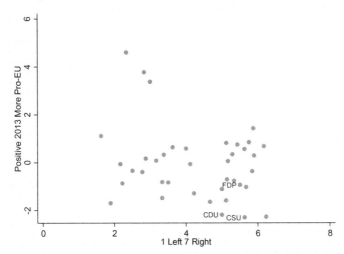

EU democracy:

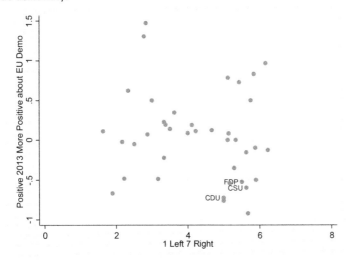

Note: Entries are mean ideology scores of parties on the x-axis (1–7); the y-axis displays change scores about EU-principles (top figure) and EU performance evaluations (bottom figure). Negative scores indicate a shift towards a critical view about the EU between 2008 and 2013.

triangulate the question whether Germany's mainstream parties are unique in their sus-tained support for the EU when compared to parties from the same ideological families elsewhere in Western Europe. To this end, we conducted several multiple regression analyses predicting party stances on EU principles and their evaluations of the EU democracy. We estimate the models using 2008–13 data for parties that were included at both surveys. We include four independent variables: a party family dummy variable which captures whether a party is a socialist, green, social democrat, liberal or Christian Democrats. These represent the party families represented in the German party system in our expert survey. Then, we added the year a survey was conducted (2008 is coded '0' and 2013 coded as '1'). Third, we included a dummy variable indicating whether parties are from Germany ('1') or from another West European country ('0'). Finally, we include a triple interaction effect between these three variables. The goal is to assess whether the position of (to name one example) the CDU/CSU in 2008 is different from Christian Democrats elsewhere in 2008; and then to see whether this *difference* has changed by 2013.

While the models are easily estimated in the pooled data (N = 180; 90 for each year), the interpretation of a triple interaction effect is quite difficult without further information. We therefore computed the predicted values for each party family within Germany (by year) and for other West European countries (Table 3). Take for example, the predicted values of the CDU/CSU. The model predicts a value of 17.3 for 2008 and a decline by 2013 to 15.1. While we observed a change in Figures 2 and 3, we now also see that the Union stays more positive than other Christian Democrats in Western Europe (2008 score = 13.7; 2013 score = 13.1). Within the

TABLE 3

PREDICTED EU PRINCIPLES AND EU DEMOCRACY EVALUATIONS FOR MAJOR PARTIES IN GERMANY AND CORRESPONDING PARTY FAMILIES ELSEWHERE IN WESTERN EUROPE 2008–13

		2008 EU principles	2013	2008 EU democracy	2013
Germany	CDU/CSU	17.3	15.1	4.6	3.9
	Liberals	18.1	17.1	4.5	4.4
	SPD	16.7	16.2	4.3	3.9
	Greens	15.3	17.1	4.1	3.1
	Die Linke	9.2	9.3	2.3	1.9
Western Europe	Christian Democrats	13.7	13.1	3.9	4.2
	Liberals	16.4	16.1	4.4	3.9
	Social Democrats	15.6	15.5	4.4	4.6
	Greens	12.2	13.9	2.8	3.2
	Socialists	7.7	8.2	2.4	2.1

Note: Cell entries are predicted values from several multi-level analyses with EU principles and performance as the dependent variables. Independent variables are: three dummy variables: year of survey (2013 vs 2008), Germany (1 yes 0 other); party family (dummy for each family analysed in separate models); and a triple interaction effect between them. We estimated two models for each party family. For example, for Christian Democrats (CD), we estimated one model with EU principles and one with EU performance as the dependent variable. Independent variables for CDs are: year, country, a dummy for CD; and an interaction effect of year*country*CD. On the basis of the coefficients, we then calculated the predicted values of EU principles for the CDU/CSU in 2008 (17.3) and 2013 (15.1). The same model estimates were also used to calculate the predicted values for Christian Democrats in Western Europe (13.7 in 2008 and 13.1 in 2013). We then estimated models for other party families analogously (e.g. for the SPD, we replace the CD dummy with a Social Democrat dummy, and calculated predicted values for the SPD and Social Democrats). We repeated this for every party family shown in Table 2.

Christian Democratic party family, therefore, the analyses suggest that the Union remains quite supportive of integration compared to its ideological cousins even though it also reduced its enthusiasm for EU principles by more than most Christian Democratic parties. In short, it has become more muted in its support but maintains its support at levels that are a bit more positive than that of other members of this party family. This shows that an analysis of change alone can be quite misleading if one were led to infer from it that the CDU/CSU has become uniquely sceptical about integration.

The SPD, in contrast, stays nearly exactly where it was in 2008 (16.7 versus 16.2 on EU principles); a pattern we also find for party stances on the EU's democracy. This pattern closely matches that of other Social Democrats in Europe which barely changed during the five-year crisis. A similar conclusion emerges about the FDP which remains positive and also duplicates the Europe-wide pattern. The one exception we noted earlier – and see confirmed here – concerns the German Greens: they are considerably more positive about EU principles than other green parties in Europe and, moreover, they have become quite sceptical about the EU's performance, again in contrast to green parties elsewhere, though we do note that the Greens were unusually positive in 2008. Overall, the Green's position on the EU's performance now closely fits with the rest of the Green European parties, though they do stay considerably more positive about EU principles than other Green parties in Western Europe.

CONCLUSION

To recap, we observe that EU stances produce a curvilinear pattern when viewed on the basis of a left–right perspective, just as elsewhere in Western Europe. The SPD is rather positive about the EU, and remains so during the crisis; the Union also remains quite positive, albeit at a more muted level. In contrast, Die Linke is fairly negative, presumably because it rejects the pro-market framework of the EU and, moreover, the austerity-based rescue packages for ailing economies. Moreover, while the AfD is not included in our expert survey, our study still suggests that it presumably entered the electoral market precisely where mainstream parties left an opening at the conservative polar end where market preferences coincide with nationalism and EU-scepticism (Schmitt-Beck, this volume).

Theoretically, our article shows that it is very difficult for mainstream parties to move towards a more sceptical position. It thus supports the reputational argument more so than the spatial perspective, at least as far as mainstream parties are concerned. For extreme parties, on the other hand, the combination of an anti-EU stance, along with a growing EU-scepticism, seems to be a winning formula, certainly for the AfD and Die Linke. So, when viewed from the mainstream perspective, the reputational mechanism appears to conflict with the spatial mechanisms; but when viewed from the perspective of extreme parties, the two mechanisms *reinforce* each other.

Finally, we would like to raise one issue that is potentially lurking behind our findings: why did the CDU/CSU begin to respond to the EU-sceptic threat of the AfD, whereas the SPD does not appear to respond at all to the EU-sceptic threat from Die Linke? We may see here the differential threat potential each party faces as a result of the novelty of a challenger. Die Linke is firmly established in the German party system, and thus has had time to develop a loyal voter clientele, as well as to develop its reputation and competence as a critic of the integrated market. This makes it difficult for the SPD to position itself as the 'original' EU-sceptic at the left end of Germany's party system. In contrast, the AfD is new and thus lacks these support pillars so that it made sense for the CDU/CSU to stem the potential defection of its own voters to the AfD on the basis of its EU-scepticism. Thus, the CDU/CSU may be better positioned to absorb EU-sceptic voters than the SPD – though whether or not this is a viable strategy for the Union, only time will tell.

DISCLOSURE STATEMENT

No potential conflict of interest was reported by the authors.

NOTES

1. A. Downs, *An Economic Theory of Democracy* (New York: Harper & Row, 1957); A. Westholm, 'Distance versus Direction: The Illusory Defeat of the Proximithy Theory of Electoral Choice', *American Political Science Review* 91 (1997), pp.865–83.
2. L. Hooghe and G. Marks, 'A Postfunctionlist Theory of European Integration: From Permissive Consensus to Constraining Dissensus', *British Journal of Political Science* 39 (2008), pp.1–23; L.N. Lindberg and S.A. Scheingold (eds), *Regional Integration: Theory and Research* (Cambridge: Cambridge University Press, 1970).
3. W.E. Paterson, 'Does Germany Still Have a European Vocation?', *German Politics* 19/1 (2010), pp.41–52.
4. For a detailed discussion of the expert surveys conducted in 27 European countries, see Robert Rohrschneider and Stephen Whitefield, *The Strain of Representation* (Oxford: Oxford University Press, 2012).
5. Hooghe and Marks, 'A Postfunctionlist Theory'.
6. M. Maier et al., 'The Impact of Identity and Economic Cues on Citizens' EU Support: An Experimental Study on the Effects of Party Communication in the Run-Up to the 2009 European Parliament Elections', *European Union Politics* 13/4 (2012), pp.580–603; M. Marsh, 'European Parliament Elections and Losses by Governing Parties', in W. Van der Brug and C. v. d. Eijk (eds), *European Elections and Domestic Politics* (Notre Dame, IN: University of Notre Dame, 2005), pp.51–72.

7. See, for example, https://en.wikipedia.org/wiki/European_Stability_Mechanism (accessed 30 June 2015) which shows that Germany committed over 190 billion Euros to the European Stability Mechanism. As a reference point, this is over half of its 2015 annual budget.
8. F. Roth et al., 'Crisis and Trust in National and European Union Institutions – Panel Evidence for the EU, 1999–2012', *RSCAS Working Papers* (Florence: European University Institute, 2013), 2013/31.
9. M.M. Bechtel et al., 'Preferences for International Redistribution: The Divide over the Eurozone Bailouts', *American Journal of Political Science* 58/4 (2014), pp.835–56.
10. This discussion relies on the theoretical account developed in Robert Rohrschneider and Stephen Whitefield, 'Responding to Growing European Union-Skepticism? The Stances of Political Parties toward European Integration in Western and Eastern Europe Following the Financial Crisis', *European Union Politics* 17/1 (2016), pp.138–61.
11. A. Wimmel and E.E. Edwards, 'The Return of "Social Europe": Ideas and Positions of German Parties towards the Future of European Integration', *German Politics* 20/2 (2011), pp.293–314.
12. F.U. Pappi and P.W. Thurner, 'Die deutschen Waehler und der Euro: Auswirkungen auf die Bundestagswahl 1998', *Politische Vierteljahresschrift* 41/3 (2000), pp.435–65; W.E. Paterson, 'Does Germany Still Have a European Vocation?', *German Politics* 19/1 (2010), pp.41–52.
13. I. Budge, 'A New Spatial Theory of Party Competition: Uncertainty, Ideology and Policy Equilibria Viewed Comparatively and Temporally', *British Journal of Political Science* 24/4 (1994), pp.443–67.
14. P. Doerschler and L.A. Banaszak, 'Voter Support for the German PDS over Time: Dissatisfaction, Ideology, Losers, and East Identity', *Electoral Studies* 87/2 (2007), pp.359–70; M.I. Vail and B. Bowyer, 'Poverty and Parisanship: Social and Economic Sources of Support for the Far Left in Contemporary Germany', *Comparative European Politics* 10/4 (2012), pp.505–24.
15. M. Wagner, 'Defining and Measuring Niche Parties', *Party Politics* 18/6 (2012), pp.845–64; J. Rovny, 'Who Emphasizes and Who Blurs? Party Strategies in Multidimensional Competition', *European Union Politics* 13/2 (2012), pp.269–92.
16. N. Berbuir, M. Lewandowsky and J. Siri, 'The AfD and Its Sympathisers: Finally a Right-Wing Populist Movement in Germany?', *German Politics* 24/2 (2015), pp.154–78.
17. F.U. Pappi, 'Sozialstruktur, gesellschaftliche Wertorientierungen und Wahlabsicht. Ergebnisse eines Zeitvergleichs des deutschen Elektorats 1953 und 1976', *Politische Vierteljahresschrift* 18 (1977), pp.195–229; M. Debus and J. Müller, 'The Programmatic Development of CDU and CSU since Reunification: Incentives and Constraints for Changing Policy Positions in the German Multi-Level System', *German Politics* 22/1–2 (2013), pp.151–71.
18. S. Roβteutscher, 'Die konfessionell-religiöse, Konfliktlinie zwischen Säkularisierung und Mobilisierung', in R. Schmitt-Beck (ed.), *Wählen in Deutschland* (Baden-Baden: Nomos, 2012), pp.111–33.
19. W. Müller and M. Klein, 'Die Klassenbasis in der Parteipräferenz des deutschen Wählers. Erosion oder Wandel?', in Schmitt-Beck (ed.), *Wählen in Deutschland*, pp.85–110; F.U. Pappi and J. Brandenburg, 'Die Politikvorschlaege der Bundestagsparteien aus Wählersicht: Zur Konstruierbarkeit von Politikräumen für das deutsche Parteiensystem', in Schmitt-Beck (ed.), *Wählen in Deutschland*, pp.276–301.
20. W. v. d. Brug and J. v. Spanje, 'Immigration, Europe, and the Cultural Dimension', *European Journal of Political Research* 48 (2009), pp.309–34; H. Kriesi, 'The Role of European Integration in National Election Campaigns', *European Union Politics* 8/1 (2007), pp.83–108.
21. The expert survey was conducted by the authors in 2007/08 and repeated in 2013 with an identical questionnaire in 24 European democracies for about 200 parties. Experts were chosen on the basis of their prior publication record which stipulated that they had to have published a book or article on their party system in the past 10 years. We aimed to have 10 completed questionnaires per country; a goal we met for Germany at both time points. See Rohrschneider and Whitefield, *Strain of Representation* and the appendix for a description of the study.
22. For West European parties in our data (N = 108), alpha = .90.
23. J. Thomassen, 'The Blind Corner of Political Representation', *Representation* 41/1 (2012), pp.13–27.
24. A. Wimmel and E.E. Edwards, 'The Return of "Social Europe": Ideas and Positions of German Parties towards the Future of European Integration', *German Politics* 20/2 (2011), pp.293–314.
25. Of course, it may be that it has moved more on domestic divisions given that Europe's integration does not constitute the most important cleavage. Additional analyses, however, indicate that the SPD has not changed its domestic issue stances by much either.

APPENDIX: THE EXPERT SURVEY

We conducted a Europe-wide expert survey in 2007–08. The CEE survey covers 94 parties in 13 Central-East European countries (all then-EU nations, plus Moldova, Russia and the Ukraine); the WE survey covers 104 parties in all EU countries minus Luxembourg. We conducted a second expert survey throughout 2013, covering many of the same parties in CEE and WE but also a number of newly founded parties. We asked experts, who were identified on the basis of their publication record on a given party system, to complete a detailed questionnaire. For each country, we strove to obtain 10 expert responses which we achieved in many instances (Table A1). We use here mostly the results from the expert survey in Germany (N = 10 in 2008; N = 9 in 2013). See appendix Table A1 for details on parties included in the West European surveys and response rates for all countries.

Indicators
Political Divisions. Question wording is presented in the main text. Respondents were shown the following card and indicated whether a cleavage is the first, second, third or fourth most important cleavage. If an expert did not select a cleavage, it was coded as '5'.

    A. Economy: redistributional issues (e.g. tax levels, welfare state spending)
    B. Economy: State-run versus market economy
    C. Democracy: strengthening democratic institutions
    D. Ethnic rights (e.g. minorities)
    E. Nationalism and Internationalism (e.g. views about the EU)
    F. Religiosity (role of church)
    G. Social rights
    H. Views of the Communist past and its legacies (issue J in 2013; was re-coded to H
        for consistency's sake)
    I. Regional divisions
    J. Urban–rural divisions

Party's left–right ideology. 'In [country], parties may be located to the left or the right of the political spectrum. In general terms, please locate each party on the ideological spectrum in [country], with 1 standing for left wing, and 7 standing for right wing.'

    West integration. Presented in text.
    Political integration. Presented in text.
    Market integration. Presented in text.
    EU democracy performance. Presented in text.

TABLE A1
PARTIES INCLUDED IN 2008 AND 2013 SURVEYS (2008 AND 2013 ENTRIES LIST THE
NUMBER OF EXPERTS WHO COMPLETED A SURVEY FOR A PARTY SYSTEM IN A GIVEN
YEAR)

Country: West	Party name in RW survey	Acronym	2008	2013	Party family
Austria	Social Democratic Party of Austria	SPO	Yes	Yes	Social-democrat
2008: 10	Austrian People's Party	OVP	Yes	Yes	Christian-democrat
2013: 9	The Greens	GRUNE	Yes	Yes	Green
	Freedom Party of Austria	FPO	Yes	Yes	Nationalist
	Alliance for the Future of Austria	BZO	Yes	Yes	Nationalist
	Team Stronach	TS	No	Yes	Nationalist
Belgium	Christian-Democratic & Flemish	CDV	Yes	Yes	Christian-democrat
2008: 10	New Flemish Alliance	N-VA	Yes	Yes	Conservative/ Separatist
2013: 8	Reform Movement	MR	Yes	Yes	Centrist
	Flemish Interest	VB	Yes	Yes	Nationalist
	Flemish Liberals and Democrats	VLD	Yes	Yes	Centrist
	Socialist Party	PS	Yes	Yes	Social-democrat
	Socialist Party. Different	SPA	Yes	Yes	Social-democrat
	Humanist Democratic Centre	CDH	Yes	Yes	Christian-democrat
	Ecologists	ECOLO	Yes	Yes	Green
	List Dedecker	LDD	Yes	Yes	Nationalist
	The Flemish Greens	GROEN	Yes	Yes	Green
	National Front	FN	Yes	No	Nationalist
Denmark	Denmark's Liberal Party	V	Yes	Yes	Conservative
2008: 9	Social Democracy	S	Yes	Yes	Social-democrat
2013: 9	Danish People's Party	DF	Yes	Yes	Nationalist
	Socialist People's Party	SF	Yes	Yes	Socialist
	Conservative People's Party	KF	Yes	Yes	Conservative
	Radical Liberals	RV	Yes	Yes	Centrist
	Unity List – The Red–Greens	EL	Yes	Yes	Socialist
	Liberal Alliance (2008: New Alliance)	NA	Yes	Yes	Conservative
Finland	Finnish Centre	KESK	Yes	Yes	Centrist
2008: 9	National Coalition Party	KOK	Yes	Yes	Conservative
2013: 8	Finnish Social Democratic Party	SDP	Yes	Yes	Social-democrat
	Left Alliance	VAS	Yes	Yes	Socialist
	Green Alliance	VIHR	Yes	Yes	Green
	Finnish Christian Democrats	KD	Yes	Yes	Christian-democrat
	Swedish People's Party in Finland	SFP	Yes	Yes	Centrist
	True Finns	PS	Yes	Yes	Nationalist
France	Union for a Popular Movement	UMP	Yes	Yes	Conservative
2008: 10	Socialist Party	PS	Yes	Yes	Social-democrat
2013: 6	Democratic Movement	MoDem	Yes	Yes	Centrist
	French Communist Party	PCF	Yes	No	Communist
	National Front	FN	Yes	Yes	Nationalist
	The Greens	VERTS	Yes	Yes	Green
	New Centre	NC	Yes	Yes	Conservative
	Radical Party of the Left	PRG	Yes	Yes	Social-democrat
	Movement for France	MPF	Yes	No	Nationalist
Merges with FDG	Communist Revolutionary League	LCR	Yes	No	Communist
	Radical Party	PR	No	Yes	Centrist
	Left Front	FDG	No	Yes	Communist
	Centrist Alliance	AC	No	Yes	Centrist
Germany	Christian Democracy Union	CDU	Yes	Yes	Christian-democrat

Continued

TABLE A1
CONTINUED.

Country: West	Party name in RW survey	Acronym	2008	2013	Party family
2008: 10	Christian Social Union	CSU	Yes	Yes	Christian-democrat
2013: 9	Social Democratic Party of Germany	SPD	Yes	Yes	Social-democrat
	Free Democratic Party	FDP	Yes	Yes	Centrist
	The Left (Party of Democratic Socialism, PDS)	DIE LINKE	Yes	Yes	Socialist
	Alliance 90/The Greens	GRUNE	Yes	Yes	Green
	Piratenpartei	Piraten	No	Yes	Centrist
Greece	New Democracy	ND	Yes	Yes	Centrist
2008: 10	Panhellenic Socialist Movement	PASOK	Yes	Yes	Social-democrat
2013: 9	Communist Party of Greece	KKE	Yes	Yes	Communist
	Coalition of the Left, the Movements and the Ecology	SYN	Yes	No	Socialist
	Popular Orthodox Rally	LAOS	Yes	No	Nationalist
	Coalition of the Radical Left	SYRIZA	No	Yes	Socialist
	Independent Greeks	ANEL	No	Yes	Nationalist
	Golden Dawn	XA	No	Yes	Nationalist
	Democratic Left	DIMAR	No	Yes	Socialist
Ireland		FF	Yes	Yes	Social-democrat
2008: 10	Fine Gael	FG	Yes	Yes	Conservative
2013: 7	Labour Party	LAB	Yes	Yes	Social-democrat
	Sinn Fein	SF	Yes	Yes	Centrist
	Green Party	GP	Yes	Yes	Green/Socialist
	Progressive Democrats	PD	Yes	No	Centrist
	Socialist	SP	Yes	Yes	Socialist
	People Before Profit Alliance	PBP	No	Yes	Communist
Italy	Left Democrats	Left_Dem	Yes	Yes	Social-democrat
2008: 10	Communist Refoundation Party	PRC	Yes	No	Communist
2013: 8	Italian Democratic Socialists	SDI	Yes	No	Social-democrat
	Italian Radicals	RI	Yes	No	Centrist
	Party of Italian Communists	PdCl	Yes	No	Communist
	Italy of Values	IdV	Yes	No	Centrist
	Green Federation	VERDI	Yes	No	Green
	Forward Italy	FI	Yes	No	Conservative
	National Alliance	AN	Yes	No	Nationalist
	Union of Christian and Centre Democrats	UDC	Yes	No	Christian-democrat
	League North	LN	Yes	Yes	Nationalist/Separatist
	The People of Freedom	PDL	No	Yes	Christian-democrat
	Union of the Centre	UDC	No	Yes	Christian-democrat
	Five Star Movement	M5S	No	Yes	Other
	Civic Choice	SC	No	Yes	Centrist
Netherlands	Christian Democratic Appeal	CDA	Yes	Yes	Christian-democrat
2008: 9	Labour Party	PvdA	Yes	Yes	Social-democrat
2013: 9	Socialist Party	SP	Yes	Yes	Socialist
	People's Party for Freedom and Democracy	VVD	Yes	Yes	Conservative
	Freedom Party	PVV	Yes	Yes	Conservative
	Green Left	GL	Yes	Yes	Green
	Christian Union	CU	Yes	Yes	Christian-democrat
	Democrats 66	D66	Yes	Yes	Centrist
	Party for the Animals	PvdD	Yes	Yes	Green

Continued

TABLE A1
CONTINUED.

Country: West	Party name in RW survey	Acronym	2008	2013	Party family
	List Rita Verdonk	VERDONK	Yes	No	Centrist
	Reformed Political Party	SGP	Yes	Yes	Christian-democrat
	50 Plus	50+	No	Yes	Centrist
Portugal	Socialist Party	PS	Yes	Yes	Social-democrat
2008: 10	Social Democratic Party	PSD	Yes	Yes	Conservative
2013: 7	Portuguese Communist Party	PCP	Yes	Yes	Communist
	Ecological Party The Greens	PEV	Yes	No	Green
	Democratic Social Centre	CDS-PP	Yes	Yes	Conservative
	Left Bloc	BE	Yes	Yes	Socialist
Spain	Spanish Socialist Workers' Party	PSOE	Yes	Yes	Social-democrat
2008: 10	People's Party	PP	Yes	Yes	Conservative
2013: 9	United Left	IU	Yes	Yes	Socialist
	Initiative for Catalonia Greens	ICV	Yes	Yes	Green
	Convergence and Union of Catalonia	CiU	Yes	Yes	Centrist
	Republican Left of Catalonia	ERC	Yes	No	Nationalist/ Separatist
	Basque National Party	EAJ-PNV	Yes	Yes	Nationalist/ Separatist
	Canarian Coalition	CC	Yes	No	Centrist/Separatist
	Galician Nationalist Bloc	BNG	Yes	No	Socialist/Separatist
	Basque Solidarity	EA	Yes	No	Nationalist/ Separatist
	Aragonese Council	CHA	Yes	No	Socialist/Separatist
	Navarre Yes	Na-Bai	Yes	No	Nationalist/ Separatist
	Union, Progress, and Democracy	UPyD	No	Yes	Centrist
	Amaiur	AMAIUR	No	Yes	Socialist
Sweden	Social Democratic Workers' Party	SAP	Yes	Yes	Social-democrat
2008: 10	Moderate Rally Party	M	Yes	Yes	Conservative
2013: 7	Centre Party	C	Yes	Yes	Conservative
	Liberal People's Party	FP	Yes	Yes	Centrist
	Christian Democrats	KD	Yes	Yes	Christian-democrat
	Left Party	VP	Yes	Yes	Socialist
	Environment Party The Greens	MP	Yes	Yes	Green
	Sweden Democrats	SD	Yes	Yes	Nationalist
UK	Labour Party	LAB	Yes	Yes	Social-democrat
2008: 10	Conservative Party	CON	Yes	Yes	Conservative
2013: 7	Liberal Democrats	LD	Yes	Yes	Centrist
	Scottish National Party	SNP	Yes	Yes	Social-democrat/ Separatist
	Plaid Cymru	PC	Yes	Yes	Social-democrat/ Separatist
	UK Independence Party	UKIP	No	Yes	Nationalist

Instrumental and Expressive Coalition Voting: The Case of the FDP in the 2009 and 2013 German Federal Elections

SASCHA HUBER

Most accounts of coalition voting are based on instrumental reasoning. However, coalition voting might also be the result of expressive motivations. Using the case of the FDP, this article studies the impact of a varying degree of coalition voting in the German federal elections of 2009 and 2013. According to theories of instrumental coalition voting, there should have been more 'threshold insurance voting' at the 2013 election, as the FDP was actually in danger of not crossing the threshold. Yet it is found that there was considerably less coalition voting in 2013 than in the 2009 election. The analysis suggests that a more comprehensive account of coalition voting is needed that considers not only instrumental reasoning but also expressive coalition voting. Taking into account expressive motivations for coalition voting helps to explain the tremendous decline of the FDP vote share in the 2013 German federal election.

INTRODUCTION

Coalition voting is almost exclusively seen as some form of instrumental reasoning. According to this logic, voters in multi-party systems of proportional representation (PR) who want to influence governmental outcomes will not only use partisan preferences but also coalition considerations. In order to achieve their preferred policy outcome they need to take into account which coalitions might be formed after the election and vote accordingly. Obviously, that is quite demanding. There is, however, another possible motivation for coalition voting: expressing one's political views by splitting the vote between two different parties. The German mixed-member proportional electoral system with two votes allows for such vote splitting and should therefore be a particularly convenient setting for expressive coalition voting.

In this article, the case of the German FDP in the two past federal elections is used to explore varying degrees of instrumental and expressive coalition voting in multi-party systems. In 2013, the FDP failed for the first time in its history to cross the electoral threshold of 5 per cent of votes. Only four years before, at the previous election, it had reached a record high of 14.6 per cent of votes. One possible factor for this tremendous decline could have been a varying degree of coalition voting in these two elections. A variety of studies have found coalition considerations of voters to be an important factor in voting for the FDP.[1] In these studies, coalition-directed voting has been attributed to instrumental reasoning and the so-called *threshold insurance strategy*. According to that strategy, supporters of big parties deviate from their first preference and vote for a small potential coalition partner in order to secure the formation of this coalition. In quite a few elections, it was mainly the FDP that benefited from this kind of strategic voting. In the 2013 election, the FDP was again massively campaigning for so-called *Leihstimmen*, trying to woo supporters of its coalition partner to 'lend' them some votes. Still, the FDP failed to get into parliament. If coalition-directed voting for the FDP was really based only on instrumental reasoning, the stark decline of the FDP in the 2013 election would seem rather odd – as the situation before the election very much resembled the ideal scenario for *threshold insurance voting*: many people wanted a CDU/CSU–FDP coalition, all polls suggested that the FDP was at risk of not getting into parliament, and both coalition partners signalled very clearly that they would want to continue their coalition.

In this study, I argue that coalition considerations are not only based on instrumental reasoning but also on expressive motivations.[2] While instrumental coalition voting would always be conditioned by outcome expectations, as it is assumed that voters want to influence the government formation process in the most efficient way, expressive coalition voting is independent of outcome expectations, as expressive voters are assumed to care less about government formation and policy outcomes than about using the vote to express their political preferences and thereby also expressing their personal identity.

A more comprehensive account of coalition voting that is not only considering instrumental reasoning may help to explain the tremendous decline of the FDP vote share in the 2013 German federal election. The next paragraphs will outline some theoretical arguments for instrumental and expressive coalition voting in Germany, before we turn to the empirical contexts of the last two elections. Based on these empirical boundary conditions of coalition voting, hypotheses will be derived about the amount of both instrumental and expressive coalition voting for the FDP in 2009 and 2013. The hypotheses will be tested using data from the German Longitudinal Election Study (GLES) of 2009 and 2013.

THEORY: INSTRUMENTAL AND EXPRESSIVE COALITION VOTING

Instrumental Coalition Voting

In multi-party systems voters face not only more difficult decisions as there are more options than in two-party systems but they are also confronted with higher uncertainty about the future government. Compared to plurality systems, where party choices translate more directly into the formation of a government, voters in PR systems are confronted with a rather complex decision environment. If they want to select a future government, voters need to take into account and evaluate coalitions that might be formed after the election. Early on Downs indicated the different decision environment that voters face in multi-party systems:

> each vote supports a party which will have to compromise its policies even if elected; hence the policies of this party are not the ones which a vote for it actually supports. Instead the vote supports the policies of whatever coalition the party joins.[3]

That is, instrumental voters should not only keep in mind what each party stands for but they should also anticipate which coalitions might be formed after an election and which compromises might be implemented by possible coalitions.[4] Downs was therefore very sceptical about the chances of instrumental voting in multi-party systems: 'In systems usually governed by coalitions, most citizens do not vote as though election were government-selection mechanisms.'[5] According to this view, voters in multi-party systems will not so much vote in order to select a government but rather in order to be represented by a party or to express a preference for a party. Being confronted with the uncertainty of various potential coalitions, they will stick to a simple calculus involving parties and candidates.

A growing literature on strategic voting in PR systems suggests that this view was probably too sceptical and that voters also apply instrumental coalition considerations in multi-party systems.[6] Bargsted and Kedar showed that coalition expectations were a significant factor of voting behaviour in Israel.[7] Carman and Johns examined elections for the Scottish Parliament and found hints for ticket-splitting based on coalition preferences.[8] Irwin and Van Holsteyn demonstrated for the Netherlands that voters adapt vote choices to different coalition scenarios.[9] For Austria, the interplay of expectations and coalition preferences was found to have an effect on voting.[10]

In Germany, it has been demonstrated that coalition considerations did have an influence on vote choices and that especially the FDP has benefited from coalition voting.[11] Coalition voting for the FDP has been mainly attributed to instrumental reasoning and the so-called 'coalition insurance strategy' that was proposed for the German party system, with two big parties and various small parties, and takes into account thresholds to enter parliament.[12] If the potential small coalition partner of a preferred larger party is in danger of not passing the threshold, supporters of the latter party may defect from their first preference and vote for the small potential partner in order to secure the formation of this coalition. This deviation from the preferred party is thus conditional on the expectations about the result of the election and the following coalition bargaining process. The FDP used that logic over decades to convince supporters of the CDU/CSU to vote for the FDP in order to get a coalition of CDU/CSU and FDP, and various studies suggest that this was quite successful.[13]

Instrumental reasoning regarding the German electoral system is not that easy. The mixed member proportional system (MMP) with two ballots combines single member district representation with proportional outcomes and is therefore often described as the 'best of both worlds'.[14] From an instrumental voter's view, however, MMP systems can be quite challenging. Voters first need to know the different meaning of the two votes: the first vote uses a majoritarian logic of choosing a local candidate and is the less important one and the second vote for a party list uses a proportional logic for determining the composition of the parliament and is the more important one. The strategic considerations for the two ballots are thus very different. For the first vote (*Erststimme*), or candidate ballot, voters need to follow the logic of a majoritarian election and assess the chances of the various candidates of winning the district. Therefore, there is the incentive to restrict choices to the viable candidates in the district, normally the candidates of the big parties. For the second or party list vote (*Zweitstimme*), voters need to follow the logic of a proportional election, keeping in mind potential thresholds and possibly considering coalition signals in multi-party systems. As outlined above, voters who want to influence government formation may not only consider which party comes closest to their political views but also try to anticipate the chances of the various parties of entering parliament and to form a specific coalition. Having considered both strategic incentives, instrumental voters should cast the two ballots independently. Having made a decision for one vote should not influence the decision for the other. As MMP is not a preference voting system, in which one might indicate the first preference with the first vote and the second preference with the second vote, it does not make sense just to split votes between the first two preferred parties. For strategic FDP voting with the more important second vote, this means that instrumental voters should not be influenced by their first vote. A CDU/CSU supporter who votes for the CDU/CSU candidate with the first vote and the FDP with the second vote will still harm their own party by the missing second vote.

Expressive Coalition Voting

Voters might not only have instrumental goals like selecting a government but they are also motivated by just expressing their preferences.[15] Expressing one's own preferences might be a good thing in itself, providing utility independent of the policy outcomes of a future government. This research argues that voting is not necessarily motivated by the wish to influence the political consequences of election results, but directly by the act of participation in the election and choosing a particular party or candidate. Expressive voting is therefore seen as a 'non-consequentialist' form of political acting whose aim is not realising certain political results.[16] Its benefit arises directly from the symbolic meaning of the action.[17]

In his account of expressive choice, Schuessler refers to public choice theories and (post-)modern social theory, arguing that the self-definition of individuals is always a reflexive act.[18] In this view, voters and consumers construct their identity as a biographical narrative by summing up all acts of choice exerted in their everyday life. By voting for a certain party, individuals assign themselves to a certain lifestyle or a reference group that is perceived to be attractive. By this act of identification, they add a subjectively meaningful personality facet to their identity. At the same time, they are also showing this facet to others. According to Schuessler, voters very much resemble consumers in modern image-intensive markets: '[M]any types of participation in collective activities – such as voting in large-scale elections and participating in the consumption of mass-produced goods – represent instances in which individuals express and reaffirm, to others and to themselves, who they are'.[19] In explaining this logic, he uses the metaphor of a jukebox which people will not only use in order to hear a song but also to establish an identity:

> Participation is not only a means for me to create the Frank Sinatra outcome on the jukebox – it is also a way for me to establish, reaffirm, demonstrate, and express my Frank Sinatra*ness* to the rest of the world, as well as to myself.[20]

Expressive voting decisions are thus seen as endeavours of individuals to reassure themselves and others about their personal identity. Theories of expressive choice are thereby focused on parties and candidates. However, expressive motives must not be restricted to parties and candidates. In multi-party contexts, one may also find it attractive to express coalition preferences.[21] Having stronger preferences for coalitions than for parties may signal that one is adapting to the changing political supply and the performance of government, that one is flexible and maybe more 'individual' and 'complex' than just sticking to one party or candidate once and for all. Take, for instance, a supporter of the CDU/CSU in Germany. She may think of herself as being 'conservative' and 'pragmatic'. As a self-concept, this may still be a bit narrow and one-dimensional. So she may also want to express that she is 'freedom-loving'. One way of demonstrating these dimensions of one's self-concept is to vote based on coalition preferences (here, for instance, CDU/CSU–FDP), because the coalition preference represents a fuller or more attractive picture of oneself.[22] Or to reformulate the metaphor of Schuessler, it may be appealing to demonstrate one's identity by playing one particular song on the jukebox all the time, but it may be even better to demonstrate a more complex or nuanced picture by sometimes choosing another artist. Or even better, if possible, one may choose two songs at the same time.

Interestingly, the German electoral system with two ballots provides for exactly this possibility – choosing two 'songs' at the same time. Voters can split their vote and choose a candidate of one party with the first vote (*Erststimme*) and another party with the second vote (*Zweitstimme*). This two-vote system should suit expressive coalition motives as voters have the easy opportunity to express themselves. If there was only one vote, a defection from the preferred party would always come with some psychological costs and voters would have to trade off the utility they would gain by expressing some coalition preference – by voting for a junior partner of the preferred party for instance – and the utility they would gain by expressing their party preference. With two votes at hand, one can easily express both, demonstrating both the identity that is associated with the party preference and the identity that is associated with the coalition partner.

Contrary to instrumental voters, expressive voters will not care too much about the institutional logic of the electoral system. They will be satisfied with the opportunity to cast two votes, thereby possibly expressing their coalition preferences, and thus possibly a more nuanced picture of their personality and identity. There is growing evidence that voters in MMP systems with more than one ballot do not cast their votes separately. Contamination effects of two votes have been shown in various countries.[23] These effects are not necessarily based on expressive motives. There might also be other reasons for these results, such as a lack of electoral knowledge. Still, contamination effects are the expected outcome if voters do mainly care about preference expression.

Before deriving hypotheses for instrumental and expressive coalition voting in the 2009 and 2013 elections, some boundary conditions of coalition voting in these two elections have to be explored. The following paragraphs will have a look at the electoral situation of the FDP before the 2009 and the 2013 elections.

EMPIRICAL CONTEXT: THE FDP AT THE FEDERAL ELECTIONS 2009 AND 2013

Before the German federal election of 2009, the FDP was part of the parliamentary opposition and wanted to form a new government together with the CDU/CSU. The partners of the Grand Coalition governing at that time both sent signals that they would be willing to govern with a smaller partner (the CDU/CSU with the FDP and the SPD with the Greens). However, it was not clear if one of these constellations would gain a majority, which led to a discussion about other coalition options.[24] During the campaign the FDP focused on addressing voters who were dissatisfied with the policies of the Grand Coalition and preferred a black–yellow coalition of the CDU/CSU and FDP. The party tried to benefit from possible doubts of the voters who did not believe in the willingness of the CDU/CSU to bring the Grand Coalition to an end. The party was thus wooing voters with a strong coalition preference to give 'at least' their second vote – which is of course the more important one in Germany – to the FDP. This pattern of argument was also echoed in the media. When analysing the different coalition options, the weekly newspaper *DIE ZEIT*, for example, concluded: 'Those who wish for a black–yellow coalition will most likely get it by giving their vote to the FDP.'[25] If one believed the statements of the CDU/CSU and FDP, who both claimed to prefer to govern together, and if one also kept in mind that according to the polls, which saw the FDP at about 10 to 12 per cent there was no danger of the FDP missing the electoral threshold of 5 per cent, this recommendation was not all that plausible from an instrumental perspective – as a CDU/CSU supporter would also get this result by voting for its preferred party and thereby also strengthening the position of the CDU/CSU within the future coalition. However, it shows possible reasons for coalition voters who just wanted to express their coalition preferences.

In the 2009 federal election the FDP achieved a record result, gaining 14.6 per cent of the vote share. As expected, it then formed a government coalition with the CDU/CSU. The so-called black–yellow coalition had a rather bumpy start. One central point of debate was a comprehensive reform of tax legislation with large tax cuts promised by the FDP during the election campaign, which could not be realised in the end. At the beginning of the parliamentary term, only individual groups like hoteliers benefited from tax relief and the FDP saw itself confronted with accusations of 'clientelistic politics',[26] even though the tax relief was also supported by the CSU. Within the FDP, there were continuing discussions about how to cope with the euro crisis and Greece, which led to a controversial members' vote and in the end to numerous withdrawals of members from the party. At the same time, the rise of *Alternative für Deutschland* (Alternative for Germany, AfD) challenged the FDP and brought another rival into German party competition. As polling figures for the FDP decreased quite significantly, the then party leader Guido Westerwelle increasingly came under attack within the party and had to fight off calls for his resignation. In 2011 he ended up being replaced by Philipp Rösler, which did not stop internal squabbles however.

Election Campaign 2013

During the election campaign of 2013, the CDU/CSU strategy was to provide as few targets as possible. It mainly focused on the popular incumbent chancellor Angela Merkel and did not particularly talk about the achievements of the coalition.[27] Moreover, it was striking that after the experiences of the 2009 federal election and the 2013 state election in Lower Saxony in which the FDP gained record results, the CDU/CSU did not tolerate the FDP's *Zweitstimmen* campaign for 'borrowed' or 'rental' votes from CDU/CSU supporters, but specifically attacked it by calling for both votes and even labelling the second vote as *Merkelstimme* (vote for Merkel). The FDP tried to underpin its electoral campaign by its performance as a government party while at the same time starting a *Zweitstimmen* campaign for second votes just as in 2009, courting CDU/CSU supporters who wanted a CDU/CSU–FDP coalition.[28] It tried to raise the spectre of a leftist red–red–green coalition of the SPD, the Greens and the Left party even though the SPD had ruled out that possibility. At the same time it tried to benefit from the popularity of Angela Merkel by arguing that any vote for the FDP might also back her chancellorship. However, for Angela Merkel it was, of course, also possible to stay chancellor with another coalition partner – as it turned out in the end, the FDP did not make it into parliament. Against this background it might have been more promising to allude to the black–yellow coalition and mobilise against the 'danger' of a possible Grand Coalition.

According to coalition signals sent out by parties, the situation was relatively clear: if the incumbent black–yellow coalition gained the parliamentary majority, this coalition would be continued; only if this was not the case would other coalition options be possible. As the SPD ruled out the possibility of forming a red–red–green coalition in the run-up to the election, most political observers considered a Grand Coalition to be the most probable alternative to a black–yellow one. The surveys before the election suggested that there would be a majority for black–yellow, but it was not certain if the FDP would pass the 5 per cent threshold so that the continuation of the black–yellow coalition depended particularly on the FDP entering the parliament. Theoretically, the situation seemed to be ideal for the FDP to propose a *threshold insurance strategy* to voters: 'Please vote for us with your second vote in order to get a CDU/CSU–FDP coalition.' In contrast to former elections in which the forecast vote share of the FDP considerably exceeded the 5 per cent threshold while the FDP nevertheless recommended strategic voting for CDU/CSU supporters, the recommendation was also plausible from a theoretical perspective. The FDP was at risk of not getting into parliament and the most efficient way of using your vote in order to have a CDU/CSU–FDP coalition was to vote for the FDP. This time, however, the CDU/CSU thwarted this strategy emphatically, pointing to the new electoral law that made it even clearer than before that a tactical second vote would hurt the actually preferred party.

HYPOTHESES

Given the recent work on voting in multi-party systems that points to the importance of coalition considerations[29] and the theoretical arguments laid out above, I expect that the FDP vote share in both 2009 and 2013 was not only a reflection of party evaluations but also of coalition considerations. In both election campaigns, the FDP was courting coalition voters to support it. Therefore, coalition evaluations should have played a role in forming vote intentions and also in translating these vote intentions into vote choices.[30]

> Hypothesis 1: Coalition evaluations had a distinct effect on the FDP vote in both 2009 and 2013 – on top of party evaluations.

From an alternative point of view, coalition evaluations are simple derivations of party evaluations and offer no distinct explanatory power. According to this view, coalition considerations should have had no effect on FDP vote intention and vote choice, once party evaluations are controlled for.

Considering the situation of the FDP before the 2009 and the 2013 elections, I expect more instrumental coalition voting in 2013 than in 2009. The situation in 2013 very much resembled the ideal conditions for *threshold insurance voting* for the FDP. First, there were clear signals from both the CDU/CSU and the FDP that they would want a coalition with each other. While this condition was also met in 2009, the second condition for *threshold insurance voting* was only met in the latest election. In 2009, the FDP was not at risk of missing the threshold. In 2013, when most polls had the FDP at just about 5 per cent, that was clearly the case. Taking into account the boundary conditions of the *threshold insurance* hypothesis, one would therefore expect instrumental coalition voting in 2013 but less so in 2009.

Hypothesis 2: There was more instrumental coalition voting for the FDP in 2013 than in 2009.

As there is no direct measure for instrumental motivation on behalf of the voters, instrumental coalition voting will be identified via interactions of coalition evaluations and outcome expectations. For expressive coalition voting, two main factors differed between 2009 and 2013. First, in 2009 the governing coalition consisted of the CDU/CSU and SPD. Voters with a strong preference for a CDU/CSU–FDP coalition may have had a particularly strong wish to express their differing political preference. By now, there is some evidence that expressive motivations have bigger effects on vote choices if one's preferences differ from the status quo government.[31] According to this view, there should have been less expressive coalition voting in 2013 as the CDU/CSU–FDP coalition was already in office. A second factor that differed between 2009 and 2013 was the behaviour of the preferred coalition partner, the CDU/CSU. In 2009, the CDU/CSU was fairly tolerant of the second vote campaign of the FDP, which was aimed at supporters of the CDU/CSU. In 2013, the CDU/CSU was distinctly arguing against that campaign and telling its supporters that every vote for the potential coalition partner would hurt the CDU/CSU. Expressive voters were thus reminded that split-ticket voting was not merely a way of expressing *coalition* preferences but that the second vote was the most important way of expressing one's *party* preferences. Interestingly, with labelling the second vote as '*Merkelstimme*' and implying that this was also about how one relates to the popular chancellor, the CDU/CSU might have successfully undermined expressive coalition voting for the FDP. Taken together, I expect less expressive coalition voting in 2013.

Hypothesis 3: There was less expressive coalition voting for the FDP in 2013 than in 2009.

Again, we have no direct measurement of expressive coalition reasoning. Still, there is the clear expectation that expressive coalition voting should be independent of outcome expectations; the direct effect of coalition evaluations on FDP voting should therefore be stronger in 2013 than in 2009. Hypothesis 3 is however by no means a simple mirror of hypothesis 2, as the amount of coalition voting, compared for instance with simple party voting, is not fixed. Theoretically, it could be possible that in one election year the boundary conditions of both instrumental and expressive coalition voting would be met, for which one would then expect more instrumental *and* more expressive coalition voting. Imagine, for instance, that in the next federal election in 2017 the FDP were again to be in danger of not crossing the threshold, that the CDU/ CSU were again signalling the wish to form a government with the FDP and that, this time, a FDP campaign for 'borrowed votes' from CDU/CSU supporters were to be tolerated and therefore an expressive logic of choice would not be undermined. In that case, one would expect more instrumental coalition voting than in 2009 *and* more expressive coalition voting than in 2013.

DATA

The analysis is based on various data sources. For the descriptive analysis of voters' party and coalition preferences and expectations the GLES pre-election face-to-face cross-sectional surveys will be used (ZA5300, ZA5700). A major advantage of the GLES studies is that all the relevant questions for our analysis were (almost) identical in 2009 and 2013, which allows for a valid comparison of the two elections. The same data sets will be used for the multivariate analysis of FDP voting intentions, which will also control for party and candidate evaluations and basic socio-demographic variables. This first multivariate analysis will be used to test the hypothesis of instrumental and expressive coalition voting. Analysing the impact of coalition evaluations of the CDU/CSU–FDP coalition on FDP vote intentions, while controlling extensively for party and candidate evaluations, will allow us to test hypothesis 1 according to which coalition evaluations had a distinct effect on vote choices in both elections. Comparing these effects between the two elections will allow us to test hypotheses 2 and 3. As instrumental coalition voting should always be conditioned by outcome expectations, interaction models of coalition evaluations and expectations of the chances of the FDP getting into parliament will be calculated. According to hypothesis 2, there should be a stronger conditionality of the impact of coalition evaluations in 2013 than in 2009. Likewise, according to hypothesis 3, there should be stronger unconditional effects of coalition evaluations on FDP vote intentions in 2013. For the dynamic analysis of vote intentions and vote choices for the FDP, the GLES rolling cross section (RCS) campaign pre–post panel studies will be used (ZA5303, ZA5703). This will allow a more detailed look at the role of coalition considerations not only on forming vote intentions but also on translating these intentions into actual voting behaviour at the two elections. In a first analysis of the panel data, aggregated vote intentions and vote choices for the FDP will be analysed in order to get some insight into potential mobilising effects during the 2009 and 2013 campaigns. A second analysis of the panel data will then investigate the role of coalition evaluations in transforming vote intentions into vote choices – controlling again for party and candidate evaluations.

RESULTS

In a first step, some descriptive analysis will shed light on the preferences and expectations of voters before the 2009 and the 2013 federal elections in Germany. Using the GLES pre-election surveys, Figure 1 presents party and coalition preferences in 2009

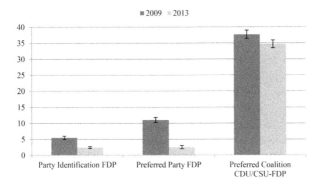

FIGURE 1
PARTY AND COALITION PREFERENCES, 2009 AND 2013

Note: Share of respondents indicating a party identification with the FDP, preferring the FDP and preferring a CDU/CSU–FDP coalition respectively, standard errors; ZA5300, ZA5700.

and 2013. For the party measures, one finds a stark decline in support for the FDP. In 2009, 5.5 per cent of voters indicated that they identify with the FDP. In 2013, this number was halved. In light of an orthodox view on party identification as a rather stable attitude which should not change so much between two elections, this is quite surprising.[32] The middle column of Table 1 presents another party measure, the share of voters who preferred the FDP over all other parties on an 11-point rating scale. This share of voters decreased from 11 per cent to only 2.5 per cent in 2013. Taken together, this suggests that a large part of the voting share loss of the FDP

TABLE 1
MARGINAL EFFECTS FDP VOTE INTENTION, 2009 AND 2013

	FDP vote intention (1/0)	
	2009	2013
Party identification FDP	+14***	+9***
Party identification CDU/CSU	−3**	+1
Party evaluation FDP	+32***	+21***
Party evaluation CDU/CSU	−9**	−5*
Leader evaluation FDP: Westerwelle (2009)/Brüderle (2013)	+5	+1
Leader evaluation CDU/CSU: Angela Merkel	+1	−1
Coalition evaluation CDU/CSU–FDP	+19***	+6***
Coalition evaluation CDU/CSU–SPD	−1	−1*
Government performance	−5*	−1
Education: high	+1	0
Female	0	0
Age	0	0
McFadden Pseudo R^2	0.40	0.42
N	1356	1463

Note: Logit models, changes of predicted probabilities (min–max), ZA5300, ZA5700.
*$p < 0.05$;
**$p < 0.01$;
***$p < 0.001$.

was due to party-related attitudes. Few voters still felt attached to the FDP or preferred the FDP over other German parties in 2013.

Interestingly, though, a very large proportion of the electorate still wanted the FDP to be part of the next government. The ruling CDU/CSU–FDP coalition was still the most popular coalition. In 2009, 38 per cent of voters wished for that coalition. In 2013, that was still the case for 35 per cent of voters. Given the sharp decline in party support for the FDP, that is quite remarkable. The second most popular coalition alternative (not shown in Figure 1) in both 2009 and 2013 was a red–green coalition of SPD and the Green party – with about 22 and 24 per cent of support. The alternative of a Grand Coalition of CDU/CSU and SPD gained some support between the two elections. In 2009, when there was a Grand Coalition in office, only 14 per cent of voters wished for a continuation of this government. In 2013, about 22 per cent wanted this coalition to be formed after the election. Thus, for both elections the CDU/CSU–FDP coalition was by far the most popular alternative. For our purpose of analysing coalition voting for the FDP, it is also interesting to have a look at those voters with a party preference for its potential coalition partner, the CDU/CSU. In 2009, 72 per cent of CDU/CSU supporters wanted a coalition with the FDP and 18 per cent wanted a coalition with the SPD. There was almost no change in 2013: 73 per cent of CDU/CSU supporters preferred a coalition with the FDP and 21 per cent preferred a coalition with the SPD. Taken together, Figure 1 presents a clear picture: the FDP lost a lot of support between the two elections but a clear majority of voters still wanted it to be part of the next government.

As outlined above, instrumental coalition voting would always be conditioned by outcome expectations. For the threshold insurance strategy, it is of particular importance whether one thinks that the smaller partner of the preferred coalition is in danger of not crossing the threshold. Figure 2 shows the shares of voters who thought that the FDP would certainly or most probably cross the parliamentary

FIGURE 2
EXPECTATIONS OF FDP AND THE CDU/CSU–FDP COALITION

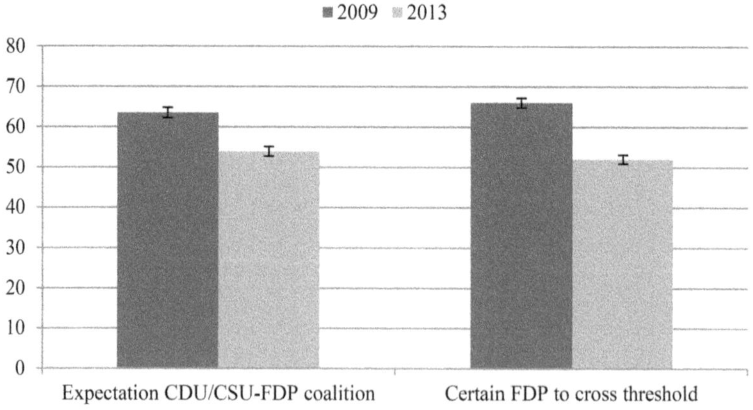

Note: Share of respondents expecting a CDU/CSU–FDP coalition and share of voters expecting the FDP to cross the electoral threshold (certainly and most probably), standard errors; ZA5300, ZA5700.

threshold of 5 per cent at the respective election. In both elections, the majority of voters were relatively certain that the FDP would cross that threshold.

Against the background of published voting polls before both elections, the small difference in expectations is quite remarkable. While polls in 2009 saw the FDP at 12 to 14 per cent of votes, well above the threshold, in 2013 most polls had the party at just 5 per cent. Those polls in 2013 suggested that it was anything but certain that the FDP would make it into parliament. Nevertheless, the share of voters who were more or less certain that the FDP would cross the threshold was only slightly lower than in 2009. This also translated into coalition expectations. A majority of voters in 2013 were expecting a CDU/CSU–FDP coalition. That was a bit less than in 2009, but it was still seen as the most likely coalition alternative. About 52 per cent of voters were expecting that coalition (28 per cent were expecting a Grand Coalition). This shows that voters were very optimistic about the chances of the FDP despite polls indicating a very close race for the threshold. This becomes even more apparent if one compares expectations about the FDP with those about another small party, the AfD. While 52 per cent of voters expected the FDP to cross the threshold, only 4 per cent expected the same for the AfD. Given that polls saw the AfD at 3–5 per cent and the FDP only slightly higher at 5 per cent, this big difference in expectations is somewhat surprising. One possible explanation is that voters did not take the uncertainty of these polling results into account. With a sample size of often no more than 1000 respondents, these commercial polls have considerable margins of error.[33] The differences between the FDP and the AfD were probably not statistically significant in most of these polls. However, polling companies had the FDP continuously just above the threshold and the AfD just under the threshold. This may have added to the overly optimistic expectations about the FDP. At the same time, voters might have taken into account that the FDP has been repeatedly in danger of not crossing the threshold but in the end it always won enough votes to get into parliament – possibly also because of successful second vote campaigns wooing rental votes.

The descriptive data shows that the FDP lost a lot of party support; but many voters still wanted it to be part of the next coalition and also expected it to be. In a next step, the effects of these evaluations and expectations on vote intentions will be analysed – using again the GLES pre-election surveys. Table 1 shows the results of logistic regressions on vote intentions in 2009 and 2013. In order to get an impression of the effect sizes, changes in predicted probabilities are reported. Since we are particularly interested in the effect of coalition evaluations, party evaluations of both the FDP and the CDU/CSU are extensively controlled for, as coalition evaluations might be simple derivations of party evaluations.

Not surprisingly, party identification with the FDP increased the likelihood of a FDP vote intention in 2009 by 14 percentage points and in 2013 by 9 percentage points. Additionally, more general party evaluations of the FDP on an 11-point rating scale had a strong effect on the likelihood of voting FDP. Candidate evaluations of the FDP candidate Westerwelle in 2009 and Brüderle in 2013 had little effect on vote intentions. Most importantly for our analysis, evaluations of the CDU/CSU–FDP coalition had significant effects on the intention to vote for the FDP in both elections. Hypothesis 1 is thus clearly supported. Even after extensively controlling for party and candidate preferences, evaluations of the CDU/CSU–FDP coalition had considerable effects on FDP vote intentions. That is, voters in the German multi-party system seemed to care not only about parties but also about coalitions when making up their mind about the coming election. There were rather large differences between 2009 and 2013, though. The influence of coalition evaluations was much stronger in 2009. Evaluating the coalition with the best possible rating increased the likelihood of a FDP vote by 19 percentage points in 2009 but only by 6 percentage points in 2013. Thus, coalition voting happened in both elections but it was much smaller in 2013. In order to assess hypothesis 2 and the conditionality of this coalition voting, the same models as in Table 1 were calculated with the addition of interactions of coalition evaluations and expectations of the chances of the FDP to cross the threshold. These interactions were not significant for both elections; additional numerical findings are not reported. Detailed interaction results are shown graphically in Figure 3.

If coalition voting was mainly driven by instrumental reasoning trying to insure the threshold for the small coalition partner, coalition evaluations of the CDU/CSU–FDP coalition should have had a particularly strong effect among those voters who were not certain that the FDP would cross the threshold. That was not the case. For both elections, there is no significant interaction between coalition evaluations and expectations. In 2009, coalition voting was even a bit more pronounced among those who were certain that the FDP would make it into parliament anyway. In 2013, the slopes for both groups were very flat for low and moderate evaluations of the CDU/CSU–FDP coalition. For voters with moderately positive evaluations of the coalition (0.6 and

FIGURE 3
PREDICTED PROBABILITIES, FDP VOTE INTENTION: INTERACTION MODELS OF
COALITION EVALUATION AND EXPECTATIONS

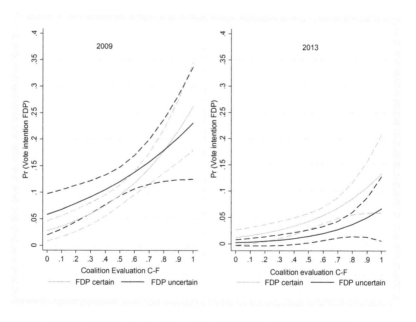

Note: Predicted probabilities (solid lines) and confidence intervals (dashed lines), ZA5300, ZA5700.

0.7), those with positive expectations were more likely to vote for the FDP than those who thought crossing the threshold was uncertain. Only for voters with very high evaluations of the coalition (starting at 0.8) does one see a bit of an interaction in the direction that you would expect from a threshold insurance strategy: the likelihood of an intention of voting for the FDP increases a bit more for those voters with low expectations. Overall, the interaction models provide no evidence for instrumentally oriented coalition voting that is conditioned by outcome expectations. For 2009, this is not so surprising as the FDP was not really in danger of missing the threshold. For 2013, this is more surprising. A possible explanation for this could be the overly optimistic expectations about the chances of the FDP as discussed above. More generally, it might just be difficult to measure voters' expectations in a valid and reliable way as voters often engage in wishful thinking when asked about election outcomes.[34] Taken together, the analysis does not provide any support for hypothesis 2, according to which there should have been more instrumental coalition voting in 2013 than in 2009. In both elections, coalition voting was unconditioned by outcome expectations, which gives support to an expressive view of coalition voting. As the comparison of direct effects of coalition evaluations in Table 1 shows, this unconditioned coalition voting was considerably stronger in 2009 and thus supports hypothesis 3.

As we have seen, coalition evaluations had direct effects on FDP vote intentions in both elections. However, they were considerably smaller in 2013 than in 2009. To shed some more light on actual voting for the FDP, the following paragraphs will analyse how vote intentions translated into vote choices. One possible explanation for the very different outcomes in 2009 and 2013 could be differing success in mobilising potential party and coalition voters of the FDP during the two campaigns. By using the pre–post panel data of the GLES RCS campaign study, vote intentions and actual voting behaviour can be compared. Figure 4 shows the simple aggregated share of respondents who intended to vote for the FDP in the pre-election wave and the aggregated share of respondents who indicated they had voted for them in the post-election wave.

FIGURE 4
VOTE INTENTION AND VOTE CHOICE, 2009 AND 2013

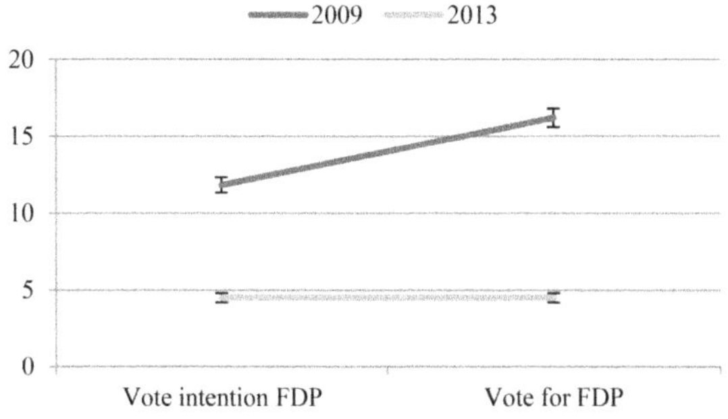

Note: Share of respondents with an intention to vote for the FDP in the pre-election wave (left side) and share of respondents indicating that they have voted for the FDP in the post-election wave, standard errors; ZA5303, ZA5703.

The analysis uses only voters who took part in both waves. In 2009 considerably more respondents voted for the FDP than intended to vote for the FDP during the campaign. Apparently, the FDP was quite successful in mobilising voters in 2009. Looking in more detail at the vote intentions of those respondents who ended up voting for the FDP in the election, there is a clear pattern (not shown in Figure 4). The FDP gained from two groups of voters in 2009. It got votes from those who intended to vote for the CDU/CSU during the campaign and from those who were then still undecided. In sharp contrast, the FDP did not gain any net support during the 2013 campaign. The share of vote intentions in the pre-election wave was about the same as the vote share in the post-election wave. Obviously, the FDP was less successful in mobilising the voters. Looking at the net changes from vote intentions to vote choices, it is particularly interesting that the FDP did not get any gains from CDU/CSU supporters. Apparently, coalition voters were not so mobilised in 2013.

The fact that the FDP gained from CDU/CSU supporters in 2009 but not in 2013 suggests that coalition considerations did play a bigger role in transforming vote intentions into actual vote choices in 2009 than in 2013. For a more direct test of the role of coalition evaluations in mobilising voters, a multivariate logit model has been calculated with the FDP vote as the dependent variable. Independent variables were FDP vote intention, party evaluations of both the CDU/CSU and the FDP, leader evaluations and most importantly evaluations of the CDU/CSU–FDP coalition. Figure 5 shows graphically the results of these models. It describes the predicted probabilities of a FDP vote conditional on evaluations of the CDU/CSU–FDP coalition on an 11-point rating (rescaled to an interval from 0 to 1). Two groups of voters are separated

FIGURE 5
PREDICTED PROBABILITIES OF VOTING FDP

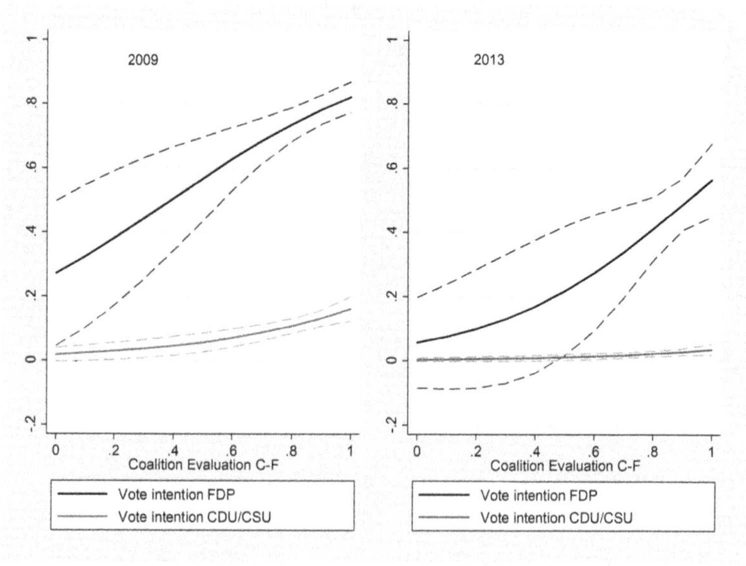

Note: Predicted probabilities (solid lines) and confidence intervals (dashed lines), ZA5303, ZA5703.

that are of particular interest to our analysis: those voters who intended to vote for the FDP in the pre-election wave and those voters who intended to vote for CDU/CSU. All other variables are held constant at their means.

In 2009, coalition considerations had a strong effect for both groups. For voters with an intention to vote for FDP, the probability of actually voting for the FDP increased from around 25 per cent for those with a very negative coalition evaluation to 80 per cent for those with a very high coalition evaluation. That is, respondents were much more likely to act on their vote intention for the FDP when they had a strong preference for the CDU/CSU–FDP coalition – controlling for party evaluations. There was also a significant effect for those voters who intended to vote for the CDU/CSU during the campaign: the more favourably the CDU/CSU–FDP coalition was evaluated, the more likely that they actually voted for the FDP in the end. Respondents with an intention to vote for CDU/CSU and a very high evaluation of the coalition had a likelihood of 18 per cent to vote for the FDP in the election. Thus, coalition evaluations were not only important for voters intending to vote for the FDP but also for those intending to vote for the CDU/CSU.

In 2013, coalition considerations played a much smaller role in transforming vote intentions into voting behaviour. First of all, respondents intending to vote FDP during the campaign had an overall much lower probability of actually voting FDP than in 2009. This is reiterating the bivariate analysis from before. The FDP was less successful in mobilising its potential voters. The multivariate analysis shows that coalition considerations played a lesser (but still statistically significant) role in 2013 than in 2009 for translating vote intentions into actual voting behaviour. Interestingly, the likelihood of voting FDP – for those who intended to – was still only at 60 per cent if someone evaluated the CDU/CSU–FDP coalition very highly. The slope of the predicted probabilities is also rather flat for lower to medium coalition evaluations. Even for voters with moderately positive evaluations of the coalition, the likelihood of voting FDP was very low. The effect of coalition evaluations was only strong for rather high evaluations. Turning to those voters who intended to vote for the CDU/CSU in the pre-election wave, there was only a very small effect of coalition evaluations in 2013. There were only few respondents with an intention to vote CDU/CSU who ended up voting for the FDP and this was only slightly moderated by coalition evaluations. This is a sharp contrast to 2009. In separate models, it was also tested whether the effects of coalition evaluations on vote choices were moderated by outcome expectations, as one would expect from a viewpoint of instrumental coalition voting. However, there were no significant interaction effects of expectations and coalition evaluation for transforming vote intentions into vote choices.

Overall, these results suggest that coalition considerations not only had an effect on vote intentions as seen before. When vote intentions are held constant, coalition evaluations still had an effect on transforming these intentions into actual voting behaviour. The panel analysis thus provides more evidence for hypothesis 1. Coalition considerations were important for both forming vote intentions and for translating these intentions into voting behaviour. The panel analysis also provides evidence for hypothesis 3 – coalition evaluations had a less direct effect on vote choice in 2013 – but no evidence for hypothesis 2, according to which there should have been more instrumental coalition voting in 2013.[35]

CONCLUSION

Coalition considerations did play a role in FDP voting decisions in both 2009 and 2013. Voters in the multi-party system of Germany were not only influenced by their party and candidate preferences but also by their coalition preferences. The analysis thus added to the growing evidence that voters do care about coalition alternatives when making up their minds on voting decisions. The size of the influence of coalition evaluations on voting decisions, however, was very different. There was much more coalition-directed voting for the FDP in 2009 than in 2013.

The descriptive analysis of this article showed that the FDP has lost a lot of party support between the two elections. The performance of the FDP in the government and internal quarrelling certainly added to the stark decline of party evaluations before the 2013 election. It was not the aim of this article to answer why the party ratings and the party identification with the FDP decreased so much during the four years, but this decrease most certainly played a big role in determining the failure of the FDP at the 2013 election. Interestingly, though, despite the strong decrease in party ratings of the FDP during the term, most voters still wanted it to be part of the next government. At the same time, voters had very optimistic expectations about the chances of the FDP getting into parliament and about the chances of the CDU/CSU–FDP coalition having another term in government.

The multivariate analysis of vote intentions and vote choices gave a clear indication that coalition considerations were very important in 2009, but less so in 2013. The influence of coalition evaluations was much stronger in 2009. The different degree of coalition voting thus contributed to both the success and the failure of the FDP at the elections of 2009 and 2013. From a viewpoint of instrumental coalition voting, this is rather surprising, as the situation in 2013 resembled very much the ideal conditions of *threshold insurance voting* for the FDP. Still, the analysis showed no evidence for this kind of reasoning. We did not find an interaction of coalition evaluations and expectations for either election. For 2009, when the FDP was at no risk of missing the threshold, this seems plausible. For 2013, when most polls had the FDP at just about 5 per cent, this was rather surprising.

Overall, our analysis suggests that coalition voting in both elections was based less on instrumental reasoning than on expressive motivations. As expected, expressive coalition voting was stronger in 2009 than in 2013. One possible reason is the different strategy of the CDU/CSU in the two elections. In 2009, the CDU/CSU more or less tolerated the second vote campaign of the FDP which was aimed at supporters of the CDU/CSU. In 2013, the CDU/CSU was distinctly arguing against that campaign and even labelling the second vote as '*Merkelstimme*'. Expressive voters were thus reminded that split-ticket voting was not merely a way of expressing *coalition* preferences but that the second vote was also the most important way of expressing one's *party* preference. Or, as the argument for a '*Merkelstimme*' goes, some may even have been convinced that the second vote was for expressing one's 'candidate' preference. Even though the CDU/CSU–FDP coalition was still by far the most popular coalition alternative, fewer voters seemed to be compelled to express their coalition preference with the second vote.

Future research on coalition voting in Germany and elsewhere should focus not only on instrumental reasoning but also on expressive motivations. As Downs already pointed out some 50 years ago, voting decisions in multi-party systems involve a lot of uncertainty and complexity. He was therefore very sceptical about the chances of instrumental voting in multi-party systems and expected voters to fall back on a simpler calculus involving parties and candidates. Voters in multi-party systems may indeed have problems with complex instrumental reasoning of coalition voting. Still, coalitions are important political objects in these systems, and voters may want to express their preferences on coalitions – independent of calculating outcome expectations. The electoral system with two ballots particularly helps to express coalition preferences. Our analysis suggests, however, that this may only work if both coalition partners tolerate vote splitting campaigns and do not appeal to a party or candidate logic of expressive choice.

DISCLOSURE STATEMENT

No potential conflict of interest was reported by the author.

NOTES

1. E.g. Susumu Shikano, Michael Herrmann and Paul W. Thurner, 'Strategic Voting under Proportional Representation: Threshold Insurance in German Elections', *West European Politics* 32 (2009), pp.634–56; Thomas Gschwend, 'Ticket-splitting and Strategic Voting under Mixed Electoral Rules. Evidence from Germany', *European Journal of Political Research* 46 (2007), pp.1–23; Sascha Huber, *Strukturen des politischen Kontexts und die demokratische Kompetenz der Wähler. Experimentelle Studien zur Urteils- und Entscheidungsbildung* (Baden-Baden: Nomos, 2012).
2. The aim of this study is not to provide a full account of the success and failure of the FDP. Using the FDP is just a case in point to explore the more general theoretical argument about different motivations of coalition voting. See also Sascha Huber, 'Coalitions and Voting Behavior in a Differentiating Multiparty System', in Bernhard Weßels, Hans Rattinger, Sigrid Roßteutscher and Rüdiger Schmitt-Beck (eds), *Voters on the Move or on the Run?* (Oxford: Oxford University Press, 2014), pp.65–87.
3. Anthony Downs, *An Economic Theory of Democracy* (New York: Harper, 1957), p.147.
4. The theoretical literature on electoral and governmental decision making in multi-party systems often assumed that voters will anticipate or react to outcomes of the coalition formation process (e.g. David Austen-Smith and Jeffrey Banks, 'Elections, Coalitions, and Legislative Outcomes', *American Political Science Review* 82 (1988), pp.405–22) and coalition and inter-branch bargaining (e.g. Alberto Alesina and Howard Rosenthal, *Partisan Politics, Divided Government, and the Economy* (Cambridge: Cambridge University Press, 1995); Torsten Persson and Guido Tabellini, *Political Economics: Explaining Economic Policy* (Cambridge: MIT Press, 2000).
5. Downs, *An Economic Theory of Democracy.*, p.300.
6. Gary W. Cox, *Making Votes Count. Strategic Coordination in the World's Electoral System* (Cambridge: Cambridge University Press, 1997); Raymond M. Duch, Jeff May and David A. Armstrong, 'Coalition Directed Voting in Multiparty Democracies', *American Political Science Review* 104 (2010), pp.598–719.
7. Matias A. Bargsted and Orit Kedar, 'Coalition-targeted Duvergerian Voting: How Expectations Affect Voter Choice under Proportional Representation', *American Journal of Political Science* 53 (2009), pp.307–23.

8. Christopher Carman and Robert Johns, 'Attitudes to Coalitions and Split-ticket Voting: The Scottish Parliament Election of 2007', Paper presented at the 'Workshop on Voters, Coalitions and Democratic Accountability 2007', Exeter, 2007.

9. Galen A. Irwin and Joop J. van Holsteyn, 'They Say It Can't Be Done? Strategic Voting in Multi-party Proportional Systems: The Case of the Netherlands', Paper presented at the 'Annual Meeting of the American Political Science Association', Philadelphia, 2003.

10. Michael F. Meffert and Thomas Gschwend, 'Strategic Coalition Voting: Evidence from Austria', *Electoral Studies* 29 (2010), pp.339–49.

11. Shikano et al., 'Strategic Voting under Proportional Representation'; Sascha Huber, Thomas Gschwend, Michael F. Meffert and Franz U. Pappi, 'Erwartungsbildung über den Wahlausgang und ihr Einfluss auf die Wahlentscheidung', in Oscar W. Gabriel, Jürgen W. Falter and Bernhard Weßels (eds), *Wahlen und Wähler. Analysen aus Anlass der Bundestagswahl 2005* (Wiesbaden: VS Verlag, 2010), pp.562–84.

12. Franz U. Pappi and Paul W. Thurner, 'Electoral Behaviour in a Two-vote System: Incentives for Ticket Splitting in German Bundestag Elections', *European Journal of Political Research* 41 (2002), pp.207–32.

13. Shikano et al., 'Strategic Voting under Proportional Representation'; Huber, *Strukturen des politischen Kontexts*.

14. Matthew S. Shugart and Martin P. Wattenberg, *Mixed-Member Electoral Systems: The Best of Both Worlds?* (Oxford: Oxford University Press, 2001).

15. Geoffrey Brennan and Loren Lomasky, *Democracy and Decision. The Pure Theory of Electoral Preference* (Cambridge: Cambridge University Press, 1993).

16. Moses Shayo and Alon Harel, 'Non-consequentialist Voting', *Journal of Economic Behaviour and Organisation* 81 (2012), pp.299–313.

17. Alan Hamlin and Colin Jennings, 'Expressive Political Behaviour: Foundations, Scope and Implications', *British Journal of Political Science* 41 (2011), pp.645–70.

18. Alexander A. Schuessler, *A Logic of Expressive Choice* (Princeton, NJ: Princeton University Press, 2000).

19. Ibid., p.ix.

20. Ibid., p.15.

21. Huber, 'Coalitions and Voting Behavior'.

22. This might be particularly important for supporters of catch-all parties like the CDU/CSU. As their political programme and image will sometimes be a bit non-specific in order to appeal to as many voters as possible, expressing a preference only for that party might also be seen as a bit non-specific or boring. Expressive voters who want to show a more nuanced picture of themselves might therefore be tempted to add another facet by also voting for a smaller coalition partner with a more specific image and policy outlook.

23. Karen E. Cox and Leonard J. Schoppa, 'Interaction Effects and Mixed-Member Electoral Systems: Theory and Evidence from Germany, Japan, and Italy', *Comparative Political Studies* 35 (2002), pp.1027–53; Jens Hainmueller and Holger L. Kern, 'Incumbency as a Source of Spillover Effects in Mixed Electoral Systems: Evidence from a Regression-Discontinuity Design', *Electoral Studies* 27 (2008), pp.213–27; Erik S. Herron and Misa Nishikawa, 'Contamination Effects and the Number of Parties in Mixed-Superposition Electoral Systems', *Electoral Studies* 20 (2001), pp.63–86.

24. Evelyn Bytzek and Sascha Huber, 'Koalitionen und strategisches Wählen', in Hans Rattinger et al. (eds), *Zwischen Langeweile und Extremen: Die Bundestagswahl 2009* (Baden-Baden: Nomos, 2011), pp.247–64.

25. *DIE ZEIT*, No. 37, 3 Sept. 2009, p.3.

26. Oskar Niedermayer, 'Aufsteiger, Absteiger und ewig "Sonstige": Klein- und Kleinstparteien bei der Bundestagswahl 2013', *Zeitschrift für Parlamentsfragen* 45 (2014), pp.73–93.

27. Richard Hilmer and Stefan Merz, 'Die Bundestagswahl vom 22. September 2013: Merkels Meisterstück', *Zeitschrift für Parlamentsfragen* 45 (2014), pp.175–206.

28. Ralf Tils and Joachim Raschke, 'Strategie zählt. Die Bundestagswahl 2013', *Aus Politik und Zeitgeschichte* 48–9 (2013), pp.20–27.

29. Duch et al., 'Coalition directed Voting in Multiparty Democracies'; André Blais, John H. Aldrich, Indridi H. Indridason and Renan Levine, 'Do Voters Vote for Government Coalitions? Testing Downs' Pessimistic Conclusion', *Party Politics* 12 (2006), pp.691–705.

30. For vote intentions and vote choices, I will look only at the more important second vote, which is the party vote. The first vote, which is the candidate vote in the plurality pillar, will not be analysed.

31. Sascha Huber and Rüdiger Schmitt-Beck, 'Expressive Wähler bei der Bundestagswahl 2013. Eine empirische Exploration', in Harald Schoen and Bernhard Wessels (eds), *Wahlen und Wähler. Analysen aus Anlass der Bundestagswahl 2005* (Wiesbaden: VS Verlag, 2016), pp.295–325.

32. Angus Campbell, Philip E. Converse, Warren E. Miller and Donald E. Stokes, *The American Voter* (New York/London: John Wiley & Sons, 1960).
33. These error terms of German polls are particularly large, if adequately calculated; see Rainer Schnell and Marcel Noack, 'The Accuracy of Pre-Election Polling of German General Elections', *MDA – Methods, Data, Analysis* 8 (2014), pp.5–24.
34. Michael F. Meffert, Sascha Huber, Thomas Gschwend and Franz Urban Pappi, 'More than Wishful Thinking: Causes and Consequences of Voters' Electoral Expectations about Parties and Coalitions', *Electoral Studies* 30 (2011), pp.804–15.
35. A look at the vote recall of participants in the 2013 survey affirms the conclusions drawn before. For many reasons, recall questions are problematic as voters might not remember their vote choices of former elections or adjust their answers to current preferences. Still, it is striking that about 40 per cent of those who said they voted for the FDP in 2009 were voting for the CDU/CSU in 2013. This indicates that many voters switched to the bigger coalition partner in the 2013 election. Part of that dynamic was probably just a normalisation from the very large defection of CDU/CSU supporters in 2009. In 2009, about 12 per cent of voters with a CDU/CSU party identification voted for the desired coalition partner FDP. In 2013, only about 4 per cent of voters with a CDU/CSU party identification voted for the FDP.

The 'Alternative für Deutschland in the Electorate': Between Single-Issue and Right-Wing Populist Party

RÜDIGER SCHMITT-BECK

The good result of the recently formed Alternative für Deutschland (AfD) was a striking outcome of the 2013 Federal Election. This article explores why AfD supporters chose this party at the 2013 Federal Election and at the 2014 European and eastern German State (Land) Elections. At the Federal Election the AfD's electorate was composed of two groups: a minority of instrumental issue-voters that were drawn to the AfD by its emphasis and positioning on the Euro crisis, and a majority of 'late supporters' that decided close to Election Day and were moved more by expressive motives, most notably xenophobic sentiments like those identified in other European countries as a main source of support for right-wing populist parties. The analysis of the subsequent elections shows that, paralleling developments in the AfD's public rhetoric, the Euro crisis ceased to be important for AfD support whereas xenophobic motives became more central.

INTRODUCTION

At the German Federal Election on 22 September 2013, two parties failed to pass the 5 per cent threshold of the electoral system by a narrow margin. One was the Free Democratic Party (FDP) which suffered a landslide loss and for the first time ever failed to win any mandates in the Bundestag. The other was the Alternative für Deutschland (Alternative for Germany, AfD), a newcomer in the German party system that had been founded just half a year before the election and immediately gained 4.7 per cent of the second votes. For a new party, this was an excellent result. In fact, never before had a newcomer or fringe party come so close to passing the 5 per cent threshold at a Federal Election. At subsequent elections the AfD drew momentum from this near success. At subsequent nation-wide and State Elections it gained enough votes to send representatives to the respective parliaments. With 7.1 per cent of the national vote share, it won seven of the 96 German seats in the European Parliament, which was elected on 25 May 2014. At the State Elections in Saxony, Brandenburg and Thuringia in August and September 2014 it obtained vote shares between 9.7 and 12.2 per cent and accordingly won substantial numbers of mandates in each of the three state parliaments. In February and May 2015 the AfD also gained mandates in the parliaments of the West German city states Hamburg and Bremen (vote shares 6.1 and 5.5 per cent). These successes were followed up with more eye-catching performances in Saxony-Anhalt, Baden-Württemberg and Rheinland Palatinate in early 2016.

The AfD emerged in early 2013 as a single-issue party criticising the policies of the federal government and the Bundestag parties on the Euro crisis.[1] However, its organisational face became somewhat ambiguous during the Federal Election campaign, as it added – although only as an aside – a variety of other issues to its profile. Due to the nature of the positions articulated by the AfD, political and scholarly observers soon began to ask whether it should be rated as a right-wing populist party comparable to the FPÖ in Austria, the *Front National* in France or the VVD in the Netherlands. To date, such enquiries have studied the AfD only from a supply-side perspective. Investigating the AfD's electoral platforms and other forms of campaign communication they focused on the party as a 'propagandiser'.[2] In spite of the party's repeated claims of pursuing policies outside the left–right spectrum systematic analyses found the AfD to be clearly leaning to the right. But overall its communication did not warrant classification as a right-wing populist party.[3]

The present article complements this research with a demand-side perspective. It studies the 'AfD in the electorate'[4] by examining why AfD supporters preferred this party at the 2013 Federal Election and at the 2014 European and regional elections. Although it takes guidance from various theories of electoral behaviour, the approach of this research is exploratory. For investigating a novel and ambiguous phenomenon like the AfD's surprising success at the 2013 and 2014 elections a wide-angle lens that covers a broad range of possible predictors of party choice appears most suitable. The article starts with a brief account of how the AfD emerged on the political stage and campaigned during the run-up to the Federal Election. It then goes on to trace how the party's electoral support crystallised during the campaign and what moved voters to support it at the polls. Moving beyond the 2013 Federal Election, the article then explores the development of the party's programmatic self-presentation and its voter support at the 2014 European and regional elections. All analyses are based on surveys conducted by the German Longitudinal Election Study (GLES).[5] To explore voting behaviour at the 2013 Federal Election, a pre–post-election panel survey is used.[6] Both waves were conducted by telephone. The pre-election wave was designed as a rolling cross-section (RCS) survey covering the entire election campaign.[7] For the analyses of voting behaviour at the 2014 European and State Elections cross-sectional data from non-representative online surveys are used.[8]

THE AFD AT THE 2013 FEDERAL ELECTION

The Euro Crisis and the Emergence of the AfD

The sovereign debt crisis in the Eurozone that resulted from the 2008 financial and economic crisis and drove some Euro member states to the verge of financial breakdown was clearly one of the most serious and far-reaching problems that the federal government of CDU/CSU and FDP had to face during the legislative period preceding the 2013 election. In connection with the bailout measures for Greece, Ireland, Portugal, Spain and Cyprus, Germany assumed very considerable financial risks. The crisis policy of the government followed the logic that financial assistance for heavily indebted Euro states should not be refused but made conditional on quite severe austerity measures.[9] Only the Left Party was clearly against this policy. The SPD and the Greens agreed to the rescue packages and supported the government's policy in parliament although over time they became more critical of the strictness of the government's austerity course.[10] Voices that on the other hand found this approach still too generous could sporadically be heard from the ranks of the FDP, but remained inconsequential in terms of actual policy.

In the indebted countries of the European South the crisis policy of the European Union (EU), the European Central Bank (ECB) and International Monetary Fund (IMF), which had been crucially influenced by the German government, led to massive legitimacy crises. The governments that were forced to implement the austerity measures came under attack from groups affected by these measures' consequences and had to face enormous losses at elections.[11] But in a donor country like Germany whose government had burdened its citizens with considerable financial risks the legitimacy of the crisis policy was also precarious.[12] It is therefore hardly surprising that the established parties shied away from thematising the Euro crisis during the 2013 election campaign. To be sure, all party manifestos included positions concerning preferred crisis policies. The government parties CDU/CSU and FDP pleaded for a continuation of the chosen course, while the SPD and the Greens wanted to soften the burden placed on the debtor countries and complement the austerity course by investment programmes. The Left demanded a complete policy reversal away from austerity. However, party manifestos remain usually unread and in the campaign communication addressed to the general public the Euro crisis was widely neglected. Campaign strategists seemed to consider this issue 'toxic'.[13] Two features thus characterised treatment of the Euro crisis in the campaigns of the Bundestag parties: *dethematisation* with regard to the saliency dimension,[14] and an only *partial coverage of the political spectrum* with regard to the position dimension,[15] ranging from restrictive and conditional to more generous financial assistance to the debtor countries, but excluding the option of refusing any support at all.[16]

It was exactly this vacancy in the political debate that the AfD aimed to fill at its foundation on 6 February 2013. Under the leadership of Bernd Lucke, a professor of macro-economics, it presented itself as a single-issue party with a rather narrow focus on the European debt crisis.[17] Its slim political agenda was dominated by liberal–conservative Euro-scepticism. Its platform demanded an 'orderly dissolution' of the European monetary zone and a return to national currencies or smaller, more homogeneous monetary associations. Germany should insist on a unilateral withdrawal from the Eurozone. The AfD thus emphasised an issue that was widely neglected in the other parties' communications and assumed a position on this issue that the established parties had left unoccupied, thereby promising, as its name indicated, an 'alternative' to the policies of the established parties.[18]

Although the Euro clearly dominated the rhetoric of the AfD, as an aside it also thematised a few other issues, although far less extensively. In its electoral platform monetary and European policy as well as fiscal and budgetary policy ranked foremost, but it also addressed themes like 'rule of law and democracy', 'old-age pensions and family' as well as education, energy and integration.[19] Some of these topics also appeared in the AfD's campaign communication, although again much less dominant than its core theme. For instance, on its campaign posters next to criticism of the monetary union voters could sometimes also encounter demands for a stricter regulation of immigration.[20] Importantly, during the campaign the AfD's messages gained considerable visibility. Generous donations from business people and other wealthy benefactors provided the party with a campaign budget that allowed it to organise a much more vigorous campaign than is usually feasible for small extra-parliamentary parties.[21] Prominent spokespersons, among them well-known renegades from established parties of the centre–right, university professors (especially economists) and talk-show celebrities also drew the news media's attention to the AfD.

Crystallisation of AfD Support during the Election Campaign

Casting a vote is the end of a more or less protracted process of decision making.[22] This section explores how the preferences of those voters that eventually chose the AfD with their second votes developed during the last 10 weeks before the 2013 Federal Election. Voters of the parties then present in the Bundestag are used as yardstick for comparison. At the beginning of the 2013 election campaign the AfD suffered the competitive disadvantage of being relatively unknown. But during the run-up to the election the party became more recognised among voters – presumably at least in part as a consequence of its professional and publicly quite visible campaign. This can be seen when inspecting how the shares of those respondents who were able to classify the AfD on thermometer scales developed over time. Early in the campaign about a third of all respondents claimed to have not enough knowledge to evaluate this party and resorted to 'don't know' answers. This changed about three weeks before Election Day on 22 September. With increasing campaign intensity the share of those unable to volunteer an opinion about the AfD decreased constantly to less than 20 per cent immediately before the election.

Figure 1 shows that, paralleling this development, the great majority of those eventually voting for the AfD made up their minds to vote for this party not until the very last days of the campaign. An advantage of the combined RCS-panel design of the survey is that the figure visualises how many of those voters eventually ending up choosing the AfD (as registered by the post-election wave) had already claimed an intention to support this party at different stages of the election campaign. It shows how the AfD's electorate built up during the campaign in a stage-wise fashion. For the sake of comparison, similar information is also given for the electorates of the CDU/CSU, the SPD, the Greens, the Left and the FDP.

Obviously, the developmental trajectories differed substantially across parties. It appears as if the TV debate between the CDU/CSU and SPD Chancellor candidates, Angela Merkel and Peer Steinbrück, on 1 September 2013,[23] had sent a signal to voters to start the process of decision making. The picture appears static up until about that date. However, the parties had no level-playing ground at that point. In July and August 70 per cent of the later voters of the CDU/CSU were already sure about their voting decision while voters of the SPD and the Greens followed closely with only slightly smaller shares of already crystallised supporters. The early support bases of the FDP and the Left were quite a bit weaker. Only less than half of their later voters already expressed a vote intention in favour of these parties. The

FIGURE 1
DEVELOPMENT OF PARTY VOTERS' VOTE INTENTIONS DURING THE 2013 FEDERAL
ELECTION CAMPAIGN

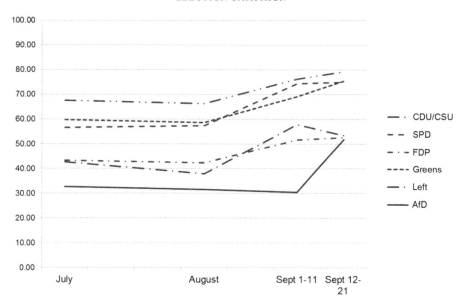

Notes: Entries are percentages of respondents expressing vote intention for respective party within each time period, to the basis of later voters of the respective party; data are weighted by education and design weight.
Source: GLES RCS/panel survey 2013.

AfD, however, was even worse off at the early phase of the campaign. Less than a third of its later voters already claimed to support this party.

At least two out of three later CDU/CSU voters had thus in July already tied themselves down to this party. During the last three weeks of the campaign support of the Christian Democrats grew further by another 10 percentage points. The electorates of the Greens and the SPD evolved similarly, although at a somewhat lower level and this pattern was less linear in the case of the Social Democrats. Among later voters of the FDP and the Left the mobilisation curves started at lower levels, but went up more steeply. Nevertheless almost half of them had not yet reached their final decisions even immediately before the election and therefore qualify as 'last-minute deciders'.[24] It is striking how different the picture yet again looks for the electorate of the AfD. Even 10 days before the election there was no increase at all in these persons' vote intentions for the AfD. Up until immediately before Election Day we see a straight line persisting at a level of just about 30 per cent.[25] But right at the end of the campaign a sudden boost occurred. The share of crystallised AfD voters increased so sharply that it caught up with the FDP and the Left. Altogether, seven out of 10 AfD voters thus arrived at their final voting decision only during the last days of the campaign or even directly on Election Day itself.

Taken together, these findings suggest that the electorate of the AfD was composed of two groups: a majority of about 70 per cent that decided only at the door of the polling station or very shortly before, and a minority of about 30 per cent that had made up their minds long before. When exactly this happened is impossible to tell for lack of data. It must have been sometime between February 2013, when the AfD emerged as a new party, and July, when the RCS survey's period of observation began. For easier distinction the two groups will in the remainder of this article be addressed as 'early supporters' and 'late supporters'. The following analyses will show that at the Federal Election these two groups choose the AfD for quite different reasons.

Backgrounds of AfD Support at the 2013 Federal Election

Dependent variables. Why did voters support the AfD at the 2013 Federal Election? Using the RCS/Panel survey of the 2013 GLES these questions will be explored by means of multivariate analyses. Two series of models are presented in Table 1 that compare supporters of the AfD to those of all other parties in order to explore which characteristics fostered preferences for the AfD. Models 1–3 focus on *vote intentions* registered by the pre-election wave of the survey. The second line of analysis consists of similarly structured panel models of *voters' actual choices* (Models 4–6). Both dependent variables are dichotomous and contrast preferences for the AfD (coded 1) with preferences for other parties (0). Non-voters are not taken into account. All estimates are derived from binary logistic regression analyses. A crucial difference between the two series of models is that analyses of vote choices include vote intentions expressed during the election campaign (1 = AfD, 0 = other party, non-voter or undecided) as an additional control variable. Whereas the cross-sectional pre-election models show which features of respondents were connected to a higher or lower likelihood to *consider voting for the AfD during the campaign*, the panel models reveal which attributes fostered a *final decision for the AfD among those voters who had not yet expressed such a vote intention in the pre-election wave*. The models for vote intentions thus indicate why *early supporters* were drawn to this party. In contrast, the panel models of vote choice reveal which factors were important for the choices of *late supporters*.

Strategy of analysis. To explore AfD support at the 2013 Federal Election a broad range of predictors is taken into account. The well-known notion of a 'funnel of causality'[26] is used as a heuristic for selecting independent variables and organising the analysis. As a model for explaining voting behaviour it links individuals' vote choices at a specific election over several steps of increasing generality to socio-political lines of conflict over material and immaterial goods. Relying on this heuristic suggests a stepwise strategy of analysis which begins with basic socio-demographic attributes of voters (Models 1 and 4). Since socio-political cleavages typically find expression in the form of general and stable political worldviews and loyalties, a set of attitudinal predispositions is included in the next step (Models 2 and 5). The specific circumstances of a particular election enter voters' calculus by way of a broad range of attitudes and beliefs that refer to currently prevalent issues and to the candidates competing for votes. Furthermore, although they are not originally included in the notion of the funnel of causality, orientations relevant for strategic voting should also be taken into account when analysing voting behaviour in a multi-party system like Germany. These short-term orientations are responsive to the current flow of events, but they are also coloured by voters' structural and

TABLE 1

PREDICTORS OF VOTE INTENTIONS AND VOTE CHOICES FOR THE AFD AT THE 2013 FEDERAL ELECTION

	Vote intentions			Vote choices		
	Model 1: socio-demographics	Model 2: plus attitudinal predispositions	Model 3: plus short-term factors	Model 4: Socio-demographics	Model 5: plus attitudinal predispositions	Model 6: plus short-term factors
Campaign time	1.76+	1.73	2.17+	–	–	–
Pre-election vote intention AfD	–	–	–	295.74***	257.13***	139.63***
Gender: male	2.34***	2.20***	2.36**	1.37	1.39	1.49+
Age	3.13	4.31^{-1}*	3.54	2.02^{-1}	1.35^{-1}	4.00^{-1}
Region: West	1.31^{-1}	1.37^{-1}	1.61^{-1}+	2.20^{-1}***	2.27^{-1}***	2.56^{-1}***
Education: completed secondary	1.23	1.39	1.41	1.12^{-1}	1.06^{-1}	1.38
Employment/occupation: worker	2.32^{-1}	2.25^{-1}	2.08^{-1}	1.04^{-1}	1.07^{-1}	1.42
Employment/occupation: new middle class	1.28^{-1}	1.22^{-1}	1.58	1.68^{-1}	1.61^{-1}	1.12^{-1}
Employment/occupation: unemployed	1.11	1.19	2.22	1.40	1.40	1.61
Employment/occupation: retired	2.27^{-1}*	2.32^{-1}*	1.19^{-1}	1.78^{-1}	1.75^{-1}	1.14^{-1}
Employment/occupation: otherwise not gainfully employed	1.49^{-1}	1.39^{-1}	1.22	3.45^{-1}*	3.45^{-1}*	2.22^{-1}
Member of trade union	1.91^{-1}*	1.48^{-1}	1.85^{-1}+	1.32	1.41	1.50+
Left–right identification		10.37***	2.21		3.69**	1.34
Party identification: CDU/CSU		7.41^{-1}***	3.23^{-1}***		4.03^{-1}***	2.22^{-1}*
Party identification: SPD		7.94^{-1}***	7.69^{-1}***		3.06^{-1}***	2.50^{-1}**
Party identification: FDP		3.03^{-1}*	3.23^{-1}+		2.10^{-1}	1.35^{-1}
Party identification: Greens		10.86^{-1}***	6.67^{-1}**		1.96^{-1}*	1.27
Party identification: Left		3.77^{-1}*	5.26^{-1}*		3.12^{-1}*	3.70^{-1}*
Most important problem: Euro crisis			2.28**			1.53+
Position issue: help countries affected by Euro crisis			11.11^{-1}***			5.26^{-1}***

Fear of Euro crisis	1.84	3.99**
Economic situation: current personal	2.07	1.30^{-1}
Economic situation: current sociotropic	1.54^{-1}	1.08^{-1}
Economic situation: retrospective sociotropic	1.21	2.13^{-1}
Economic situation: prospective sociotropic	8.33^{-1}**	2.78^{-1} +
Most important problem: economy general	1.13	1.34
Most important problem: labour market	1.32^{-1}	1.59^{-1}
Most important problem: social justice	1.54^{-1}	1.13
Most important problem: 'NSA' scandal	1.37^{-1}	1.14^{-1}
Most important problem: energy policy	1.27^{-1}	1.54^{-1}
Most important problem: education policy	1.67^{-1}	1.45^{-1}
Most important problem: immigration policy	1.33	1.19
Most important problem: family policy	1.12^{-1}	4.76^{-1}*
Position issue: government should redistribute	2.38^{-1}*	2.56^{-1}*
Position issue: immigrants should adapt	1.06	5.13***
Performance federal government	9.09^{-1}***	1.39^{-1}
Chancellor preference: Merkel (CDU/CSU)	1.04^{-1}	2.13^{-1}*
Chancellor preference: Steinbrück (SPD)	1.05^{-1}	1.59^{-1}

(Continued)

TABLE 1
CONTINUED.

| | Vote intentions | | | Vote choices | | |
	Model 1: socio-demographics	Model 2: plus attitudinal predispositions	Model 3: plus short-term factors	Model 4: Socio-demographics	Model 5: plus attitudinal predispositions	Model 6: plus short-term factors
Likelihood of AfD passing 5 per cent threshold			57.00***			6.45***
Following media polls			1.62+			1.09
Campaign interest			1.15^{-1}			4.35^{-1}**
McKelvey & Zavoina's Pseudo-R^2	.10	.29	.55	.23	.29	.51
(N)	(4078)	(4078)	(4078)	(3546)	(3546)	(3546)

Notes: Entries are odds ratios; all independent variables transformed to range 0–1; unweighted data. ***$p < .001$; **$p < .01$; *$p < .05$; +$p < .10$.
Source: GLES RCS/Panel survey 2013.

attitudinal dispositions which serve as perceptual screens.[27] Together, they form the third block of predictors which is included in the final steps of the respective analyses (Models 3 and 6). Proceeding in three stages of growing complexity allows not only to understand which factors increased the odds of voters favouring the AfD instead of another party, but also how more specific factors mediated the impact of more distant and general ones.

Independent variables. All independent variables are taken from the pre-election wave. Models 1 and 4 include only predictors located at the distant end of the funnel of causality. They encompass a variety of basic socio-demographic characteristics, including respondents' gender (1 = male, 0 = female), residential region (1 = West Germany, 0 = East Germany), age, level of education (1 = completed secondary education, 0 = less), occupational status (dummy variables for workers, new middle class, unemployed persons, pensioners and persons for other reasons not included in the workforce; reference category: old middle class) as well as trade-union membership (dummy variable). In addition, Model 1 also includes a time variable (derived from the dates of interviews) in order to capture the trajectory of AfD support during the election campaign. Models 2 and 5 build on Models 1 and 4 by adding measures of stable attitudinal predispositions. Ideological left–right positions have been shown to be important structuring factors for German voters' electoral preferences.[28] Partisanship exerts an even more powerful influence on electoral behaviour.[29] For both vote intentions and vote choices respondents' self-placement on 11-point left–right scales as well as a set of dummy variables indicating their party identification (CDU/CSU, SPD, FDP, Greens and Left; reference category: apartisans including 'don't know') are therefore added at the second stage of modelling.

The block of independent variables most proximate to the vote in the funnel of causality concerns short-term orientations relating to the specific circumstances of the 2013 Federal Election. It is added in Models 3 and 6. An important type of such situational factors are voters' orientations towards the issues and themes prevalent at the time of the election. The central topic of the AfD's rhetoric during the 2013 campaign was the Euro crisis and the way it was handled by the government of the CDU/CSU and the FDP and the opposition parties in the Bundestag. It is therefore of predominant interest whether and how AfD support was responsive to perceptions and attitudes concerning the Euro crisis as well as to more general economic assessments. Several indicators allow assessing whether the AfD profited from voters' concern about the Euro crisis. In spite of the low attention the Bundestag parties paid to this issue in their campaign communication, almost 20 per cent of the voters mentioned it spontaneously when asked which was, in their opinion, the most important problem facing the country. The analyses therefore include a dummy variable that indicates whether respondents saw the Euro crisis as one of Germany's two most important political problems.[30] Moreover, respondents were asked to position themselves with reference to Germany's policy in the Euro crisis, using a five-point Likert scale on the following statement: '[i]n times of the European sovereign debt crisis Germany should grant financial help to EU member states that have strong economic or financial problems'. Respondents were also invited to indicate how the Euro crisis affected them emotionally, using a five-point scale from 'no fear at all' to 'extremely great fear'.

Furthermore, the analysis includes a standard set of perceptions commonly referred to in analyses of economic voting:[31] retrospective, prospective and current sociotropic evaluations of the economy as well as assessments of respondents' current personal economic situation (all measured on five-point scales).

Although the Euro crisis was the dominant theme of the AfD in the months after its foundation, it occassionally also addressed other topics. It is therefore of interest whether support of the AfD was also spurred by other issue orientations than scepticism on the European common currency and perhaps more general economic worries. The analysis includes a series of dummy variables indicating other policy areas mentioned by respondents in response to the most important problems' question as well as respondents' positions on core issues of the two basic cleavages of German politics.[32] To elicit positions on the socio-economic cleavage, respondents were asked to indicate their position on redistribution, using a Likert scale refering to the statement: '[t]he government should take measures to reduce income disparities'. The immigration issue was chosen to indicate positions on the libertarian–authoritarian dimension, and the statement read: '[i]mmigrants should be obliged to adapt to the culture of Germany'. In addition to specific position and valence issues, parties' electoral prospects may also be influenced by more general valence assessments. The analysis therefore includes retrospective evaluations of the performance of the federal government (11-point thermometer scale from -5 to $+5$).

Besides specific or generalised issue and policy-related orientations, party preferences may also be influenced by voters' perceptions and evaluations of the candidates nominated by the parties and competing for their esteem and sympathy. The most important candidates under the German electoral regime are the Chancellor candidates of the two large parties the CDU/CSU and the SPD.[33] The final models for vote intentions and choices therefore take respondents' Chancellor preferences into account. They include a set of two dummy variables indicating whether respondents named the incumbent Chancellor Angela Merkel (CDU/CSU) or her challenger Peer Steinbrück (SPD) as their preferred future head of government (reference category: undecided or none of the two candidates).

For a number of reasons, most prominently its origin in the American two-party system, the heuristic of the funnel of causality neglects the possibility that electors might cast their votes strategically. However, in recent years electoral research has become more sensitive to the fact that in multi-party systems electoral choices must not always be sincere, but can also take the form of strategic responses to expectations of how parties will fare at the election.[34] These expectations depend on two factors – persons' assumptions about other voters' likely behaviour at the polls, and their understanding of how electoral rules transform votes into parliamentary mandates. A crucial element of German electoral law is the 5 per cent threshold that parties need to pass in order to obtain seats in the Bundestag. Assuming that electors wish to avoid 'wasted votes', it should make a difference for small parties like the AfD whether they are expected to pass the 5 per cent threshold or not.[35] It is therefore of interest to explore if and how electoral support for the AfD also depended on voters' expectation about whether or not it would pass the 5 per cent threshold. As up-to-date information about the electorate's support of particular parties is a crucial basis for such expectations the models not only take these expectations into account, but also whether the respondents followed the results from opinion polls (dummy variable), and whether they were generally interested in the election campaign (five-point scale from 'very interested' to 'not interested at all').

FINDINGS

The first line of Table 1 confirms the descriptive finding of Figure 1 that voters' likelihood to consider voting for the AfD increased during the election campaign (although only with $p < .10$). Socio-demographic background attributes explain support for the AfD overall only to a limited extent. The effect patterns of Models 1 and 4 show a mix of similarities and differences. For instance, the AfD gained more support among men than among women. Moreover, it also was preferred more often by voters from the new states of East Germany. However, the gender effect was much more pronounced for vote intentions, whereas the reverse was true for voters' region of residence. According to Model 1, pensioners were less prone to consider voting for the AfD. Regarding vote choices, on the other hand, persons not gainfully employed for other reasons than being unemployed or retired appeared rather less inclined to support this party (Model 4). However, these relationships disappear once short-term orientations are taken into account. Regarding vote intentions, trade-union membership decreased voters' likelihood to favour the AfD, but the effect reversed its sign for the AfD's late supporters.

Inspecting Models 2 and 5 we see that with regard to both vote intentions and vote choice AfD support had a clear ideological profile. Matching the party platform's ideological profile, voters that placed themselves right of centre were more strongly than others drawn to the AfD. For early supporters this relationship was more pronounced than for late supporters. However, its evaporation for both vote intentions and choices indicates that support for the AfD rooted in general ideological leanings was mediated by more specific orientations (Models 3 and 6). Party identification, by way of contrast, mostly remains a significant predictor even when controlling for short-term factors. Persons expressing a vote intention for the AfD during the campaign as well as those casting their ballot for it on Election Day came predominantly from the ranks of apartisans.

Short-term factors were much more important for both vote intentions and vote choices than socio-demographic and attitudinal predispositions. As is to be expected in view of the AfD's core issue, beliefs and attitudes concerning the Euro crisis appear very influential on whether or not voters preferred this party. In close correspondence to its strong emphasis on this issue, voters who mentioned it spontaneously as the country's most important problem were more strongly attracted by the AfD. However, this concerns especially early supporters, whereas the relationship is weaker and only marginally significant for late supporters. The first panel of Figure 2 visualises the substantial implications of the difference between the effects of these problem perceptions on AfD vote intentions (dotted lines) and vote choices (solid lines) by means of average marginal effects,[36] computed on the basis of Models 3 and 6.[37] Viewing the Euro crisis as Germany's most important problem increased the likelihood to develop a vote intention for the AfD by about two

FIGURE 2
PREDICTED PROBABILITIES OF AFD SUPPORT AT THE 2013 FEDERAL ELECTION FOR
SELECTED BELIEFS AND ATTITUDES

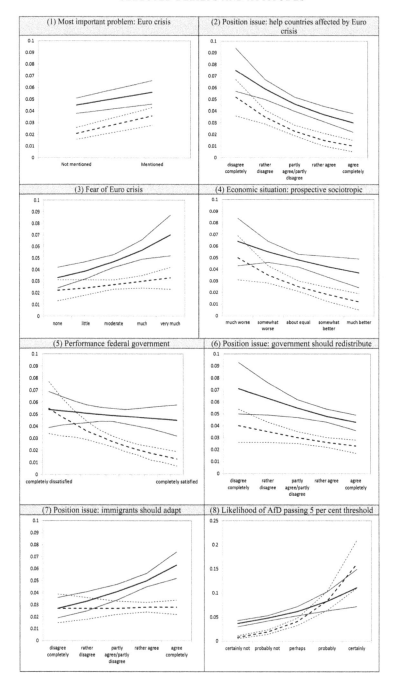

Notes: Predicted probabilities of vote intentions (dotted lines) and voting decisions (solid lines) in favour of AfD with 5 per cent confidence intervals, unweighted data.
Source: GLES RCS/panel survey 2013.

percentage points, whereas the corresponding effect on vote choices was only about half as large. Closely corresponding to the AfD's rhetoric, scepticism or outright opposition to financial help for indebted Euro countries on the part of voters also led to strongly increased odds of preferring that party at the polls. Although this relationship was of considerable strength also for late supporters, it was again more pronounced for those voters that already early on had decided to vote for it. According to the estimates displayed in the second panel of Figure 2, a strict refusal of financial help resulted in a five-fold increased chance of a vote intention in favour of the AfD than strong support for a generous crisis policy.

Affective responses to the Euro crisis also had some impact on AfD support, although – in stark contrast to the valence and position-based issue effects of saliency perceptions and policy opinions – only with regard to those voters that flocked to this party late in the campaign. For early vote intentions fearful reactions to the crisis made no difference. In contrast, the probability for voters that found the crisis emotionally disturbing to switch to the AfD late in the campaign amounted to 7 per cent and was thus four percentage points higher than for carefree voters (see the third panel of Figure 2). Among the four dimensions of general economic evaluations included in Models 3 and 6 only prospective sociotropic assessments were relevant for support of the AfD. Regardless of orientations specifically related to the Euro crisis, the party thus also took advantage of economic pessimism among voters. Prior to the 2013 Federal Election only a few citizens expected a deterioration of the country's economic situation in the year to come.[38] But those who did were strongly drawn to the AfD, although especially early in the campaign. Model 3 predicts a probability of 5 per cent to prefer the AfD for very pessimistic voters compared to only 1 per cent for very optimistic voters. Regarding vote choices the difference between voters with negative and positive economic expectations are much smaller and statistically only marginally significant (see the fourth panel of Figure 2).

Besides orientations related to the AfD's core topic, several other beliefs and opinions concerning the material substance of politics were also relevant for voters' inclination to support this party. For early supporters two further policy-related relationships appear significant in Model 3. Persons dissatisfied with the performance of the federal government of the CDU/CSU and the FDP and socio-economically conservative persons that were opposed to redistribution policies tended to consider voting for the AfD during the campaign. Compared with completely satisfied voters, extremely discontented voters' probability to express a vote intention for the AfD was four percentage points higher (see the fifth panel of Figure 2). However, retrospective performance evaluations did not play a role for voters who found their way to the AfD only late (Model 6). This was different for socio-economic conservatism. As can be seen in the sixth panel of Figure 2, the difference between strict opponents and ardent supporters of redistributive policies amounted to two to three percentage points for both vote intentions and voting decisions. Moreover, preferences for the AfD were considerably fostered by immigration-sceptical attitudes, although only among voters that made up their minds late in the campaign. Compared with fervent proponents of a multiculturalist immigration policy, the vehement opponents' probability of switching to the AfD immediately before the election increased by about four percentage points. In striking contrast, the seventh panel of Figure 2 shows only a flat line for vote intentions. For the preferences of the AfD's early supporters immigration policy was completely irrelevant.

Candidate-related attitudes were important for late supporters, but not for early supporters, and they concerned only Angela Merkel of the CDU/CSU. According to Model 6, those who disliked the prospect of the incumbent Chancellor continuing in office more often chose the AfD. Lastly, we see evidence in both Models 3 and 6 that strategic considerations were important for AfD support. In line with the 'wasted vote' hypothesis, voters' expectation that the AfD would make it across the 5 per cent threshold emerges as an extremely powerful predictor of the party's early support, and to a lesser extent also of late support. To be sure, only a few voters (about 8 per cent) expected the AfD to enter the Bundestag at least 'probably', but among these persons the party found remarkable support during the election campaign as well as in the final spurt that led it close to actually passing the electoral threshold. The last panel of Figure 2 shows that voters who were certain that the AfD would pass the 5 per cent threshold had a probability of 11 per cent to switch to the AfD compared to 4 per cent for those being convinced that it would not gain any seats in the parliament. For early support, the impact of these expectations was even larger.

Opinion polls are a useful source of information that helps voters to develop expectations on likely election outcomes.[39] However, in line with the AfD's low support in the electorate during most of the campaign that is evident from Figure 1, the data published by pollsters did not give any reason to expect the party to pass the 5 per cent threshold.[40] Correspondingly, Model 6 does not show a significant connection between AfD votes and voters' attention to media polls. Moreover, it is quite remarkable that late switches to the AfD happened much more likely among those with no or only little interest in the election campaign than among those that followed it closely. For its early support, campaign interest did not make a difference.

The AfD emerged in early 2013 as a single-issue party, but in view of its campaign communication the question soon was raised whether it should rather be classified as a right-wing populist party. Its campaign communications appeared ambiguous in this regard. Right-wing populist motives, in particular scepticism about immigration, were increasingly present in the party's public rhetoric, although the Euro crisis remained clearly dominant throughout the pre-election period. According to the data presented above as 'party in the electorate' the AfD was similarly two-faced. It started out with an instrumental single-issue electorate that was mainly drawn to it by the high saliency it placed on the Euro crisis and its liberal–conservative position with regard to how it should be dealt with. However, close to Election Day these early supporters were supplemented with a major influx of voters responsive to a motive that in other countries has been identified as a mainspring of support for right-wing populist parties – an exclusivist stance on immigration.[41] Although this motive was not central in the party's campaign rhetoric, it was one of the main predictors of late supporters' votes for the AfD. And this group of voters, in turn, contributed many more votes to the AfD's favourable outcome than the early supporters for whose choices immigration-sceptical attitudes were entirely irrelevant.

TABLE 2
PREDICTORS OF VOTE INTENTIONS FOR THE AFD AT THE 2014 EUROPEAN ELECTION AND
STATE ELECTIONS

	European Election	State Elections Saxony, Brandenburg, Thuringia
Gender: male	1.63	1.19^{-1}
Age	2.94^{-1}	3.30
Region: West	2.50^{-1*}	–
Education: completed secondary	1.08^{-1}	1.20
Employment/occupation: worker	1.57	1.24^{-1}
Employment/occupation: new middle class	1.69	$2.05^{-1}+$
Employment/occupation: unemployed	1.29	1.37^{-1}
Employment/occupation: retired	2.09	$2.53^{-1}+$
Employment/occupation: otherwise not gainfully employed	1.77^{-1}	2.11^{-1}
Member of trade union	1.01	1.47
Left-right identification	17.95**	17.67***
Party identification: CDU/CSU	6.33^{-1**}	5.10^{-1***}
Party identification: SPD	4.50^{-1**}	6.02^{-1***}
Party identification: FDP	–	5.71^{-1*}
Party identification: Greens	–	18.25^{-1**}
Party identification: Left	10.64^{-1*}	5.08^{-1***}
Most important problem: Euro crisis	3.42+	1.16
Position issue: help countries affected by Euro crisis	–	1.88^{-1}
Position issue: exclude indebted countries from Euro zone	5.38*	–
Position issue: reintroduce D-Mark	4.01*	–
Economic situation: current personal	2.88	1.22
Economic situation: current sociotropic	1.96	5.60^{-1*}
Economic situation: retrospective sociotropic	20.66**	3.52*
Economic situation: prospective sociotropic	12.55^{-1*}	4.46^{-1*}
Position issue: government should redistribute	–	1.72^{-1}
Position issue: immigrants should adapt	–	2.86*
Position issue: restrict immigration	6.02+	-
Performance state government	10.71^{-1**}	1.79^{-1}
Preferred head of state government: CDU	–	1.27^{-1}
Preferred head of state government: SPD	–	1.61^{-1}
Preferred head of state government: Left	–	1.25^{-1}
Likelihood of AfD passing 5 per cent threshold	–	2.65*
Campaign interest	–	1.10^{-1}
Political interest	15.68**	–
McKelvey & Zavoina's Pseudo-R^2	.62	.39
(N)	(671)	(1118)

Notes: Entries are odds ratios; all independent variables transformed to range 0–1; unweighted data. PId FDP and Greens excluded for European Election due to insufficient numbers of cases. ***$p < .001$; **$p < .01$; *$p < .05$; +$p < .10$.
Source: GLES tracking survey T24; cumulated GLES State Election boosts Saxony, Brandenburg, Thuringia 2014.

THE AFD AT THE 2014 EUROPEAN AND STATE ELECTIONS

The AfD's Self-Presentation after the 2013 General Election

At the Federal Election of September 2013 the AfD failed to gain seats in the Bundestag. However, the campaign gave it a lot of publicity and the margin of its failure was small enough to send a signal to voters that the party might be a viable competitor at future elections. Partly as a self-fulfilling prophecy (due to the facilitating role of voters' expectations concerning the party's likelihood to surpass the electoral threshold), history confirmed this view. In all six parliaments elected until 2015, the AfD gained mandates.

In the immediate aftermath of the Federal Election, it had been unclear whether the AfD would continue to present itself as a single-issue party mainly concerned about European monetary policies or whether it would rather move towards a stronger and more general commitment to right-wing populist topoi.[42] Impressionistic evidence suggests that the AfD gradually opted for the latter course. Accompanied by quite intense struggling within the party leadership it abandoned its near exclusive focus on the Euro crisis and broadened its thematic spectrum. It now addressed a wider set of issues and shifted its emphasis towards views that more closely resembled the typical menu of right-wing populist ideas and arguments, although it still never went so far that it unequivocally qualified as a right-wing populist party.[43]

'Courage for Germany' was the slogan the AfD adopted for its European Election campaign. It expressed a more general commitment to re-nationalising European politics, although stopping short of taking the step from 'soft', that is, sectoral, to 'hard', that is, fundamental and principled Euroscepticism by requesting the European Union to be dismantled or Germany to terminate its membership.[44] While retaining its previous emphasis on domestic implications of European unification, this allowed the AfD to broaden its outlook. At the three East German State Elections four months later, the Euro crisis was finally relegated to the background. Instead, the AfD mainly campaigned on a range of issues more or less directly related to general themes of open borders and immigration, such as dangers for German society presumably resulting from Islam, trans-border crime as well as 'unregulated' immigration and the presumed overload of the German welfare system resulting from it. It also thematised issues of life-style politics, for instance by denouncing gay marriage and advocating the 'three-child family'. At the same time, anti-establishment rhetoric paired with demands for more direct democracy to give 'the' people more say – another typical element of right-wing populism[45] – gained ground in the party's communication.[46]

Backgrounds of AfD Support at the 2014 Elections

How did voters respond to this shift in the party's self-presentation? A look at vote intentions at the four elections that took place in 2014 concludes our exploration of AfD support. It is based on online surveys conducted in the GLES project prior to these elections. The surveys are not based on random samples, but this should not seriously distort statistical relationships between voters' preferences and background attributes in multivariate models.[47] The models displayed in Table 2 are set up in such a way that they correspond as closely as possible to Model 3 in Table 1. This could be achieved somewhat more completely for the State Elections than for the European Election. Still, important predictors are missing in both models so that the analyses are not fully comparable and have therefore primarily heuristic value. To obtain sufficient numbers of cases the data for the three State Elections have been merged into one integrated data set that covers the three elections about equally.

In important, yet varying respects, the backgrounds of AfD support at the 2014 European and State Elections resembled the profile of AfD preferences at the 2013 Federal Election. Apartisans yet again emerged as the strongest source of AfD support. Moreover, at the European Election East Germans were yet again more strongly inclined to vote for the AfD than West Germans. More importantly, the effect of ideological leanings on vote intentions for the AfD appears not only relevant but indeed far stronger at all 2014 elections than at the Federal Election in the previous year. Most notably, in stark contrast to the Federal Election it does not evaporate once short-term attitudes are taken into account. Even in the full model that includes all short-term predictors, rightist voters appear very strongly drawn to the AfD. However, these differences should be interpreted with caution due to the variation in survey modes and coverage.

At the Federal Election, early support for the AfD had appeared mainly as a consequence of instrumental issue-voting pertaining to the Euro crisis and the economy more generally. Voting behaviour at the 2014 European Election displayed a similar pattern, whereas this was not the case for the East German State Elections. At the European Election, but not at the three State Elections, viewing the Euro crisis as Germany's most important problem yet again seems to have stimulated votes for the AfD. Likewise, Euro-related policy positions were important at the European Election, but not at the State Elections. The State Election surveys contained the same item as the 2013 Federal Election survey which registered respondents' position on helping indebted Euro countries. According to Table 2, its effect is negative like the one displayed in Table 1, but it attains not even marginal statistical significance. The European Election survey included different items to register attitudes on the European common currency. Their effects on AfD preferences are strong and statistically significant. Persons in favour of excluding indebted countries from the Eurozone and of returning to the D-Mark as national currency were considerably more likely to vote for the AfD.

Pessimistic assessments of the general economic prospects played a role at both elections, but much more strongly at the European Election than at the State Elections. In a similar vein, assessments of the federal government's performance were important only at the European Election, but not at the State Elections. Voting behaviour at the European Election thus bore resemblance to the AfD's early supporters' behaviour at the 2013 Federal Election in its rather instrumental and issue-focused character, whereas these motives were almost or completely irrelevant at the State Elections in Saxony, Brandenburg and Thuringia. Economic concerns were important at these elections, but only generally, whereas considerations specifically pertaining to the Euro crisis seem to have disappeared from the calculus that led voters to support the AfD.

To elicit the role of immigration-sceptical attitudes at the East German State Elections the same item as at the Federal Election could be used. According to Table 2, it is much more strongly related to AfD preferences than opinions and beliefs concerning the Euro crisis. In the European Election survey again, a different instrument was used for measuring attitudes on immigration, but it is similarly strongly related to AfD support. Voters who were in favour of limiting immigration displayed a strong inclination to prefer the AfD. Hence, whereas AfD support at the European Election resembled early supporters' preferences at the Federal Election quite strongly with regard to its issue-specific instrumentality, it was also to some extent responsive to xenophobic attitudes which had emerged late in the Federal Election campaign as a new important predictor of choices for the AfD. At the East German State Elections, AfD support was even more clearly determined by such orientations. In essence,

AfD votes at the three State Elections held in 2014 appear primarily as expression of a general ideological tendency towards the right, a negative current and prospective assessment of the overall economic situation and immigration-scepticism. Compared to the beginning of the AfD's electoral history early in the 2013 Federal Election campaign the background of this party's support has thus changed considerably – paralleling and presumably responding to the party's redefinition of its programmatic profile. With regard to the AfD's development after the 2013 Federal Election, demand-side changes thus corresponded to those on the supply side.

CONCLUSION

Against the background of the European sovereign debt crisis, the AfD appeared on the political stage early in the election year 2013 as a single-issue party. Its manifesto was slim and primarily focused on criticism of the European currency union. However, during the Federal Election campaign its public rhetoric as an aside also alluded to right-wing populist motives, most notably a critical stance on immigration. After the 2013 Federal Election it moved further in that direction, downplaying the Euro crisis and focusing its campaign communication more strongly on xenophobic topoi and other motives from the repertoire of right-wing populism. Systematic analyses of its rhetoric found it inappropriate to categorise the AfD as a full-fledged right-wing populist party.[48] Rather, the party seems to have presented itself sufficiently ambiguously to open up the possibility of being seen differently by different voters. The analysis of voting behaviour at the 2013 Federal Election presented in this article suggests that the party profited from this ambiguity at the polls. As 'party in the electorate' the AfD's appearance matched the two-faced character displayed by the party in its public communication – although already with reversed weights at the 2013 Federal Election, and with a clear trend further away from Euro concerns to more general xenophobic motives thereafter.

That the 2013 electorate of the AfD consisted of two groups – a smaller group of voters who already at an early stage of the campaign were determined to choose the AfD, and a much larger group of late supporters that made up their minds in favour of this party only during the final days of the campaign or even on Election Day itself – is a striking outcome of this research. Just as important is the fact that early and late supporters preferred the AfD for quite different reasons. Of course, like any new party the AfD drew advantage from the increasing electoral availability of voters.[49] Weakly anchored voters were an important source of its support. It obtained considerably more votes from apartisans than from individuals with firm party attachments. Likewise, voters from the states of post-socialist East Germany were more strongly drawn to the AfD than voters from the 'old' Federal Republic. But beyond these similarities the 'two electorates' of the AfD differed considerably.

Right from the start of the election campaign, the AfD was supported by a small but stable group of voters that preferred it mainly because of its core issue. In several respects, these early supporters appear as instrumental issue voters. Findings suggest that they found the AfD appealing because of its self-presentation as a single-issue party predominantly concerned about the Euro crisis and its domestic economic implications. As the Bundestag parties remained mostly silent about this issue, the AfD became attractive for voters for whom it was highly salient. Moreover, the party gained strong support from voters that preferred a much more restrictive policy course with regard to financial aid for indebted countries of the Eurozone than advocated by any of the parties in the Bundestag. In a situation where these parties almost unanimously agreed on the necessity of financial help and only discussed its conditions, the AfD – true to its name – became an attractive alternative for voters that were opposed to any such help. From both a valence and a positional point of view[50] the AfD thus appeared as an attractive choice for voters concerned about its central theme, the crisis of the European common currency.

The impact of general economic pessimism was also more pronounced among persons who knew very early that they would vote for the AfD. That early rather than late moves towards the AfD were more likely among persons dissatisfied with the performance of the federal government also fits into this picture. Voters more generally displaying a liberal–conservative mindset on socio-economic issues also tended to express a vote intention in favour of the AfD. This suggests that attitudes on the Euro issue were not unrelated to the traditional cleavages of German politics. Importantly, there also seems to have been a pronounced strategic component to early supporters' vote intentions for the AfD, since their preferences depended very strongly on the party's perceived electoral viability. Given what polls indicated with regard to the size of the AfD's support base, voters had little reason to expect the party to surpass the 5 per cent threshold. But some did nonetheless, and within their ranks early support for this party was especially probable.

Overall, however, the early supporters of the AfD made up only about a third of the party's electorate. Its good result at the polls was mainly brought about by the second group of voters which was twice as large and joined its ranks only immediately before or even on Election Day itself. These late supporters' ultimate conversion towards the AfD seems to have been driven mostly by other, arguably rather expressive motives. To begin with, while valence and positional considerations concerning the Euro crisis were not irrelevant for these voters' choices, they were clearly less important. At the same time, fearful reactions to this event brought the AfD votes from late supporters while they made no difference for early supporters.

Even more importantly, immigration-sceptical attitudes contributed significantly to late supporters converting to the AfD, whereas they were completely irrelevant for its early supporters. This suggests that the AfD's campaign rhetoric made voters aware of the immigration-sceptic stances that the party assumed alongside its economically couched, 'soft' Euroscepticism, even though it put much more emphasis on the latter. This let the AfD appear an attractive choice for persons averse to inclusivist immigration policies. In a range of studies xenophobic attitudes of this kind have emerged as the most powerful predictor of support for right-wing populist parties in Europe.[51] It appears that the AfD was able to tap into a voter reservoir that just like in comparable countries exists in Germany as well, but could thus far not express its sentiments at the polls because the legacy of German history prevented a party of that type taking root in the party system.[52] Also paralleling findings from studies of electoral support of right-wing populist parties, the AfD was more attractive for male voters and for voters with right-of-centre ideological leanings.[53] The influence of the latter, however, was mediated by short-term attitudes. That AfD late supporters' choices at the Federal Election were expressive rather than instrumental is further underlined by the finding that last-minute conversions to this party were more likely for voters who had little or no interest in the election campaign. Importantly, the findings of this study indicate that this group contributed many more votes than the early supporters for whose choices immigration-sceptical attitudes were entirely irrelevant.

When the AfD first stepped onto the electoral stage in early 2013, it presented itself as a single-issue party concerned about the policies of the Bundestag parties with regard to the Euro crisis. However, during the Federal Election campaign it added right-wing populist themes, particularly immigration-sceptical motives, to its rhetoric, although it still retained its main focus on the Euro crisis. After the Federal Election, it more clearly began to shift its emphasis, and at the three State Elections held in East Germany about a year after the Federal Election, the AfD eventually campaigned mainly on xenophobic topoi whereas the Euro crisis and even European unification more generally no longer played a prominent role. Presumably responding to these changes on the supply side the driving forces of AfD support in the electorate gradually shifted as well. From instrumental issue-oriented voting based on voter concerns about the Euro crisis that were insufficiently addressed by the Bundestag parties, the basis of its support moved to xenophobic attitudes and thus over time came to resemble even more clearly the profile of electoral support for right-wing populist parties in neighbouring countries. At the 2013 Federal Election, the influx of late-deciding supporters of this type was the main reason for the favourable result of the AfD. At the European Election in May 2014 concerns about both the Euro crisis and xenophobic motives were important sources of votes. At the three eastern German State Elections, at long last, the former source of electoral support vanished whereas the latter dominated. Over four stages and with regard to both the party organisation and the 'party in the electorate' the AfD has covered a considerable distance on the road from single-issue to right-wing populist party.

However, not only in its public rhetoric, but also as 'party in the electorate' at least up until 2015 it did not yet qualify as a full-fledged right-wing populist party. For one, xenophobic attitudes were not the only source of its support. It also was considered an attractive choice by voters with liberal–conservative views on socio-economic issues. In some respects the AfD's support profile also did not correspond to expectations from extant research on the typical demand-side conditions of votes for right-wing populist parties.[54] In particular, this concerns the demographics of AfD voters. Neither workers nor unemployed persons were markedly more likely than other voters to choose this party. We also found no effect of lower levels of formal education. While xenophobic attitudes are often seen as the attitudinal core of electoral support for right-wing populist parties, authoritarian and populist attitudes are also considered important ingredients of such behaviour.[55] Whether orientations of this kind also played a role for the AfD's support at the 2013 and 2014 elections could not be examined for lack of appropriate data.

After its electoral successes in 2014 the AfD mainly made it into the news through bitter infighting about its future course. In July 2015, an extraordinary party convention finally brought the split of the organisation. The founding leader Bernd Lucke was voted down by a clear majority of the present party members, and replaced by the chairwoman of the Saxon party branch Frauke Petry, a staunch advocate of a 'national–conservative' course. Tellingly, when polled about the 'major problems of the country' attendees of the party conference placed 'uncontrolled immigration' ahead of the Euro crisis. Leading proponents of a 'liberal' agenda, among them the AfD's founder Lucke himself, immediately left the party to found a new one, labelled ALFA, the 'Allianz für Fortschritt und Aufbruch' ('Alliance for Progress'). The AfD's new leadership's quickly asserted that the party will not move to the right and its platform will remain unchanged. But in all likelihood the schism will ultimately lead to a clarification of the party's profile. It is bound to lose the programmatic ambiguity from which it profited at the 2013 Federal Election and the 2014 European Election, and consequently also (at least) one of its two electorates. Like the proverbial sorcerer's apprentice, by covertly appealing to xenophobic sentiments the AfD's founding leaders raised the spectre of right-wing populism which eventually they were unable to keep under control. It remains to be seen whether the AfD will go all the way and transform itself into a full-fledged right-wing populist party, and whether it will be able to maintain a stable base of electoral support among German voters.

ACKNOWLEDGEMENTS

I am indebted to Klaus Armingeon, Josephine Hörl, Oskar Niedermayer, Julia Parthey-müller and Robert Rohrschneider for advice and constructive comments on a previous version of this article. I gratefully acknowledge the hospitality of the Research School of Social Sciences of the Australian National University Canberra which allowed me to complete work on this article during a Visiting Fellowship.

DISCLOSURE STATEMENT

No potential conflict of interest was reported by the author.

NOTES

1. See Robert Grimm, 'The Rise of the German Eurosceptic Party Alternative für Deutschland, between Ordoliberal Critique and Popular Anxiety', *International Political Science Review* 36/3 (2015), pp.264–78.
2. On the notion of 'party as propagandiser', see Paul Allen Beck, *Party Politics in America* (New York: Longman, 1997), p.14.
3. See Nicole Berbuir, Marcel Lewandowsky and Jasmin Siri, 'The AfD and Its Sympathisers: Finally a Right-Wing Populist Movement in Germany?', *German Politics* 24/2 (2015), pp.154–78; Simon Tobias Franzmann, 'Die Wahlprogrammatik der AfD in vergleichender Perspektive', *MIP* 20/1 (2014), pp.115–24; Kai Arzheimer, 'The AfD: Finally a Successful Right-Wing Populist Eurosceptic Party for Germany?', *West European Politics* 38/3 (2015), pp.535–56; Oskar Niedermayer, 'Eine neue Konkurrentin im Parteiensystem? Die Alternative für Deutschland', in Oskar Niedermayer (ed.), *Die*

Parteien nach der Bundestagswahl 2013 (Wiesbaden: Springer VS, 2015), pp.175–207; Marcel Lewandowsky, 'Eine rechtspopulistische Protestpartei? Die AfD in der öffentlichen und politikwissenschaftlichen Debatte', *Zeitschrift für Politikwissenschaft* 25/1 (2015), pp.119–34.

4. On the notion of 'party in the electorate', see Beck, *Party Politics in America*, pp.12–13.
5. The GLES is funded by the Deutsche Forschungsgemeinschaft (German Research Foundation, DFG) under its long-term programme. All GLES data are freely available from http://www.gesis.org/gles. For general information on the project, see http://www.gles.eu and Rüdiger Schmitt-Beck, Hans Rattinger, Sigrid Roßteutscher and Bernhard Weßels, 'Die deutsche Wahlforschung und die German Longitudinal Election Study (GLES)', in Frank Faulbaum and Christof Wolf (eds), *Gesellschaftliche Entwicklungen im Spiegel der empirischen Sozialforschung* (Wiesbaden: VS-Verlag für Sozialwissenschaften, 2010), pp.141–72.
6. Hans Rattinger, Sigrid Roßteutscher, Rüdiger Schmitt-Beck, Bernhard Weßels and Christof Wolf, *Rolling Cross-Section-Wahlkampfstudie mit Nachwahl-Panelwelle* (GLES 2013; GESIS Datenarchiv, Köln, 2014: ZA5703 Datenfile Version 1.0.0, doi:10.4232/1.11803) (pre-election wave: N = 7882, post-election wave: N = 5353). For further information on this survey, see Julia Partheymüller, Rüdiger Schmitt-Beck and Christian Hoops, *Kampagnendynamik bei der Bundestagswahl 2013: Die Rolling Cross-Section-Studie im Rahmen der 'German Longitudinal Election Study'*, MZES Working Paper No. 154 (Mannheim: Mannheim Centre for European Social Research, 2013), available from http://www.mzes.uni-mannheim.de/publications/wp/wp-154.pdf (accessed on 1 March 2015).
7. See Richard Johnston and Henry E. Brady, 'The Rolling Cross-Section Design', *Electoral Studies* 21/2 (2002), pp.283–95. Data collection started on 8 July 2013 and ended on 21 Sept. 2013. Random samples of on average about 104 voters were interviewed every day.
8. Hans Rattinger, Sigrid Roßteutscher, Rüdiger Schmitt-Beck, Bernhard Weßels and Christof Wolf, *Langfrist-Online-Tracking*, T24 (GLES) (GESIS Datenarchiv, Köln, 2014: ZA5724 Datenfile Version 1.0.0, doi: 10.4232/1.11963) (N = 1044; conducted 9–23 May 2014); *Langfrist-Online-Tracking zur Landtagswahl in Sachsen 2014* (GLES) (GESIS Datenarchiv, Köln, 2014: ZA5738 Datenfile Version 1.0.0, doi: 10.4232/1.12047) (N = 503; conducted 15–30 Aug. 2014); *Langfrist-Online-Tracking zur Landtagswahl in Brandenburg 2014* (GLES) (GESIS Datenarchiv, Köln, 2014: ZA5738 Datenfile Version 1.0.0, doi:10.4232/1.12054) (N = 507; conducted 29 Aug.–13 Sept. 2014); *Langfrist-Online-Tracking zur Landtagswahl in Thüringen 2014* (GLES) (GESIS Datenarchiv, Köln, 2014: ZA5740 Datenfile Version 1.0.0, doi: 10.4232/1.12057) (N = 504; conducted 29 Aug.–13 Sept. 2014). The author is indebted to Rebecca Steffen for cumulating the three State Election datasets.
9. See Simon Bulmer, 'Germany and the Eurozone Crisis: Between Hegemony and Domestic Politics', *West European Politics* 37/6 (2014), pp.1244–63.
10. See Hubert Zimmermann, 'A Grand Coalition for the Euro: The Second Merkel Cabinet, the Euro Crisis and the Elections of 2013', *German Politics* 23/4 (2014), pp.322–36; Grimm, 'The Rise of the German Eurosceptic Party'.
11. See Hanspeter Kriesi, 'The Political Consequences of the Financial and Economic Crisis in Europe: Electoral Punishment and Popular Protest', *Swiss Political Science Review* 18/4 (2012), pp.518–22; Michael S. Lewis-Beck, Marina Costa Lobo and Paolo Bellucci, 'Economic Crisis and Elections: The European Periphery', *Electoral Studies* 31/3 (2012), pp.469–642; Sonja Alonso, 'Wählen ohne Wahl. Demokratie und die Staatsschuldenkrise in der Eurozone', in Wolfgang Merkel (ed.), *Demokratie und Krise* (Wiesbaden: Springer VS, 2015), pp.245–74.
12. See Fritz W. Scharpf, *Legitimacy Intermediation in the Multilevel European Polity and Its Collapse in the Euro Crisis*, MPfG Discussion Paper No. 12/6 (Köln: Max-Planck-Institut für Gesellschaftsforschung, 2012).
13. Daniel Brössler, 'Merkels Gift wirkt', *Süddeutsche Zeitung*, 11 Aug. 2013, p.4.
14. See Hans-Dieter Klingemann, Richard I. Hofferbert and Ian Budge, *Parties, Policies, and Democracy* (Boulder, CO: Westview, 1994).
15. See Anthony Downs, *An Economic Theory of Democracy* (Boston, MA: Addison Wesley, 1965).
16. See Robert Rohrschneider and Stephen Whitefield, 'Party Positions about European Integration in Germany: An Electoral Quandary?', this issue.
17. See Niedermayer, 'Eine neue Konkurrentin im Parteiensystem?'.
18. Grimm, 'The Rise of the German Eurosceptic Party'.
19. See http://www.Alternativefuer.de/partei/wahlprogramm/ (accessed 20 Dec. 2013); see also Berbuir et al., 'The AfD and Its Sympathisers'; Niedermayer, 'Eine neue Konkurrentin im Parteiensystem?'.
20. See Berbuir et al., 'The AfD and Its Sympathisers'.
21. See Mona Krewel, 'Die Wahlkampagnen der Parteien und ihr Kontext', in Rüdiger Schmitt-Beck, Hans Rattinger, Sigrid Roßteutscher, Bernhard Weßels, Christof Wolf et al., *Zwischen Fragmentierung und Konzentration: Die Bundestagswahl 2013* (Baden-Baden: Nomos, 2014), pp.35–45.

22. See Paul F. Lazarsfeld, Bernard Berelson and Hazel Gaudet, *The People's Choice: How the Voter Makes Up His Mind in a Presidential Campaign* (New York/London: Columbia University Press, 1968); Richard Johnston, André Blais, Henry E. Brady and Jean Crete, *Letting the People Decide: Dynamics of a Canadian Election* (Stanford, CA: Stanford University Press, 1992); Andrew Gelman and Gary King 'Why Are American Presidential Election Campaign Polls So Variable When Voters Are So Predictable?', *British Journal of Political Science* 23/4 (1993), pp.409–51; Robert S. Erikson and Christopher Wlezien, *The Timeline of Presidential Elections: How Campaigns Do (and Do not) Matter* (Chicago, IL: University of Chicago Press, 2012); Thomas Plischke, *Wann Wähler entscheiden. Abläufe von Entscheidungsprozessen und der Zeitpunkt der Wahlentscheidung* (Baden-Baden: Nomos, 2014).
23. See Jürgen Maier, Thorsten Faas and Isabella Glogger, 'Das TV-Duell', in Schmitt-Beck et al., *Zwischen Fragmentierung und Konzentration*, pp.281–92.
24. See Steven H. Chaffee and Rajiv Nath Rimal, 'Time of Voting Decision and Openness to Persuasion', in Diana C. Mutz, Paul M. Sniderman and Richard A. Brody (eds), *Political Persuasion and Attitude Change* (Ann Arbor, MI: University of Michigan Press, 1996), pp.267–91.
25. Thirty-five per cent of those not yet supporting the AfD intended to vote for another party (CDU/CSU: 10 per cent; SPD, FDP and the Left: 6 per cent each; Greens: 4 per cent; other parties: 3 per cent), 5 per cent contemplated abstaining, 28 per cent were undecided.
26. See Angus Campbell, Philip E. Converse, Warren E. Miller and Donald E. Stokes, *The American Voter* (New York: Wiley, 1960), pp.24–32; Warren E. Miller and J. Merrill Shanks, *The New American Voter* (Cambridge, MA: Harvard University Press, 1996), pp.189–211; Michael S. Lewis-Beck, William G. Jacoby, Helmut Norpoth and Herbert F. Weisberg, *The American Voter Revisited* (Michigan: University of Michigan Press, 2009), pp.22–8.
27. See Larry Bartels, 'Beyond the Running Tally: Partisan Bias in Political Perceptions', *Political Behavior* 24/2 (2002), pp.117–50.
28. See Anja Neundorf, 'Die Links-Rechts-Dimension auf dem Prüfstand: Ideologisches Wählen in Ost- und Westdeutschland 1990–2008', in Rüdiger Schmitt-Beck (ed.), *Wählen in Deutschland, PVS-Sonderheft 45* (Baden-Baden: Nomos, 2012), pp.227–50.
29. See Harald Schoen and Cornelia Weins, 'Der sozialpsychologische Ansatz zur Erklärung von Wählerverhalten', in Jürgen W. Falter and Harald Schoen (eds), *Handbuch Wahlforschung* (Wiesbaden: VS-Verlag, 2005), pp.206–25.
30. The variable was generated by means of an automatic analysis of verbatim answers. If they contained one or several of the following strings as words or word parts they were attributed to the category 'Euro crisis': *Euro*; *Schulden*; *Finanz*; *Griechen*; *Rettung*; *Banken*; *Waehrungsunion*; *Haushalt*; *Krise*.
31. See, for example, Charlotte Kellermann and Hans Rattinger, 'Wahrnehmungen der Wirtschaftslage und Wahlverhalten', in Hans Rattinger, Oscar W. Gabriel and Jürgen W. Falter (eds), *Der gesamtdeutsche Wähler. Stabilität und Wandel des Wählerverhaltens im wiedervereinigten Deutschland* (Baden-Baden: Nomos, 2007), pp.329–56.
32. See, for example, Hanspeter Kriesi, Edgar Grande, Romain Lachat, Martin Dolezal, Simon Bornschier and Timoteos Frey, *West European Politics in the Age of Globalization* (Cambridge: Cambridge University Press, 2008).
33. See Franz U. Pappi and Susumu Shikano, 'Personalisierung der Politik in Mehrparteiensystemen am Beispiel deutscher Bundestagswahlen seit 1980', *Politische Vierteljahresschrift* 42/3 (2001), pp.355–87; on candidate assessments at the 2013 Federal Election, see Aiko Wagner, 'Spitzenkandidaten', in Schmitt-Beck et al., *Zwischen Fragmentierung und Konzentration*, pp.267–80.
34. See, for example, Paul R. Abramson, John H. Aldrich, André Blais, Matthew Diamond, Abraham Diskin, Indiri H. Indridason, Daniel J. Lee and Renan Levine, 'Comparing Strategic Voting under FPTP and PR', *Comparative Political Studies* 43/1 (2010), pp.61–90.
35. See Thomas Gschwend, 'Ticket-Splitting and Strategic Voting under Mixed Electoral Rules: Evidence from Germany', *European Journal of Political Research* 46/1 (2007), pp.1–23; Sascha Huber, Thomas Gschwend, Michael F. Meffert and Franz Urban Pappi, 'Erwartungsbildung über den Wahlausgang und ihr Einfluss auf die Wahlentscheidung', in Oscar W. Gabriel, Bernhard Weßels and Jürgen W. Falter (eds), *Wahlen und Wähler. Analysen aus Anlass der Bundestagswahl 2005* (Wiesbaden: VS-Verlag, 2009), pp.561–84.
36. See Michael Hanmer and Kerem Ozan Kalkan, 'Behind the Curve: Clarifying the Best Approach to Calculating Predicted Probabilities and Marginal Effects from Limited Dependent Variable Models', *American Journal of Political Science* 57/1 (2013), pp.263–77.
37. Because of the large share of late supporters within the actual electorate of the AfD the chances calculated for voting decisions are on average higher than for vote intentions.
38. See Markus Steinbrecher, 'Wirtschaftliche Entwicklung und Eurokrise', in Schmitt-Beck et al., *Zwischen Fragmentierung und Konzentration*, pp.225–38.

39. See Thorsten Faas, Christian Mackenrodt and Rüdiger Schmitt-Beck, 'Polls That Mattered: Effects of Media Polls on Voters' Coalition Expectations and Party Preferences in the 2005 German Parliamentary Election', *International Journal of Public Opinion Research* 20/3 (2008), pp.299–325.
40. See Krewel, 'Die Wahlkampagnen der Parteien und ihr Kontext', p.37.
41. See Pippa Norris, *Radical Right: Voters and Parties in the Electoral Market* (Cambridge: Cambridge University Press, 2005); Cas Mudde, *Populist Radical Right Parties in Europe* (Cambridge: Cambridge University Press, 2007); Kai Arzheimer, *Die Wähler der extremen Rechten 1980–2002* (Wiesbaden: VS-Verlag, 2008); Hanspeter Kriesi, Edgar Grande, Martin Dolezal, Marc Helling, Dominic Höglinger, Swen Hutter and Bruno Wüest, *Political Conflict in Western Europe* (Cambridge: Cambridge University Press, 2012).
42. See Niedermayer, 'Eine neue Konkurrentin im Parteiensystem?'.
43. See Arzheimer, 'The AfD'.
44. See Arzheimer, 'The AfD'; Grimm, 'The Rise of the German Eurosceptic Party'.
45. See Mudde, *Populist Radical Right Parties*.
46. See Matthias Lohre, 'Die Angst-Partei', *Die Zeit*, 7 Aug. 2014, p.6; Josef Joffe, 'Protest- statt Prof-Partei', *Die Zeit*, 18 Sept. 2014, p.12; Grimm, 'The Rise of the German Eurosceptic Party', pp.272–3.
47. See Ina E. Bieber and Evelyn Bytzek, 'Online-Umfragen: Eine geeignete Erhebungsmethode für die Wahlforschung? Ein Vergleich unterschiedlicher Befragungsmodi am Beispiel der Bundestagswahl 2009', *Methoden-Daten-Analysen* 6/2 (2012), pp.185–211.
48. Berbuir et al., 'The AfD and Its Sympathisers'; Franzmann, 'Die Wahlprogrammatik der AfD'; Arzheimer, 'The AfD'.
49. See Stefano Bartolini and Peter Mair, *Identity, Competition and Electoral Availability* (Cambridge: Cambridge University Press, 1990).
50. See Donald E. Stokes 'Spatial Models of Party Competition', *American Political Science Review* 57/2 (1963), pp.368–77; Donald E. Stokes, 'Valence Politics', in Dennis Kavanagh (ed.), *Electoral Politics* (Oxford: Clarendon Press,1992), pp.141–64.
51. See Norris, *Radical Right*; Mudde, *Populist Radical Right Parties*; Arzheimer, *Die Wähler der extremen Rechten*; Kriesi et al., *Political Conflict in Western Europe*.
52. See Berbuir et al., 'The AfD and Its Sympathisers'; Arzheimer, 'The AfD'.
53. See Mudde, *Populist Radical Right Parties*; Arzheimer, *Die Wähler der extremen Rechten*.
54. See Norris, *Radical Right*; Mudde, *Populist Radical Right Parties*; Arzheimer, *Die Wähler der extremen Rechten*.
55. See Mudde, *Populist Radical Right Parties*.

If You Don't Know Me by Now: Explaining Local Candidate Recognition

HEIKO GIEBLER and BERNHARD WEßELS

For the personal vote to be cast in a meaningful way it is a minimal condition that voters recognise candidates. However, from earlier studies we know that there is huge variation in the number of candidates recognised. Little to nothing is known about candidate recognition and its determinants. This study explores the sources of candidate recognition from three different angles: candidates; citizens; and context. Furthermore, it enables the distinction of campaign-related from other factors. A unique multi-level within-subject design was set up for the analyses of the 2013 German Federal Election to ensure a meaningful validation of our theoretical framework. Our results suggest that, indeed, many factors lead to recognition but as well that earlier studies overestimated the effects of political interest or incumbency status. Moreover, we show that a good campaign makes a difference for recognition – as does the context in which it takes place.

INTRODUCTION

Why it is relevant to know what triggers candidate recognition? There are at least three reasons. The first reason relates to the normative ideas behind an electoral system like that of the Federal Republic of Germany. A second reason is the connection between recognition and the vote. Third, knowledge about the factors contributing to candidate recognition is very limited – not only in Germany.

Turning to the first point, candidate recognition has 'long been used in surveys to test political knowledge'.[1] It seems plausible that candidate recognition may be necessary in order to be prepared to make a reasonable choice – reasonable in the sense of the normative core of each specific electoral system. However, to which degree candidate knowledge is necessary certainly depends on the character of choices and, thus, the electoral system. Holding a representative elected in the district accountable or making a reasonable choice between candidates to be elected by personal vote in the first place requires, at least, the recognition of individual candidates. Hence, candidate recognition can be described as the necessary and minimal condition of accountability in majoritarian electoral systems.

Furthermore, research from various countries and types of elections shows a strong relationship between candidate recognition and vote choice. This has been shown for the USA, Britain and even Germany. Results seem to support that recognition contributes to a reasonable choice because only with recognition there is evaluation. Thus, there is a relationship between candidate recognition and the vote which in general terms fits to the idea of a personal vote and the normative expectations regarding the mechanism of accountability and representation.

The third reason to investigate candidate recognition is that little to nothing is known about the factors that are conducive for candidate recognition. The German case constitutes no exception to this rule. Although there is much more research in and about the USA and Great Britain because of their majoritarian electoral systems, clear and systematic knowledge is not available for those countries either. As candidate recognition plays an important role both in constituency-level account-ability and as a personal vote choice, this situation is not satisfying. This contribution aims at increasing our knowledge about the genesis of candidate recognition by using a unique combination of data from a candidate survey and two election surveys of the 2013 German Federal Election to explore the whole variety of factors that matter in prior research on candidate recognition – from candidates' characteristics and cam-paign efforts to citizens' characteristics and campaign perceptions to contextual factors of the district.

The article is organised as follows: section two gives an overview of earlier studies explaining candidate recognition and introduces three different blocks of explanatory variables: candidate-related; voter-related; and context-related. Next, we present our data sources as well as the measurement of variables used, and the design of our empirical analyses. The results section is divided into three parts: we start with some descriptive findings which are followed by an in-depth discussion of our causal model. We complete this section by presenting the relative importance of each block of explanatory variables. The article concludes by summarising our find-ings, discussing them in relation to earlier studies, and putting them into context in terms of the function of candidate recognition in democracies. We show that concep-tualising the sources of candidate recognition in a more encompassing way as well as applying an appropriate estimation model is not just fruitful but necessary.

THEORETICAL BACKGROUND: EXPLAINING CANDIDATE RECOGNITION

As Pattie and Johnston wrote almost two decades ago, much is known about the elec-toral consequences of local campaigns, but the impact of local campaigns on voters' knowledge of candidates and parties still has to be discovered.[2] This certainly is a result of undervaluing the relevance of local candidates and campaigns. Even in single-member district systems like the USA, for a long time, electoral research did not figure that candidate recognition was of particular relevance. In *Voting*, the seminal book of Berelson and colleagues, the demand was that 'the democratic citizen is [...] supposed to know [...] what alternatives are proposed, what the party stands for'[3] and in Downs' *Economic Theory of Democracy* the need to know about alternatives was acknowledged, but seen as party-centred: '[t]hus before he can make a voting decision, a voter must acquire for example information about the date of the election, the number of parties running, their names, and voting pro-cedure'.[4] Research regarding candidate recognition as political knowledge relevant for political choices has developed slowly and due to the insight that local and person-alised campaigning may matter. As Norris summarises, 'name-recognition is a signifi-cant indirect indicator of broader awareness of electoral choices, [...] and it is important as a minimal criteria before citizens can evaluate the record of elected members'.[5]

In Germany, it took even longer until local campaigning gained attention. This was partly due to the general impression of researchers on electoral systems and voting behaviour that voters in the constituency choose candidates almost completely according to party labels and not according to personal campaign efforts, personal performance or other individual characteristics of the candidate. That this view was only partly true, if at all, was shown by an analysis of Klingemann and Weßels pointing out that satisfaction with constituency work and performance in the parliament contributed considerably to the choice made with the personal vote.[6] They found that the difference in personal vote share of candidates perceived as performing poorly compared to candidates performing very well was 17.5 percentage points. Since then, the ignorance concerning local candidates has vanished and research on local campaigning in Germany receives more and more scholarly attention.[7]

The mixed-member proportional electoral system of Germany allocates half of the 598 parliamentary seats by list votes and half by personal first-past-the-post voting. The mixed-member electoral system is the result of a compromise in the parliamentary council in 1948 between those favouring a pure proportional system and those favouring a majoritarian electoral system.[8] The combination of the two visions of liberal democracy implies that the actors, that is, the represented and the representing, cope with two different normative ideas and different demands at the same time.[9] In a majoritarian electoral system, citizens elect individual politicians in single-member districts. In a proportional electoral system, citizens elect representatives by voting for party lists and parties determine by candidate selection how those lists are composed. The link between citizens and representatives differs clearly between the two procedures. The mandate in the majoritarian model is given to a person and this person is held accountable in the next elections for her performance. In the proportional model, the mandate is given to a party and the party is held accountable in the next elections.[10] Thus, voters have to generate different types of accountability: person-oriented in the majoritarian, party-oriented in the proportional model. But although there is more information available on parties than on individual constituency MPs, even the party-oriented accountability mechanism is not always easy to apply as, for example, research on economic voting has shown.[11]

Factors contributing to an informed personal vote, however, are manifold. A logical precondition is certainly the recognition of the candidate. This may again depend on a set of factors as complex as that for an informed personal vote. Personal characteristics and campaign efforts of the candidates may be relevant as well as the personal characteristics of the voters and their individual exposure to campaign efforts as well as the particular local context in the constituency. In the literature, positive findings can be found on all three general aspects: candidate-related, voter-related and context-related, although all three have been rarely included in one analysis.

The general theoretical frame or the model of candidate recognition thus considers three explanatory blocks of factors: candidate-related; voter-related; and context-related. The two actor-related blocks are further divided into (a) factors linked to personal characteristics and (b) campaign-related factors. Regarding candidates, these latter factors include campaign efforts; regarding voters, campaign exposure (see

FIGURE 1
A MODEL OF CANDIDATE RECOGNITION

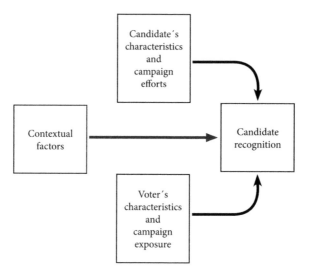

Figure 1). Thus, three general blocks of variables, two of them split into sub-blocks, will be considered in our analysis.

Regarding candidate-related factors, the first aspect are candidates' personal characteristics. In general, so-called personal vote-earning attributes providing informational shortcuts can be the birthplace or electoral experience of the candidate.[12] More generally, the local ties of a candidate may contribute to her recognition as well as her electoral profile in terms of experience or even success with candidacy. If asked for their preference, 17.8 per cent of German voters said they like to see a representative to be of the same generation, 22.4 per cent of the same social class and 24.4 per cent of the same region.[13] It is important to note that incumbency may only be a proxy for other factors connected or even leading to incumbency. Research shows that incumbency adds little to recognition if factors like visibility, evaluation advantages and media access of candidates are controlled for.[14] In their normal vote analysis, Goldenberg and Traugott did therefore not include incumbency in their model predicting deviations from normal vote because its contribution was effectively captured by the other variables in the model.[15] Thus, electoral experience of a candidate may stand as an indicator for more general advantages or disadvantages that might make her known or to be made known by others like by endorsements of interest groups.

Second, general efforts of the candidates and, at election times, specific campaign efforts are of relevance. Research on campaign effects on candidate recognition is rare in comparison to the rich literature on campaign effects on voting. However, Pattie and Johnston found for Britain, that intensity of local campaigning is associated with improved knowledge of the voters referring to who is standing for election in a constituency.[16] The relationship between campaign efforts and citizens' learning as well as candidate recognition has been confirmed for the USA by Wolak, who found that name recognition increases with campaign effort.[17] For Germany, however, Gschwend and Zittel could show a strong impact of campaign exposure but no significant effects of campaign intensity, campaign content or campaign organisation.[18]

The effect of campaign efforts on electoral success depends on resources. Research results suggest that money, time, the size of the team and media access matter a lot – the more of these resources, the higher the chance of electoral success.[19] As direct evidence on candidate recognition is limited, these findings on the relevance for electoral success are analogously transferred to the recognition of candidates. The close relationship between candidate recognition and vote choice makes such an expectation not too far-reaching. Goldenberg and Traugott concluded in their book on the USA that 'a campaign's net effect on individual voters' choices is a consequence of whether the voters recognise one or both opponents and how evaluations of them compare'.[20] Even in experimental studies and field experiments at the local level in the USA, the strong effect of candidate recognition on candidate support could be shown.[21] In Great Britain, Pattie and Johnston found that 'electors who know the identity of a party's constituency candidate are more likely to vote for that candidate than are electors who do not know the candidate's identity'.[22] Last not least for Germany, Gschwend and Zittel could confirm that candidate recognition – they coined it 'cognitive personalisation' – had a rather large effect on the personal vote in the 2009 German Federal Election.[23]

However, recognition is not a one-sided process. Whether campaign efforts get through to the voters may depend on citizens' characteristics and whether campaign efforts of candidates have succeeded in reaching citizens, which may again depend on citizens' characteristics. Goldenberg and Traugott found that the likelihood of candidate recognition rises if citizens are attentive to campaign news and better educated.[24] Furthermore, Wolak showed that general political knowledge and campaign interest matter as well.[25] Gschwend and Zittel confirmed for Germany the effect of political knowledge.[26] Thus, a general political interest, following the (local) news, a certain degree of political knowledge and the discussion of politics are conducive for candidate recognition. All the mentioned factors may contribute to an increased likelihood of campaign exposure; that is, to getting actually in touch with parties or candidates by different means. Goldenberg and Traugott stressed that any campaign activity reaching citizens such as rallies, coffee klatches, mailings and ads contributed to increased candidate recognition.[27] However, the effects of campaign exposure may be conditioned by partisanship. The degree of campaign exposure does not matter for candidate recognition of voters highly identifying with the party of the candidate, but it matters a lot for voters without party identification.[28] In the US case, however, campaign exposure showed to have a persistent effect on candidate recognition even under the control of the strength of partisanship.[29] Additionally, the ability to recognise a candidate might also be a function of general mobilisation and attention levels. Knowing a candidate's name already long before or still long after Election Day should be more difficult than close to the election.

Finally, the specific district context can certainly have an impact on candidate recognition. One aspect is to which degree a district can be described as 'personal and local'. Rural electoral districts or those in smaller towns differ considerably from those in the big cities or city conglomerates. Anonymity is higher in highly populated districts. Geographically, the size of such a district will be smaller, but high population density will make a community-like personalisation of politics at the local level unlikely. A second contextual aspect is the general political climate or ideology prevailing in the district. If a particular party has the sympathy of most voters in a district, it may well be that its candidate will be more recognised than the others. A similar mechanism may be at work at the candidate level. If only one or two candidates get most of the votes or if many candidates have more or less the same share of the votes, it makes a difference for the need to recognise candidates. If there is hegemony in the district, efforts for recognising as many candidates as possible do not pay off from a cost–benefit perspective.

Review of research shows that candidates' and voters' characteristics as well as context-related factors clearly play a role in explaining candidate recognition. Voters' characteristics seem to be most important. However, also campaign-related factors matter a lot. This can be taken as a positive message: evidence suggests that local campaigning can make a difference. Thus, local campaigning and its reception may play a crucial role in providing the necessary conditions of personalisation and the personal vote that, to be meaningful, should both be dependent on candidate recognition. However, prior studies do not allow a full picture and may have run the risk of overestimating the impact of certain factors, for example political interest or incumbency, as they did not consider a comprehensive set of explanatory factors or were not able to do so by data limitations. Furthermore, most research designs do not or cannot take care of the hierarchical structure of the complex set of factors, quite often because of the lack of comprehensive data. In particular, most studies do not have integrated voter- and candidate-level data. Research often concentrated on either voters' characteristics or campaign characteristics, did not deal with these two levels at the same time or only in an under-complex manner. A complete and integrated analysis of the factors of candidate recognition and their relation is necessary in order to understand and evaluate better the state of accountability and to identify how it can be improved. This is what our study provides.

DATA, METHODS AND MEASUREMENT

Conducting our study makes it necessary to link data taken from a mass survey, an elite survey and contextual data. Fortunately, the German Longitudinal Election Study (GLES; http://www.gles.eu) provides all the necessary data and means to link the different study components. We use the combined pre- and post-election cross-sectional dataset[30] for information on candidate recognition, campaign exposure and other characteristics of the citizenry.[31] Data on candidates and their campaign efforts are taken from the GLES candidate survey that also provides all information needed on the contextual level.[32] We had to delete all candidates of the 'Alternative for Germany' (AfD) and the Pirate Party because the voter surveys only asked about the recognition of candidates running for CDU/CSU,[33] SPD, FDP, the Left or the Greens. Obviously, we also had to delete all candidates only running on party lists. All in all, we cover 233 of 299 constituencies and, after dropping all cases with missing values, we ended up with 3381 citizens and 478 candidates.[34] The parties covered in this study put forth 1194 constituency candidates which means we cover more than 40 per cent – a very impressive figure if we consider the problems often accompanying elite surveys. Linking citizens and candidates results in 6841 citizen–candidate combinations.

The structure of the data is hierarchical and there are various ways to address this. Unfortunately, earlier studies on the determinants of candidate recognition, while making a valid conceptual contribution, applied insufficient constraints to their empirical models in terms of clustering which sheds doubts on the reliability of their results.[35] We apply a three-level structure with candidates nested in citizens nested in constituencies. In other words, we set up a within-subjects design on the lower levels. Each individual (citizen) is compared against her baseline allowing the researcher to control for unobserved individual characteristics which are estimated as the level-two random intercept. By asking the same individual about the recognition of all candidates running for major parties, we can assess, for each individual, how candidate-specific factors (for example, exposure to a candidate's campaign or campaign resources) affect the probability to recognise the specific candidate. At the same time, we can estimate the constant effect of a citizen's characteristics on candidate recognition (e.g. political knowledge) and the effect of constituency characteristics, like the level of electoral competition. As our dependent variable is binary (recognised candidate yes/no), we ran a three-level logistic regression with unconstrained random intercepts. Log-likelihood ratio tests as well as the respective Intra-Class Correlation Coefficients of 0.54 for level two (citizens) and 0.33 for level three (constituencies) support our model specification.

The measurement of our dependent variable is very much straightforward. In both pre- and post-election surveys respondents were asked to report all candidates by name as well as their party affiliation.[36] Interviewers had a pre-coded list of names for the constituency where the interview took place and were told to accept abridgements. We deem a candidate to have been recognised if a respondent was able to recall name and party affiliation.

As we have argued above, candidate recognition has many sources. To save space for the analysis, we provide all information on the variables used in our analysis in Table A1 in the appendix.

RESULTS

We argue that candidate recognition is affected by different blocks of factors belonging to different subjects and objects. In addition, we claim that we can deal with all these factors simultaneously due to a unique multi-level dataset, in contrast to prior studies which either could not include all factors due to data and design limitations or did not provide fully satisfying models of candidate recognition. Before going into the model explaining candidate recognition, the relevance of district representation and, thus, candidates and their recognition is discussed on the basis of some descriptive figures. This includes first insights into the distribution of our dependent variable. It is followed by the presentation of results from the causal analysis. This section ends with an analysis of the explanatory power of the different blocks of explanatory factors; that is, candidate-, voter- and context-related.

Descriptive Results

Above, arguments have been made regarding the relevance of candidate recognition given the normative ideas of vote choice and representation embedded in the German electoral system. The institution of a personal vote resulting in a representative responsible for a district does not just result from an idea of the inventors of the electoral rules but finds strong support within the electorate (Figure 2). About 80 per cent of the voters regard it as important or very important that an MP elected in the district represents her voters in the district, about 70 per cent that she represents all voters in the district. These perceptions are quite independent from the fact whether voters recognise their own candidates in the district.

Candidate recognition depends in part on the visibility of the candidates that may – beyond their party's national popularity – have to do with the fact of whether a candidate served the constituency during the term before the election. This would imply very different chances for being recognised depending on the candidate's party. The Christian Democrats, for example, held 72.9 per cent of all 299 constituency mandates before the 2013 Federal Election, the Social Democrats 21.4 and the Left 5.4 per cent. The Greens held only one mandate, the Liberals none. On this background, it comes as a surprise that while recognition is clearly skewed in favour of the two bigger parties with the higher proportions of district mandates the difference is much less pronounced than incumbency would suggest. A total of 47.4 per cent of the voters recognised candidates of the Christian Democrats, only a little less those of the Social Democrats and about 20 per cent knew candidates of the Liberals, the Left and the Greens. This is clearly an indication of the importance of other factors than incumbency and the sheer number of district mandates won by a party.

The results presented in Figure 3 confirm this expectation. In total, 62.7 per cent of the voters recognise at least one candidate, 42.4 per cent two or more, including a low proportion of 7.8 per cent recognising five candidates. These proportions of recognition may be regarded as too low for providing the preconditions for a reasoned

FIGURE 2
RELEVANCE OF FOCUS OF CONSTITUENCY REPRESENTATION AND CANDIDATE
RECOGNITION

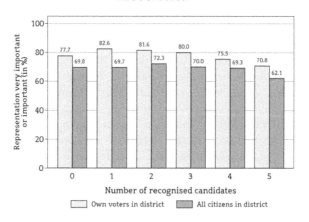

FIGURE 3
NUMBER OF RECOGNISED CANDIDATES

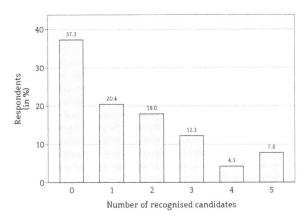

choice between candidates and thus a reasonable personal vote. However, in a comparative perspective, these figures are not low at all. Although they are varying in their specific calculations, both Holmberg and Norris showed a medium to high rank of Germany's proportion of candidate recognition even compared to countries with plurality or majority systems.[37]

Causal Model

Which factors enable citizens to recognise a constituency candidate? To answer this question, we estimated a three-level random intercept logistic regression. The results are presented in Table 1.[38] Before going into detail, the first observation is that the large number of significant predictors underlines our argumentation on the manifold sources of candidate recognition.

On the lowest level, representing candidate-specific variables, findings suggest that it pays for candidates to try to get in touch with voters; those voters reporting that they had been contacted by a candidate keep that politician's name in mind better than others. The same is true if the respondent likes the candidate's party.

Turning to candidates' characteristics, we find the probability of recognition increases for candidates who already won a mandate in the prior election in comparison to new candidates. Having already run a campaign in 2009 but unsuccessfully does neither contribute positively nor negatively to recognition. Money and time spent during a campaign are highly relevant resources for a candidate if she wants to be recognised by citizens. The mere size of the campaign team can be neglected.

Neither campaign diversity, that is, using a large number of different campaign means, nor addressing local issues nor having media access increases the probability to be recognised for a candidate. The same is true for the campaign focus. It is not really relevant for recognition whether a candidate runs a campaign stressing herself as a person or stressing her party. What matters, however, is campaign style. The more classical the style is, for example, if the candidate uses canvassing or sends out letters and leaflets, the more successful it is in making a candidate known.

TABLE 1
MULTI-LEVEL LOGIT MODEL PREDICTING CANDIDATE RECOGNITION

Dependent variable: Candidate recognition
Candidate level (citizen–candidate combinations): N = 6841
Respondent level: N = 3381; Constituency level: N = 233

Candidate level	
Campaign contacts	.57*** [.04]
Party like–dislike	.28*** [.02]
Candidate profile (base category: did not run in 2009)	
ran without winning a seat in 2009	−.23 [.17]
successful campaign in 2009	.90*** [.18]
Residence	−.19 [.17]
Endorsement	.03 [.13]
Time	.22** [.08]
Team	−.00 [.00]
Money	.02*** [.00]
Campaign diversity	.02 [.01]
Campaign style	1.01** [.35]
Campaign focus	.04 [.02]
Local topics	.03 [.19]
Media access	−.11 [.16]
Intercept	−12.08*** [1.50]
Respondent level	
Political interest	.04 [.16]
Political knowledge	.66*** [.10]
Reading local newspaper	.80*** [.80]
Discuss politics	.50** [.15]
Proximity to election	.12*** [.03]
Constituency level	
Party popularity	.03** [.01]
Effective number of electoral candidates	1.13** [.42]
Population density	−.31** [.11]
Random part	
Error variance, respondent level	4.28*** [.56]
Error variance, constituency level	4.22*** [.67]
Log-likelihood	−2,723.1

Notes:
We present results as usual for multi-level models by sorting the independent variables based on their level of measurement. We ran a second model including a dummy variable differentiating between the pre- and post-elections survey. There are no significant differences except that the variable measuring the proximity to the election becomes insignificant. The dummy itself is negative and significant at the 1 per cent level indicating that the probability to recognise a candidate is about 5.2 per cent lower if a respondent was interviewed after the election.
$^*p < .05$; $^{**}p < .01$; $^{***}p < .001$; standard errors in brackets.

On the respondent level, all variables except political interest are crucial. A citizen with a higher level of political knowledge who reads at least one local newspaper and discusses politics has a much higher probability to recognise a candidate. Our finding on political interest is striking at first hand as most other studies on candidate recognition find a significant effect. Taking a second look, however, this is not surprising at all. First of all, we are able to measure citizens' characteristics in a more detailed way than the other studies. Political interest can be regarded as a summary measure of more specific indicators of political involvement like reading newspapers and discussing politics. Second, several studies presenting a significant effect of political interest on candidate recognition use insufficient estimation procedures. By neglecting the nested data structure, standard errors of higher-level predictors are deflated which then leads to only seemingly significant effects.

Finally, turning to the block of context-related factors, our model predicts a better chance to get recognised if the candidate's party is more popular in the constituency – even controlling for all other factors. Furthermore, citizens living in more urban and densely populated districts tend to not know electoral candidates. This is consistent with the argument on the anonymity of cities and a stronger communal orientation in less densely populated cities or villages. Political competition matters as well. As expected from the cost–benefit argument made above, investment in knowledge about candidates pays off only if there is no hegemony in the district. Consequently, the model predicts a positive effect of electoral competition: the higher the effective number of electoral candidates, the higher the probability for them to be recognised.

Substantive interpretation of logit coefficients is rather difficult. Therefore, we present the average marginal effect of a one-unit change in terms of probability changes for each predictor.[39] Figure 4 displays the marginal effects of those predictors which show at least significant on the 5 per cent level of confidence. The predictors are ordered by block (candidate-related, voter-related and context-related) and their effect

FIGURE 4
AVERAGE MARGINAL EFFECTS OF SIGNIFICANT PREDICTORS

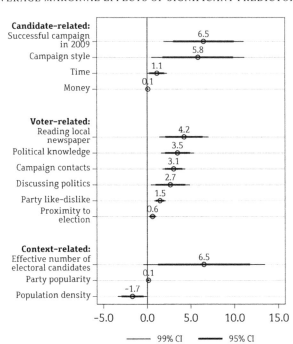

size. In addition to the probability change, we present also the 95 and 99 per cent confidence intervals.

We calculate the baseline probability of recognising a candidate if all independent variables are set on their empirical mean. The predicted probability equals 5.7 percentage points. This helps us to evaluate the impact of each of the indicators because we can compare the respective effect to the baseline probability. The results show that if competition in the district increases by one effective electoral candidate chances to get recognised are more than doubled in comparison to the baseline probability. Having been a successful candidate in the 2009 election has the same effect. Switching from an all postmodern campaign style to an equally balanced campaign or from the latter to an all classic campaign increases the probability to get recognised by 5.8 percentage points. Reading a local newspaper or not (4.2) and discussing politics or not (2.7) have rather small effects while one additional point on the political knowledge scale increases the probability by 3.5 percentage points. Campaign contacts prove to have a very large effect: for each time a respondent was contacted by the candidate or her party, the model estimates an increase of 3.1 points, while the average number of such contacts is close to 2.5. The same can be said about the party like– dislike scale (1.5 for each increase on the 11-point scale). In contrast to earlier studies, we find rather small effects for campaign resources. Twenty-four hours of campaigning per week increase the probability by only 1.1 percentage points and spending an additional amount of €1000 on the local campaign only adds .1 percentage points. Interestingly, running for a popular party is also not very relevant because it needs a 10-percentage-point increase in the vote share to get recognised with a 1-percentage-point higher probability. Population density seems to play a more important role as the predicted probability decreases by 1.7 percentage points for each additional 1000 inhabitants per square kilometre – in other words, the difference between a rural and a rather urban constituency easily adds up to more than 10 points. Last but not least, we find a rather moderate effect of proximity to the election. As a one-unit change represents that the interview was conducted one additional week before or after the Election Day, a probability change of 0.6 is moderate at best.

Explanatory Power of Different Variable Blocks

All in all, the probability changes presented in Figure 4 further support our claim that candidate recognition depends on many factors and all explanatory blocks – candidate-related, voter-related and context-related – are not just helpful but also necessary. The remaining question is how important the different blocks of explanatory variables are in comparison.

The difficulty in answering this question is that there are no uncontested standard procedures in non-linear multi-level set-ups to calculate the contribution of a single independent variable or even a group of variables in regard to explanatory power. Hence, we have to develop a procedure to determine the relative contribution of each variable group. We do so by, first, standardising each non-binary independent variable by dividing it by two standard deviations following an approach by Gelman.[40] In a second step, we calculate the average marginal effect of a one-unit change for each independent variable identically with the calculation described above. We then add up all these marginal effects. This figure represents the total probability change caused by our standardised independent variables if each of them increases by one unit. Finally, we sum up all marginal effects for indicators in a specific block or, as we distinguish the actor-centred blocks further by individual character-istics and campaign factors, sub-block and divide this number by the total probability change. In other words, we calculate the relative proportion of the total probability change for each group of variables. While these values should not be interpreted in absolute terms, we get the relative effect of each variable group in comparison to the other groups on candidate recognition.

Figure 5 depicts the relative effect of each group of variables. Obviously, there are differences in terms of relevance. However, the results emphasise – similar to the regression results in Table 1 – that none of the blocks should be neglected because all contribute considerably to candidate recognition. The effect of the least important sub-block (candidate characteristics) is still more than one tenth of the overall effect of the model and larger than one-third of the most influential sub-block (citizen characteristics).

In relative terms, the most important explanatory block is voter-related. Adding the effect of campaign exposure and citizen characteristics results in roughly 50 per cent of the overall effect – with the latter constituting the most important group of indepen-dent variables. Second comes the block of candidate-related variables (characteristics and campaign effort) making up for 28 per cent, followed by context-related variables contributing a little more than one-fifth.

Contextual effects and campaign exposure of citizens have more or less the same effect on candidate recognition which emphasises the importance of contextual factors like competition. Clearly, campaign exposure, especially in terms of campaign con-tacts, should have a large effect on an individual's ability to recognise a candidate. However, our results also show that this ability is structured by the level of electoral competition – good news for accountability. What about the object of recognition, the candidates? Their characteristics have the smallest relative effect. This is notable because this explanatory block includes whether a candidate was an MP prior to the election or not, a characteristic which in prior research showed to be very important.

FIGURE 5
RELATIVE RELEVANCE OF EXPLANATORY BLOCKS

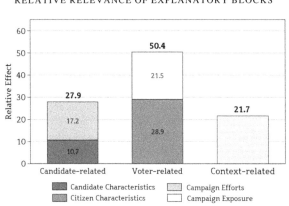

Here, with more detailed measures of campaign efforts, results show that these efforts are more important than the status or profile of a candidate. Campaign efforts account for about one-sixth of the overall effect. Showing more effort and choosing a favourable strategy can indeed make a difference because, as other studies have shown, recognition translates into a higher probability to get elected. Finally, if we only look to candidate- and voter-related factors and compare the overall effect of campaigns, the effect size of campaign-related variables is as big as of personal characteristics. Disregarding context, this means that local campaigning contributes about half of the effect for candidate recognition, which is 38.7 per cent of the overall effects.

CONCLUSION

Candidate recognition has found much less scholarly attention than the relationship of local campaigning and candidates' success. This emphasis on success neglects that an informed personal vote implies candidate recognition if the accountability mechanism in single-member districts and its normative idea of delegation is taken seriously. In the German case, the electoral system has implemented both visions of democracy: the proportionate-influence vision and the majority-control vision of democracy, the latter needing candidate recognition for accountability.

This analysis is an attempt to explain candidate recognition in full. Prior research falls short of an integrated analysis because of design restrictions or other shortcomings. Here, we made use of a unique data source combining candidate- and voter-related as well as context-related factors in a multi-level data structure which allows us to address questions concerning the impact of personal characteristics of candidates and voters, campaign characteristics and context in an integrated way. Analysing candidate recognition in the 2013 German Federal Election, our goal was three-fold: first, we wanted to offer an integrated perspective demonstrating the complexity of contributing factors and, thus, showing that none of the blocks of variables which can be found in research can be neglected. Second, we intended to identify the relative relevance of blocks of determinants and, third, by doing so, to come up with a yardstick as to which degree accountability mechanisms can be assumed in the personal vote.

In descriptive terms, results show that almost two-thirds of the citizens recognise at least one candidate knowing her name and party. Whether they do or not depends on factors relating to all three blocks of variables – candidate-, voter- and context-related. Out of 22 variables, 14 showed significant effects. The traditional way of explaining political knowledge – to which candidate recognition belongs – is looking at individual characteristics at the voter level. This one-sided perspective neglects that the supply-side may be relevant for citizens in order to decide whether they care or not. Moreover, supply-side efforts make it easier to acquire the necessary information – or not. At the same time, one may argue that the effect of supply-side efforts is conditioned or restricted by individual characteristics of the addressees. Results show in fact that the effect of voters' characteristics is the most important block of variables. However, we did not find any effect of political interest on recognition. We argue that this is the result of our more comprehensive set of predictors which encompasses several independent variables often subsumed in other studies under the label 'political interest'. Being informed and involved makes a big difference but is much less than half of the story. The campaign efforts of the candidates make a big difference, too, because they are also contributing to the big effect of campaign exposure at the voters' level. Characteristics of candidates matter less than expected. Comparable literature on personal voting finds an enormous effect of incumbency which we detected regarding candidate recognition in terms of statistical significance but not regarding size. That we did not identify such a strong effect has certainly to do with the fact that we measure campaign efforts with a more differentiated set of instruments indicating that incumbency may just be a proxy for a more complex set of factors. In contrast to Gschwend and Zittel who could not find significant effects of campaign intensity, campaign content or campaign organisation,[41] we find significant effects of time and money. Again, differentiation seems to be the reason that in our integrated design we determine an effect which others could not observe, defining intensity, style and organisation basically all by money. However, effects of time and money seem to be small in our analysis in comparison to other factors. One may assume that all this helps to increase campaign exposure of citizens, which has a huge relative effect on recognition and does hold even under control of liking of the candidate's party. That the constituency context and, for accountability of major interest, the competitive situation of the candidates have a strong impact shows that it is relevant to consider all three blocks of variables in the explanation of candidate recognition.

That campaign-related factors play a major role among the relevant factors, contributing close to 40 per cent to the overall explanation, can be taken as a positive message: this is clear evidence that local campaigning can make a difference. Local campaigning and its reception are important for facilitating the necessary conditions of personalisation and the personal vote. It shows, at the same time, that holding politicians accountable by the personal vote can work given the fact that neither partisanship nor other characteristics of individual voters determine candidate recognition from the very beginning or even primarily.

In more general terms, our study illustrates the complexities of the democratic process. The working of core elements of modern democracy – elections and, as their result, representation – does not depend on political elites or citizens, not on the supply and demand side of politics alone. It depends on the interaction of these two groups as well as individual efforts and characteristics creating and interpreting these interactions. What is more, the democratic process does not take place in a vacuum but is strongly influenced by contextual factors. They facilitate or restrict different forms of information seeking, decision making and behaviour – also in the context of candidate recognition. Some might prefer parsimony when it comes to cause and effects in political science and they might be disappointed with our conclusion. However, we see these interdependencies and the subsequent complexity in a positive light because it represents the inherent logic of democracy. Its functioning depends on the actions and commitment of many and not just a few and the explicit corrective mechanism, free and fair elections, ensures adaptability to contextual changes.

DISCLOSURE STATEMENT

No potential conflict of interest was reported by the authors.

NOTES

1. Pippa Norris, *Electoral Engineering: Voting Rules and Political Behavior* (Cambridge: Cambridge University Press, 2004), p.238.
2. C.J. Pattie and R.J. Johnston, 'Party Knowledge and Candidate Knowledge: Constituency Campaigning and Voting and the 1997 British General Election', *Electoral Studies* 23/4 (2004), pp.795–819.
3. B.R. Berelson, P.F. Lazarsfeld and W.N. McPhee, *Voting: A Study of Opinion Formation in a Presidential Campaign* (Chicago, IL: University Press of Chicago, 1954), p.308.
4. A. Downs, *An Economic Theory of Democracy* (New York: Harper & Brothers, 1957), p.215.
5. Norris, *Electoral Engineering*, p.238.
6. H.-D. Klingemann and B. Weßels, 'Political Consequences of Germany's Mixed-Member System: Personalization at the Grass-Roots?', in M.S. Shugart and M.P. Wattenberg (eds), *Mixed Member Electoral Systems: The Best of Both Worlds?* (Oxford: Oxford University Press, 2001), pp.279–96.
7. H. Giebler, B. Weßels and A.M. Wüst, 'Does Personal Campaigning Make a Difference?', in B. Weßels, H. Rattinger, S. Roßteutscher and R. Schmitt-Beck (eds), *Voters on the Run or on the Move?* (Oxford: Oxford University Press, 2014), pp.140–64; H. Giebler and A.M. Wüst, 'Campaigning on an Upper Level? Individual Campaigning in the 2009 European Parliament Elections in Its Determinants', *Electoral Studies* 30/1 (2011), pp.53–66; T. Gschwend and T. Zittel, 'Machen Wahlkreiskandidaten einen Unterschied? Die Persönlichkeitswahl als interaktiver Prozess', in R. Schmitt-Beck (ed.), *Wählen in Deutschland. Special Issue 45 of Politische Vierteljahresschrift* (Baden-Baden: Nomos, 2012), pp.371–92; T. Gschwend and T. Zittel, 'Do Constituency Candidates Matter in German Federal Elections? The Personal Vote as an Interactive Process', *Electoral Studies* 39 (2015), pp.338–49; A.M. Wüst, H. Schmitt, T. Gschwend and T. Zittel, 'Candidates in the 2005 Bundestag Election: Mode of Candidacy, Campaigning and Issues', *German Politics* 15/4 (2006), pp.420–38; T. Zittel and T. Gschwend, 'Individualised Constituency Campaigns in Mixed-Member Electoral Systems: Candidates in the 2005 German Elections', *West European Politics* 31/5 (2008), pp.978–1003.
8. S.E. Scarrow, 'Germany: The Mixed-Member System as a Political Compromise', in M.S. Shugart and M.P. Wattenberg (eds), *Mixed Member Electoral Systems: The Best of Both Worlds?* (Oxford: Oxford University Press, 2001), pp.55–69.
9. J.D. Huber and G.B. Powell, 'Congruence between Citizens and Policymakers in Two Visions of Liberal Democracy', *World Politics* 46/3 (1994), pp.291–326; G.B. Powell, *Elections as Instruments of Democracy: Majoritarian and Proportional Visions* (New Haven, CT: Yale University Press, 2000).
10. W.C. Müller, 'Political Parties in Parliamentary Democracies: Making Delegation and Accountability Work', *European Journal of Political Research* 37/3 (2000), pp.309–33.
11. C.J. Anderson, 'Economic Voting and Political Context: A Comparative Perspective', *Electoral Studies* 19/1 (2000), pp.151–70; R.M. Duch, 'Comparative Studies of the Economy and the Vote', in C. Boix and S.C. Stokes (eds), *The Oxford Handbook of Comparative Politics* (Oxford: Oxford University

Press, 2009), pp.805–44; E. Parker-Stephen, 'Clarity of Responsibility and Economic Evaluations', *Electoral Studies* 32/3 (2013), pp.506–11; G.B. Powell and G.D. Whitten, 'A Cross-National Analysis of Economic Voting: Taking Account of the Political Context', *American Journal of Political Science* 37/2 (1993), pp.391–414; A. Wagner and H. Giebler, 'It's the Responsibility, Stupid! Determinanten der Verantwortlichkeitszuschreibung zwischen Europäischer Union und nationaler Regierung für die wirtschaftliche Lage', *Zeitschrift für Vergleichende Politikwissenschaft* 8/Supplement 2 (2014), pp.123–42.

12. M.S. Shugart, M.E. Valdini and K. Suominen, 'Looking for Locals: Voter Information Demands and Personal Vote-Earning Attributes of Legislators under Proportional Representation', *American Political Science* 89/2 (2005), pp.327–43.

13. H. Rebenstorf and B. Weßels, 'Wie wünschen sich Wähler ihre Abgeordneten? Ergebnisse einer repräsentativen Bevölkerungsumfrage zum Problem der sozialen Repräsentativität des Deutschen Bundestages', *Zeitschrift für Parlamentsfragen* 20/3 (1989), pp.408–24, p.416.

14. E.N. Goldenberg and M.W. Traugott, 'Congressional Campaign Effects on Candidate Recognition and Evaluation', *Political Behavior* 2/1 (1980), pp. 61–90.

15. E.N. Goldenberg and M.W. Traugott, 'Normal Vote Analysis of U. S. Congressional Elections', *Legislative Studies Quarterly* 6/2 (1981), pp.247–57, p.253.

16. Pattie and Johnston, 'Party Knowledge and Candidate Knowledge'.

17. J. Wolak, 'The Consequences of Concurrent Campaigns for Citizen Knowledge of Congressional Candidates', *Political Behavior* 31/2 (2009), pp.211–29.

18. Gschwend and Zittel, 'Do Constituency Candidates Matter'.

19. R.K. Carty and M. Eagles, 'Do Local Campaigns Matter? Campaign Spending, the Local Canvass and Party Support in Canada', *Electoral Studies* 18/1 (1999), pp.69–87; D. Denver, G. Hands and I. MacAllister, 'The Electoral Impact of Constituency Campaigning in Britain, 1992–2001', *Political Studies* 52/2 (2004), pp.289–306; T.M. Holbrook and A.C. Weinschenk, 'Money, Candidates, and Mayoral Elections', *Electoral Studies* 35 (2014), pp.292–302; R. Johnston and C. Pattie, 'Candidate Quality and the Impact of Campaign Expenditure: A British Example', *Journal of Elections, Public Opinion and Parties* 16/3 (2006), pp.283–94; R.J. Johnston and C.J. Pattie, 'The Impact of Spending on Party Constituency Campaigns at Recent British General Elections', *Party Politics* 1/2 (1995), pp.261–73; C.J. Pattie, R.J. Johnston and E.A. Fieldhouse, 'Winning the Local Vote: The Effectiveness of Constituency Campaign Spending in Great-Britain, 1983–1992', *American Political Science Review* 89/4 (1995), pp.969–83.

20. E.N. Goldenberg and M.W. Traugott, *Campaigning for Congress* (Washington, DC: Congressional Quarterly Press, 1984), p.145.

21. C.D. Kam and E.J. Zechmeister, 'Name Recognition and Candidate Support', *American Journal of Political Science* 57/4 (2013), pp.971–86.

22. Pattie and Johnston, 'Party Knowledge and Candidate Knowledge'.

23. Gschwend and Zittel, 'Do Constituency Candidates Matter'.

24. Goldenberg and Traugott, 'Congressional Campaign Effects'.

25. Wolak, 'The Consequences of Concurrent Campaigns for Citizen Knowledge of Congressional Candidates'.

26. Gschwend and Zittel, 'Do Constituency Candidates Matter'.

27. Goldenberg and Traugott, 'Congressional Campaign Effects'.

28. Gschwend and Zittel, 'Do Constituency Candidates Matter'.

29. Wolak, 'Consequences of Concurrent Campaigns'.

30. H. Rattinger, S. Roßteutscher, R. Schmitt-Beck, B. Weßels, C. Wolf, A. Wagner, H. Giebler, I. Bieber and P. Scherer, *Vor- und Nachwahl-Querschnitt (Kumulation) (GLES 2013)* (Köln: GESIS Datenarchiv, 2014. ZA5702 Datenfile Version 2.0.0, 10.4232/1.12064).

31. Obviously, mixing pre- and post-election surveys is not completely unproblematic. However, we deem it more important to cover as many constituencies as possible and to catch as many citizens per constituency as possible. As both surveys use independent sampling procedures, both quantities increase tremendously if one uses the combined dataset. Moreover, and in contrast to, for example, party choice, we assume that candidate recognition is less biased by bandwagon effects.

32. H. Rattinger, S. Roßteutscher, R. Schmitt-Beck, B. Weßels, C. Wolf, A. Wagner and H. Giebler, *Kandidatenstudie 2013: Befragung, Wahlergebnisse und Strukturdaten (GLES)* (Köln: GESIS Datenarchiv, 2014. ZA5716 Datenfile Version 3.0.0, 10.4232/1.12043).

33. Although the CDU and the CSU officially are two different parties, they do not compete against each other and are often described as 'sister parties'. The CSU only stands for election in Bavaria while the CDU runs in all other regions. Hence, we consider them to be interchangeable in the sense that we use information on the CSU (candidate) in Bavaria and the CDU (candidate) in all other regions.

34. We refrained from imputing missing values with the exception of the candidates' campaign budgets. Similar to mass surveys, money is a rather sensitive issue causing a larger quantity of missing information. Hence, we used a multiple imputation approach for all cases without missing values on any of the other variables in use. The latter, in addition to party dummies, were used as regular variables for the imputation procedure. We set up a multiple imputation procedure using verified party positions with 500 iterations for all parties not fulfilling the criteria described in step one. We applied a truncated regression for a continuous variable with a restricted range as the imputation equation. As a result, the imputed values have to be elements of the original range of empirical values. The imputed values for money spent are calculated as the mean of all 500 iterations. All in all, 52 values were calculated by this procedure. For a similar approach, see S.A. Banducci, H. Giebler and S. Kritzinger, 'Knowing More from Less: How the Information Environment Increases Knowledge of Party Positions', *British Journal of Political Science* (2015) available from http://dx.doi.org/10.1017/S0007123415000204 (accessed 23 May 2016).
35. Gschwend and Zittel, 'Do Constituency Candidates Matter'; Pattie and Johnston, 'Party Knowledge and Candidate Knowledge'.
36. Beyond the tense used in the questions, there were no differences between the pre- and post-election surveys. The original question translates as 'Do you remember the name and party affiliation of one or more electoral candidates in your constituency which stand for election at the Federal Election on 22 September 2013? Please, tell me the name as well as his or her party affiliation.'
37. S. Holmberg, 'Candidate Recognition in Different Electoral Systems', in H.D. Klingemann (ed.), *The Comparative Study of Electoral Systems* (Oxford: Oxford University Press, 2009), pp.58–70; Norris, *Electoral Engineering*.
38. As there is no valid equivalent to R^2 values in non-linear multi-level set-ups, we calculated the ROC value for our model which basically looks at sensitivity and specificity values of estimations under varying cut-off conditions. See C.E. Metz, 'Basic Principles of ROC Analysis', *Seminars in Nuclear Medicine* 8/4 (1978), pp.283–98. The model results in an ROC value of .88 which represents a very good model fit.
39. In non-linear models, these probability changes depend on the values of all other independent variables in the model. Moreover, because we run a hierarchical model, they are also dependent on the cluster-specific intercepts. We decided to calculate the average marginal effect setting all other independent variables to their empirical mean controlling for the unequal size of clusters. For both higher levels in our model, the intercept variances are estimated with a mean of zero. We used this feature by estimating the average marginal effects for the 'average' citizen in the 'average' constituency represented by random intercepts of zero on both levels.
40. See A. Gelman, 'Scaling Regression Inputs by Dividing by Two Standard Deviations', *Statistics in Medicine* 27 (2008), pp.2865–73. Rescaling by two standard deviations makes a one-unit change of non-binary variables comparable to the effect of binary predictors. He also suggests subtracting the mean before the division. However, this is only necessary if a model includes an interaction which is not the case here.
41. Gschwend and Zittel, 'Do Constituency Candidates Matter'.

APPENDIX

Variable name	Description	Measurement
Pre- and post-election surveys[a]		
Dependent variable		
Candidate recognition	Respondents were asked to report all names and party affiliations of candidates of the CDU/CSU, SPD, FDP, the Left and the Greens running in their district.	Dummy; 1 = candidate recognised, 0 = otherwise
Voters' characteristics		
Representational norm: own voters in district	Respondents were asked how important it was for them that an MP represents her voters in the district.	Dummy; 1 = very important, important, 0 = otherwise
Representational norm: all citizens in district	Respondents were asked how important it was for them that an MP represents all citizens in the district.	Dummy; 1 = very important, important, 0 = otherwise
Party like–dislike	Respondents were asked to rate all parties on a like–dislike scale.	11-point scale; 1 (strongly dislike) to 11 (strongly like)
Political interest	Respondents were asked to report their degree of interest in politics on a five-point scale.	Dummy; 1 = very strong, strong, 0 = otherwise
Political knowledge	Respondents were asked two questions about the electoral system applied in Federal Elections (threshold to win seats based on the proportional tier and which of the two ballots is more important for the electoral result).	Sum score; 0 (no correct answer) to 2 (both questions answered correctly)
Reading local newspaper	Respondents were asked about their media consumption, including a question on whether they read a local newspaper.	Dummy; 1 = yes, 0 = no
Discuss politics	Respondents were asked whether they discuss political issues with family members, friends or colleagues.	Dummy; 1 = yes, 0 = no
Voters' campaign exposure		
Campaign contacts	Respondents were asked to report all party-specific campaign contacts during the campaign. All in all, contact via 14 different means and instruments (ranging from e-mails to canvassing) were measured.	Sum score of all means and instruments per party; 0 (no contact) to 14 (contacted via all means and instruments)
Proximity to election	This indicator measures the absolute distance to the election date (22 September 2013)	Continuous measure in weeks rescaled so that low values indicate larger distance to election; min = −13.14, max = −.14

Continued

TABLE A1
CONTINUED.

Variable name	Description	Measurement
Candidate surveys[b]		
Candidates' characteristics		
Candidate profile	Respondents were asked whether they ran in the 2009 Federal Election and whether they won a seat.	Categorical measure; 1 = did not run in 2009, 2 = ran without winning a seat in 2009, 3 = successful campaign in 2009
Residence	Respondents were asked whether they were living in the constituency they were running in.	Dummy; 1 = yes, 0 = no
Endorsement	Respondents were asked whether they were publicly endorsed by an organisation (e.g. trade unions, religious organisations or clubs).	Dummy; 1 = yes, 0 = no
Candidates' campaign efforts		
Time	Respondents were asked how much time they spent for campaigning per week during the last month before the election.	Continuous measure in days; min = .08, max = 7
Team	Respondents were asked about the size of their individual campaign team.	Continuous measure; min = 0, max = 150
Money	Respondents were asked how much money they spent for their individual campaign.	Continuous measure in €1000; min = 0, max = 120
Campaign diversity	Respondents were asked to report all different means and instruments they used for their campaign.	Sum score of all means and instruments; 0 (no use of campaign means and instruments) to 20 (use of all campaign means and instruments)
Campaign style	Constructed variable to measure the campaign style in terms of classic and postmodern means and instruments.	Two sum scores were constructed, one for classic and one for post-modern means and instruments. Due to the different number of items used to construct the two scales, we rescaled both to values from 0 to 1. Campaign style is measured as the difference between classic and postmodern means and instruments; high values indicate the usage of more classic means and instruments; −1 (sole usage of postmodern means and instruments) to 1 (sole usage of classic means and instruments)
Campaign focus	Respondents were asked about the focus of their campaign in terms of attracting as much attention as possible to themselves or to their party	11-point scale; 1 (focus on party) to 11 (focus on candidate)
Local topics	Respondents were asked whether they emphasised any local topic during their campaign	Dummy; 1 = yes, 0 = no

Continued

TABLE A1
CONTINUED.

Variable name	Description	Measurement
Media access	Respondents were asked how often they featured in the media during the campaign on a five-point scale	Dummy; 1 = very often, often, 0 = otherwise
Contextual information[b]		
Party popularity	This variable measures party popularity as the average vote share (proportional ballot) of the 2009 and 2013 constituency result in percentage points	Continuous measure; min = 3.07, max = 55.2
Effective number of electoral candidates	This variable measures the effective number of electoral candidates based on the constituency ballot using the Laakso and Taagepera formula.[c] Only the electoral results for the CDU/CSU, SPD, FDP, the Left and the Greens are taken into account. Averages were calculated of the values for 2009 and 2013	Continuous measure; min = 2.17, max = 4.97
Population density	This variable measures population density in 1000 inhabitants per square kilometre for each constituency	Continuous measure; min = 38, max = 12842.9

Sources:
[a]Rattinger et al., *Vor- und Nachwahl-Querschnitt (Kumulation) (GLES 2013)*.
[b]Rattinger et al., *Kandidatenstudie 2013. Befragung, Wahlergebnisse und Strukturdaten (GLES)*.
[c]See M. Laakso and R. Taagepera, '"Effective" Number of Parties: A Measure with Application to West Europe', *Comparative Political Studies* 12/1 (1979), pp.3–27.

169

Correct Voting at the 2013 German Federal Election: An Analysis of Normatively Desirable Campaign Effects

BEN CHRISTIAN

This article studies campaign effects at the 2013 German Federal Election. It analyses whether and how the 2013 campaign contributed to electors' ability to cast votes in line with their political preferences – 'correct' votes in the terminology of Lau and Redlawsk. The article takes a novel perspective at correct voting by analysing its dynamic development during the course of an election campaign, using observational data collected by means of a rolling cross-section survey. It finds that voters' likelihood to choose correctly significantly increased during the election campaign. Two campaign-induced processes in particular contributed to explaining this development: voters' growing involvement with electoral politics and their decreasing indifference with regard to the parties competing for their votes. These findings suggest that by stimulating citizens to engage more intensively with electoral politics campaigns can strengthen the linkage between voters' preferences and their actual voting behaviour. Despite much criticism of how they are conducted, election campaigns can exert normatively desirable effects, thereby improving the quality of representative democracy.

INTRODUCTION

Election campaigns have a bad reputation. They are widely considered to be no more than a boring and sometimes even annoying side aspect of representative democracy without any normatively desirable impact. Some argue, for instance, that political parties shy away from open debate and only concentrate on their own issues, thus preventing a well-balanced debate with healthy effects on the formation of public opinion.[1] Others criticise recent campaigns' tendency towards personalisation and negativism. With a special focus on the news media, 'horse-race journalism'[2] is found to be symptomatic for current campaign coverage, leading to an 'entertainization of politics'.[3]

The present article looks at election campaigns from a more positive angle. It investigates whether despite (or perhaps even because of) these features campaigns may have consequences for citizens' decision making that are desirable from a normative point of view. It does not deal with any of the many details characterising the conduct of modern campaigns, but is interested in their overall effects on electoral behaviour. It seeks to explore electoral implications of the 'campaign as such', defined as an overall communication process taking place over time before Election Day.[4] Is there a relationship between campaigning and the quality of voting decisions? If so, which? And how does it come about? These are the questions that will be answered by this research.

Powell's notion of the 'chain of responsiveness' is a useful conceptual tool to contextualise these questions (see Figure 1).[5] In a representative democracy, citizens delegate their preferences to political representatives and thus give them the mandate to make public policies in accordance with the will of the people. According to Powell's model, this process can be differentiated into four stages and three so-called 'linkages' that connect them. Each of these linkages indicates a crucial step in the logic of democratic delegation from citizens to policy-makers, but also illustrates a specific challenge representative democracies have to meet. In an ideal representative democracy, all these linkages work perfectly well so that citizens' preferences are transformed into political outcomes in an unbiased way. Whether and to what extent this is the case in any real system of democratic representation, however, is open to question. Concentrating on the first linkage, the *structuration of voter's choices*,[6] the present article investigates whether and how election campaigns help citizens to transform their political preferences into voting decisions that are in line with these preferences. It seeks to discern whether election campaigns have normatively desirable effects by enabling voters to pick the party corresponding best to their political preferences in the variety of electoral alternatives offered to them, thus improving the quality of their voting decisions.

Normative issues of this kind are rarely addressed in studies of voting behaviour. An exception is the concept of *correct voting* developed by Lau and Redlawsk[7] which explicitly focuses on the quality of voting decisions as a criterion for the normative evaluation of democracies.[8] Recognising ordinary voters' well-known deficiencies in political knowledge and understanding, these authors define a party or candidate choice as 'correct' if it 'is the same as the choice which would have been made under conditions of full information'.[9] The higher the share of voters that cast correct votes, the better the first linkage of Powell's chain of responsiveness works. Correct voting thus implies a standard for evaluating the normatively desirable functioning of a representative democracy.

Correct voting and its backgrounds have been quite intensely analysed. Several studies have investigated how attributes of individual citizens as well as their

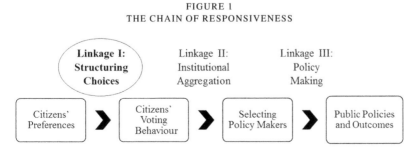

FIGURE 1
THE CHAIN OF RESPONSIVENESS

Source: Adapted from Powell, 'Chain of Responsiveness', p.92.

institutional and social contexts contribute to correct voting.[10] However, although Lau and Redlawsk see their research as a contribution to the study of election campaigns, the question whether and how campaigns impact citizens' likelihood of voting correctly has rarely been addressed.[11] If campaigns are beneficial with regard to correct voting, electors' odds of casting a correct vote should increase during the run-up to an election, and the share of correct votes in the electorate at large should accordingly grow. Investigating whether this is the case is the first aim of the present article. If this expectation can be confirmed, the article's second aim is to explore the mechanism through which election campaigns improve the odds of voting correctly. By using a rolling cross-section survey to analyse the development of correct voting intentions in the course of an election campaign, the study applies a novel methodological approach to the study of this phenomenon. To my knowledge, it is the first study using observational data for studying correct voting from a dynamic perspective.

The article starts with a theoretical discussion that leads to a set of testable hypotheses. Based on the 2013 German Federal Election as a test case, the following sections introduce data, measurements and the strategy of analysis to test these hypotheses. The subsequent section presents the findings of the empirical analyses. They demonstrate that in the course of the 2013 Federal Election campaign correct voting intentions became significantly more widespread. Several factors contributed to this development, most notably voters' growing political involvement and their decreasing indifference towards the political parties.

CAMPAIGNS AND CORRECT VOTING: THEORETICAL CONSIDERATIONS AND HYPOTHESES

According to Lau and Redlawsk, and in line with Powell's idea of a chain of responsiveness, a democracy cannot work well if voters' preferences are not accurately expressed in their vote decisions.[12] Vote choices, therefore, should be made in such a way that they correspond to the choices made under the hypothetical condition of full information.[13] However, referring to the discrepancy between the normative ideals of thinkers like Mill or Rousseau concerning responsible and well-informed citizens on the one hand, and empirical evidence on the other, they conclude: '[f]ive decades of behavioural research in political science have left no doubt, however, that only a tiny minority of the citizens in any democracy actually live up to these ideals'.[14] Based on this insight, Lau and Redlawsk try to answer the following question: are voters – in spite of their deficiencies with regard to political knowledge – capable of selecting the candidates that they would have chosen in an 'ideal world of fully informed preferences'?[15] Using experimental and observational methods, they find that many, but by no means all voters are capable of doing so, and they identify a number of attributes and conditions that are advantageous for achieving this goal.[16] What remains unclear, however, is whether and how election campaigns contribute to correct voting.

Lau and Redlawsk do not formulate any hypotheses concerning the impact of campaigns. In the literature on campaign effects, however, arguments suggesting a positive role for campaigns in correct voting have been made. In support of such an expectation, particularly Gelman and King's work on the 'enlightening' role of campaigning can be called in evidence. According to these authors, the parties' media and campaign strategies can help voters to arrive at voting decisions that are 'enlightened', which means that they are strongly determined by so-called 'fundamental variables'; that is, voters' political predispositions and the economy. According to these authors, '[t]he function of the campaign is to inform voters about the fundamental variables and their appropriate weights'.[17] They are able to show that for all groups of voters, candidate preferences are gradually becoming enlightened in this sense during election campaigns, as the statistical relationships between fundamental variables and vote intentions become stronger over time.[18]

Obviously, Gelman and King's concept of enlightened choices is leaner than the more encompassing notion of correct voting proposed by Lau and Redlawsk, but the two concepts are similar in implying a normative perspective. They both suggest a desirable basis for vote choices which allows distinguishing between choices of high and low quality. When Gelman and King speak about 'enlightened preferences',[19] they refer to choices that correspond to voters' political predispositions and the state of the economy, whereas Lau and Redlawsk's notion of 'fully-informed preferences'[20] encompasses a much broader range of considerations of potential electoral relevance. What they have in common, however, is the idea that a vote choice should be considered as normatively desirable if it is not biased due to an incomplete or wrong informational background. With regard to enlightened choices, research indicates that election campaigns have normatively desirable effects. Studies by Gelman and King, but also by other authors have shown that enlightened choices become indeed more frequent as election campaigns progress.[21] It appears likely, therefore, that the same is true for choices that are correct in the sense of Lau and Redlawsk. They should be made more frequently in the course of election campaigns so that it can be hypothesised:

> H1: The share of correct voting intentions increases during the election campaign.

This hypothesis only proposes an answer to the 'whether' question, but does not say anything about the 'how' or 'why'. If campaigns indeed have the effect on correct voting proposed by this hypothesis, how does it come about? One possible line of explanation concentrates on political involvement and political communication. According to Lazarsfeld's classic idea of electoral activation, campaigns increase voters' political involvement which in turn increases their attention for electoral information.[22] Norris proposes similar ideas in her contribution to the debate on media malaise and mobilisation, captured in the concept of a 'virtuous circle'.[23] It postulates a dynamic 'two-way interaction process'[24] of increasing media attention and involvement: voters get politically involved through information obtained from the mass media, and thereby become motivated to search for even more information which, in turn, improves their political knowledge and understanding. Norris evaluates the effect of this circle as beneficial for electoral politics, but also states more generally: '[a] virtuous circle represents an iterative process gradually exerting a positive impact on democracy'.[25]

With regard to enlightened voting, Gelman and King also emphasise the important mediating role of political involvement. They expect election campaigns to be helpful for people in order to clarify their fundamental preferences – a process which is not possible without some kind of involvement: '[t]his process then depends on the media to provide information [...] and the voters to pay attention'.[26] Once people become engaged with the upcoming election and start to think about it, they will increase their political knowledge and it should be more likely that they vote correctly. It can therefore be hypothesised that the positive campaign effect proposed by H1 evolves due to an increasing political involvement of voters which is spurred by the election campaign.

> H2a: During the election campaign, election-related interest increases, and this in turn leads to an increased likelihood of correct voting intentions.
> H2b: During the election campaign, political knowledge increases, and this in turn leads to an increased likelihood of correct voting intentions.

According to these lines of reasoning, the positive effects of campaigns do not only come about as a consequence of increasing political involvement during the campaign, but also of increased attention to media coverage and other sources of electoral information. Besides the news media, interpersonal communication can also be an important source for people in order to catch up on political topics. Their influence might in fact be even more powerful than the impact of the news media.[27] One can imagine that in election campaigns in which political topics are omnipresent, people are also talking more about politics – whether this happens at the workplace or at the dining table. It can therefore be hypothesised that positive campaign effects on correct voting may evolve due to people's increasing attention to political communications from both media and personal sources.

> H3a: During the election campaign, the frequency of political discussion increases, and this in turn leads to an increased likelihood of correct voting intentions.
> H3b: During the election campaign, the frequency of media consumption increases, and this in turn leads to an increased likelihood of correct voting intentions.

Another line of reasoning refers to electors' perceptions of the parties that compete for their votes. Enabling voters to differentiate among the parties may be an important achievement of campaigning. Before a campaign starts, it may be hard for voters to discern what distinguishes parties from one another. Many different party positions on a broad range of different issues circulate through the general public – 'something for everyone'.[28] Throughout the course of the campaign, voters are challenged by the difficult task of making up their minds about which one of the many competing parties to choose. In this situation, they may find it helpful that the election campaign reduces the many controversial issues 'into one big residual difference of opinion'.[29] Through their campaigning, parties may become more distinctive so that it becomes easier for voters to see their differences which in turn should lead to a decrease of their indifference against the parties. In the end, they should know better what each party stands for – or does not stand for. This in turn should facilitate the development of voting preferences according to voters' political preferences and thus increase the likelihood to vote correctly. It can hence be hypothesised:

H4: During the election campaign, voters' indifference towards parties decreases, and this in turn leads to an increased likelihood of correct voting intentions.

DATA AND MEASUREMENT

To study dynamic developments in voters' preferences, attitudes and beliefs during campaign periods, data structured in time are needed. All analyses in this article are based on data from a survey conducted by telephone according to the *rolling cross-section (RCS) design* as part of the German Longitudinal Election Study (GLES) 2013.[30] The specific feature that makes RCS data particularly useful for the present purpose is the random stretching of interviews on a daily basis over the entire campaign period. Thus, the interviews collected on each day constitute small random samples of the population of citizens eligible to vote.[31] This allows for a flexible analysis of dynamic developments during the election campaign on a fine-grained day-to-day basis and without the methodological problems often produced by using panel data (i.e. panel mortality, panel conditioning). In contrast to panel surveys, RCS studies only allow studying change at the aggregate level, but this constraint is no drawback for the purpose of the analyses presented below. The RCS data used in the present article span the entire campaign of the 2013 German Federal Election, from 8 July to 21 September, the day before the election. Slightly more than 100 respondents were interviewed every day.[32]

Measuring the dependent variable, *correct voting*, implies considerable challenges. The phenomenon of correct voting has been mostly studied in the United States, and by means of experimental methods. Neither transferring the measure to another political context nor to (observational) survey data is trivial. For studying correct voting using survey data, Lau and Redlawsk have themselves developed an approach, the so-called 'normatively naïve' strategy of measurement.[33] The basic idea is to compare the individual preferences of each respondent with the objective positions of the parties and thus determine for which party this individual *should* vote if he or she followed his or her preferences. Referring to a range of different dimensions of beliefs and attitudes of known relevance for vote choices, an overall score for every party is calculated, and a personal rank order of parties is then established for each respondent.[34] Based on this, the voting intention of a respondent is defined as correct if he or she intends to vote for the party with the highest score in this ranking. The underlying premise is that this party reflects the respondent's preferences best. It therefore represents his or her correct choice. For the German context, there are three adaptations of this logic so far: one by Lau et al.,[35] one by Rudi and Schoen[36] and one by Kraft.[37]

The first task in constructing a measure of correct voting is to decide which attitudes and beliefs should be included in the overall ranking score. For their analyses of American Presidential Elections, Lau and Redlawsk have taken more than 20 different orientations into account.[38] The German adaptation by Kraft includes a similar number of elements.[39] However, the relative scarcity of measures contained in the data used for the present study precludes such a detailed and complex operationalisation. Since RCS surveys cannot be conducted by means of extensive face-to-face interviews, there is an inescapable trade-off: their dynamic character – which is an essential precondition of the present study – necessarily comes at the expense of relative short-age with regard to measures of electoral beliefs and attitudes. However, previous studies relying on similarly restricted datasets successfully measured correct voting using a smaller number of dimensions. In a comparative study of correct voting in 33 democracies, Lau et al., for example, were faced with a similar problem when relying on CSES data.[40] They focused on three dimensions of electoral attitudes to gen-erate overall party scores: (1) party performance ratings; (2) left–right placement; and (3) party identification.[41] The present article takes guidance from this approach, although with modifications in some important details.

Two small adjustments are necessary due to the nature of the data. The measure-ment of party performance is based on parties' attributed problem-solving competence. Moreover, instead of left–right placements of parties (that are not contained in the RCS data of the 2013 GLES), a somewhat more specific issue scale is used which measures respondents' socio-economic left–right self-placement and perceptions of party positions (taxes vs social welfare). The other modification is motivated by sub-stantial considerations and concerns party identification. The inclusion of this construct does not seem convincing with reference to the present article's normative perspective because its orthodox understanding[42] does not postulate that a voter always has to vote in line with his or her party identification. However, including it in the overall score presupposes the implicit assumption that it is desirable and normatively correct to vote always in correspondence to one's party identification. In the present study, party identification will therefore be replaced by candidate evaluation, an attitude used in many of Lau and Redlawsk's own analyses.[43] This goes well with its normative premise: a voter should opt for the candidate he or she perceives as being most capable.[44]

In the first step of constructing the measure of correct voting, for each of the three dimensions – parties' perceived problem-solving competence, socio-economic left-right placements and candidate evaluations – a score is generated, based on the general logic of relating respondents' preferences to the respective party attributes. Sub-sequently, an overall score for every party is calculated through averaging across these three dimensions. On this basis, parties can then be ranked for each respondent. In the next step of the procedure, the voting intention of each respondent is classified as correct or incorrect, depending on whether the party he or she intended to choose (with the second vote of the German Mixed Member Proportional (MMP) system) was the one scoring highest in his or her personal ranking order. The final step of oper-ationalising the correct voting variable considers the fact that under the German MMP system, voters often take strategic considerations into account when deciding which party to support at the ballots. For instance, if the SPD were the correct alternative for a respondent, a vote for the Greens could under certain circumstances also be counted as a correct choice. The same applies to the CDU/CSU and FDP. The basic strategy for this final step of the operationalisation is simple: 'vote borrowing' for small coalition partners is considered acceptable in the sense of casting a correct vote if a respondent at the same time states a corresponding coalition preference.[45]

Although it is clear that the share of correct votes registered by a study depends strongly on the operationalisation it has chosen, analyses of correct voting are typically – and for understandable reasons – very interested in determining the share of correct votes cast by a population or at a particular election. The measurement procedure used in the present article leads to an overall share of 65 per cent of respondents classified as having voted correctly. However, it must not be overlooked that other ways of measuring this complex construct might lead to different levels. More important in view of the present article's research question is the fact that this number is based on a simple averaging across the full sample that is insensitive to time. Thus, only values generated by the same measurement technique are compared in the present study. As will be shown later on, the share of correct voters was indeed not stable during the campaign period.

Turning to the independent variables, the most crucial one is time. The variable *campaign duration* results from a count of the 76 days of data collection. Hence, this variable indicates at which point in time a respondent was interviewed between 8 July and 21 September 2013. Two measures register political involvement. *Election-related interest* consists of an index which was constructed by averaging across the original two variables *interest in the election campaign*[46] and *interest in the outcome of the election*[47] (both measured on five-point scales). The second measure is a dummy variable indicating *political knowledge*. It registers whether respondents gave the correct answer (second vote) to the question which of the two votes of the German MMP system is the more important one with regard to allocating seats in the Bundestag.[48] To assess the role of political communication, both *usage of news media* and *everyday discussion about politics* are taken into account (measured in days during the previous week, scale 0–7). For measuring news media exposure, several indicators are used. In a first step, various media (newspapers, TV newscasts, news on the Internet) are analysed separately. Based on initial findings, some of them are also combined into an averaging index for the further analyses (Internet news and newscasts of the two public broadcasters ARD and ZDF). The measure for the *indifference between parties* is derived from sympathy thermometers for parties (range +5 to −5). It indicates the size of the difference between the first most liked and second most liked party. If it is zero, the respondent is highly indifferent. The larger the distance between the two parties, the lower the respondents' indifference between parties.[49] Besides these substantially interesting independent variables, a number of socio-demographic variables – age, gender and education – are included as controls in the multivariate models.

STRATEGY OF ANALYSIS

The first question to be answered by the following analyses is *whether* the likelihood of voting intentions to be correct has indeed, as expected by H1, been increasing in the course of the 2013 German Federal Election campaign. This will be checked by graphic analysis and confirmed by means of a simple bivariate (logistic) regression analysis. Since this analysis indeed detects growth in the amount of correct voting during the campaign, it is to be asked *why* this might have been the case. Obviously, people do not have more correct voting intentions in September than in June just because it is September. Time itself cannot suffice as explanation. Rather, it is necessary to identify independent variables whose impact can explain the change observed for correct voting intentions over time. Mediation analysis[50] is used to answer this question. Three conditions must be fulfilled for an independent variable in order to be considered relevant for the temporal development of correct voting. First, since constants cannot explain change, it must not be static during the campaign, but has to develop dynamically itself as Election Day comes closer. Second, it must be related to correct voting at the individual level. Third, when included in a multivariate model in addition to time, the effect of the latter on a voter's likelihood to vote correctly should diminish, indicating that it is more or less strongly mediated by the development of the independent variable in question.

For the sake of comparability, the following regression tables show 'full-dose' effects.[51] Technically, this means that all variables are re-scaled to range 0 to 1, and the tables display average marginal effects (AME).[52] These coefficients indicate the change in the probability of a correct vote intention caused by a shift in the respective independent variable over its entire range, from its lowest to its highest value. For the time variable, for instance, this indicates the estimated difference in respondents' likelihood of correct voting between the start and the end of the campaign. Data are weighted by combined design (household size) and socio-demographic weight (region, gender, age, education) and all regression models are estimated using robust standard errors clustered by survey days.

FINDINGS

Figure 2 visualises the development of correct voting intentions during the 2013 German Federal Election campaign. It clearly shows the expected positive trend. The share of correct voting intentions has significantly increased in the course of the campaign. According to the AME estimated by means of a bivariate regression

FIGURE 2
DEVELOPMENT OF CORRECT VOTING INTENTIONS DURING THE CAMPAIGN (PER CENT)

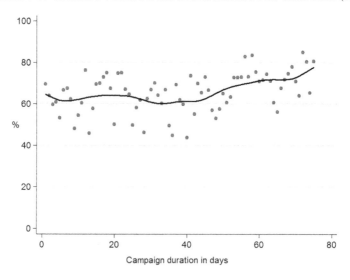

Note: Data are weighted, trend line is smoothed (Lowess, bandwidth = .40).

analysis, the growth in correct voting amounted to 11 percentage points ($p < .01$). The basic hypothesis H1 – that the 2013 election campaign had the normatively desirable effect of increasing the share of correct vote intentions – is thus confirmed. It appears that election campaigns can indeed improve the quality of voting decisions. In 2013, as the campaign progressed the likelihood for voters to express correct voting intentions increased. During the campaign, the share of correct voting intentions was around one-sixth higher than its initial amount. This may not seem particularly dramatic, but changes when looked at from another angle: between the start and the end of the 2013 campaign, one out of four voters who initially expressed an incorrect voting intention switched to a correct one.

How can the growing quality of voting decisions in the course of the election campaign be explained? By which mechanism did the campaign enable voters to cast correct votes? If the positive relationship between campaign duration and correct voting should be explained, variables that may have mediated the relationship between time and correct voting need to be identified. Since constants cannot explain change, only factors that also altered during the campaign can have contributed to voters' increased likelihood of voting correctly. The bivariate (ordinary least squares (OLS); for political knowledge: logit) regression analyses displayed in Table 1 test all potential campaign-related predictors of correct voting identified by our hypotheses for whether or not and in which direction they changed during the campaign.

The two dimensions of political involvement have indeed been developing during the campaign: both voters' election-related interest and political knowledge were significantly increasing as Election Day came closer. Obviously, the longer the campaign lasted, the more people got involved and the more they learned about politics. Similarly, some of the voters' political communication activities became more intense during the campaign. People talked more often about politics, and they also used some news media more frequently to inform themselves about political topics.

TABLE 1
DEVELOPMENT OF POTENTIAL PREDICTORS OF CORRECT VOTING DURING CAMPAIGN

	Election-related interest	Political knowledge	Political discussions	Tabloid newspaper (BILD)
Campaign duration	.11***	.08***	.20***	.00

	Broadsheet newspapers	News on the Internet	Public TV: ARD news	Public TV: ZDF news
Campaign duration	.03	.04*	.06**	.05*

	Private TV: RTL news	Private TV: SAT.1 news	Index of media consumption	Indifference
Campaign duration	.02	.00	.05***	−.03**

Notes:
***$p < .001$; **$p < .01$; *$p < .05$.
Entries are unstandardised regression coefficients (political knowledge: average marginal effect), constants are not shown; all variables are rescaled to range 0–1; data are weighted; minimum N = 7120; regression models calculated with robust standard errors.

Specifically, this was the case for the news on both public TV channels (ARD and ZDF) and for news in the Internet, but not for newspapers and news on commercial channels (RTL and SAT.1). To simplify the next steps of the analysis, the three dynamic media variables are combined in an index of media consumption by averaging across the three original variables. Table 1 shows the AME of this index as well, and of course it is very similar to those of its ingredient variables. Lastly, the amount of voters' indifference also changed during the campaign. According to Table 1, it decreased which means that it became easier for voters to identify favourites among the parties that they clearly liked better than even their closest competitors.

Table 1 establishes a necessary, but not sufficient condition for hypotheses H2a/b, H3a/b and H4 to be true. Both dimensions of political involvement as well as exposure to sources of both personally communicated and mediated political information went up over the course of the election campaign, whereas indifference between parties diminished. The following analysis tests whether and how these variables were related to correct voting and to which extent they indeed mediated the effects of time on correct voting. To this end, a series of multivariate regression analyses is performed whose results are shown in Table 2. The baseline model (Model 1) once again, but now controlling for demographics, confirms the significant positive effect of time on correct voting. It deserves noting that the results for the control variables resemble the relationships found by Lau and Redlawsk for American voters: older and better educated respondents have a higher likelihood to vote correctly.[53]

Let us now test the hypotheses H2a/b to H4 one by one. The modelling strategy follows a stepwise logic which is derived from the heuristic assumption of a sequential process. It posits that the campaign first leads to increased political involvement on the part of citizens. This in turn leads people to search for more political information: they start talking about politics with their partners, friends and colleagues as well as informing themselves using the mass media. As a result, voters learn to discern parties more clearly which enables them to identify a personal favourite. Ultimately, these processes lead to an increasing ability of voters to make choices that are the right ones for them: correct votes, in line with their political preferences. It needs to be reiterated that this line of reasoning is understood as a heuristic guideline to organise the analyses and not a fully developed theory. In particular, it is highly likely that some processes could also work the other way round – as expressed, for instance, in Norris' notion of the 'virtuous circle'[54] which implies that media consumption is not only an effect, but also a cause of political involvement.

As evidenced by Model 2, both dimensions of political involvement – election-related interest and political knowledge – had significant effects on correct voting intentions. The more people were interested in the election campaign and the more they knew about politics, the higher their likelihood to vote correctly, although in direct comparison the impact of interest was much more powerful than the effect of knowledge. Importantly, in Model 2, the effect of time is nearly halved compared to the baseline model. This suggests that the expansion of correct voting intentions in the course of the campaign can to a considerable extent be explained by the people's growing political involvement. This is in line with H2a and H2b: the positive campaign effect evolved due to an increasing political involvement among voters during the election campaign. Whereas it is well known from previous research that

TABLE 2
MEDIATORS OF THE TIME EFFECT ON CORRECT VOTING

	1 Baseline	2 Political involvement	3 Political communication	4 Involvement & communication	5 Indifference	6 Involvement & communication & indifference
Campaign duration	.12**	.07*	.08*	.06	.10**	.05
Election-related interest		.49***		.45***		.42***
Political knowledge		.04*		.04*		.03
Political discussions			.16***	.08*		.07
Media consumption			.14**	.06		.06
Indifference					-.55***	-.47***
Age	.20***	.09	.11	.06	.20***	.06
Education	.07**	.02	.04	.01	.08**	.02
Gender (male=1)	.06**	.04**	.04*	.04*	.05**	.04*
N	4798	4798	4798	4798	4798	4798
McFadden-R^2	.01	.05	.02	.05	.03	.06

Notes:
***$p < .001$; **$p < .01$; *$p < .05$.
Entries are average marginal effects; all variables are rescaled to range 0–1; data are weighted; regression models calculated with robust standard errors.

political involvement can be a powerful predictor of correct voting,[55] the combined findings of Tables 1 and 2 provide the new insight that political involvement increases during the campaign and thus improves voters' likelihood to cast correct votes on Election Day.

Model 3 tells a similar story: both voters' political discussions with others and their attention to mass media – although only for newscasts on public TV and the Internet – had significant effects on correct voting intentions during the 2013 campaign, and at the same time they reduced the time effect visibly. The more people talked and informed themselves about politics by using certain news media, the higher the likelihood that their voting intentions were correct. Since these communication activities increased during the election campaign, correct voting intentions also become more frequent. This is in line with hypotheses H3a and H3b: the positive development concerning correct voting intentions was related to people's intensifying communication activities during the election campaign.[56]

Model 4 changes the picture, though. It combines political involvement and communication, taking into account the presumably close relationship between these factors. Political involvement clearly appears as the stronger background of correct voting in this model. When controlling for political involvement, political discussion still has an autonomous and significant effect on the likelihood of correct voting intentions, although its size is considerably diminished. Media consumption, however, loses its relevance so H3b cannot be confirmed by this more complex model.

Model 5 shows that a full-dose change of indifference (covering the entire span between the lowest and highest value) very strongly decreased the likelihood of a voter expressing a correct voting intention, and this effect is highly significant. Moreover, adding the indifference variable to the baseline model reduces the effect of campaign time, although not by a large margin. As people developed clearer stances towards the parties during the campaign, their indifference diminished which in turn facilitated the evolution of voting intentions according to their political preferences, so that the likelihood of correct votes was ultimately increased, as expected by H4.

Model 6 finally shows what happens when all dynamic predictors are simultaneously taken into account. Here one can see that election-related interest and indifference regarding the parties are of great importance. Prior to the 2013 Federal Election, they had a very sizable impact on the likelihood of voting correctly whereas the effects of all communication variables as well as political knowledge evaporate. Strikingly, when including all predictors in the model, the baseline effect of campaign time is more than halved and becomes insignificant. In the full model, time as such no longer plays a role as predictor of correct voting. This strongly suggests that especially voters' growing interest in the election and their decreasing indifference against the parties over the course of the campaign were the decisive factors that lead to the empirically observable and normatively desirable campaign effect of an increasing share of correct voting intentions. Ultimately, only two hypotheses about the mechanism by which election campaigns influence voters' odds of correct voting are therefore sustained. H2a and H4 are in line with the data. But H2b as well as H3a and H3b are no longer supported, once all relevant predictors are taken into account.

In sum, based on the analyses discussed above, the two questions raised by this article, concerning the 'whether' and the 'why' of election campaigns' contribution to correct voting, can now be answered. First, for the case of the 2013 German Federal Election, it could be shown that correct voting intentions indeed became more widespread as Election Day came closer. H1 was thus confirmed by this study. Second, the mediation analysis demonstrated that especially two factors contributed to this phenomenon: political involvement and party differentiation. While none of the hypotheses postulated above appeared irrelevant in the partial models, the full model made clear that H2a and H4 describe best why election campaigns lead to higher rates of correct voting. Findings suggest that the campaign stimulated political involvement, most notably the interest in the election, and that it helped voters to better distinguish parties from one another, leading to clearer favourability profiles. Together, these two processes nourished the spread of correct voting.

CONCLUSION

Slightly at odds with much recent criticism of election campaigns, this article started with the question whether election campaigns have a normatively desirable impact on the politics of democratic representation. More specifically, it asked whether campaigns contribute to correct voting; that is, vote choices that are in line with voters' political preferences. Similar questions have already been raised and answered affirmatively for the related concept of enlightened voting based on fundamentals.[57] But no study has yet analysed with observational data in a dynamic perspective how correct voting is developing during an election campaign, and how the campaign contributes to bringing about this outcome.

During the 2013 German Federal Election campaign, the share of correct voting intentions increased significantly, as expected. For any election campaign, this is a highly welcome outcome from a normative point of view. The 2013 campaign tightened the connection between voters' preferences and their actual voting behaviour. It thus contributed to the process of 'structuring choices', the first step within the multi-stage process of electoral democracy's 'chain of responsiveness'.[58] Despite the criticism often waged against how campaigns are conducted in modern democracies, they seem to have something valuable to contribute to the quality of democracy. By helping voters to arrive at correct choices, they exert a normatively desirable effect. Campaigns apparently deserve better than merely being disdainfully criticised as being annoying and useless. They may be mostly 'shows', but still they constitute an important learning arena for many citizens.

Thus, the fundamental hypothesis of this article could be confirmed. How did the campaign induce this outcome? Why were more people able to transform their political preferences into correct voting intentions at the end of the campaign than at its beginning? The findings presented above suggest that election campaigns work like a stimulus for the citizens to deal more intensively with politics: during the campaign, people get more involved, communicate more frequently and learn to differentiate better between the political parties. In this way, voters become both more informed and motivated and thus are better able to delegate their political will to the appropriate party at the ballot box. Fostering voters' interest in electoral politics and enabling them to discern parties more clearly seem to be the most powerful processes through which campaigns contribute to the quality of voters' electoral choices.

ACKNOWLEDGEMENTS

I am indebted to Rüdiger Schmitt-Beck, Robert Rohrschneider, Neil Hatton, Louisa Plasberg, Christoph Diringer and Elisabeth Christian for valuable advice and constructive comments on previous versions of this article as well as to Josephine Hörl for her careful language editing.

DISCLOSURE STATEMENT

No potential conflict of interest was reported by the author.

NOTES

1. Sascha Huber, 'Politisches Lernen im Wahlkampf bei der Bundestagswahl 2009', in Thorsten Faas, Kai Arzheimer, Sigrid Roßteutscher and Bernhard Weßels (eds), *Koalitionen, Kandidaten, Kommunikation* (Wiesbaden: Springer Fachmedien, 2013), p.173.
2. Thomas E. Patterson, 'The 1976 horserace', *The Wilson Quarterly* 1/3 (1977), pp.73–9.
3. Christina Holtz-Bacha, 'Entertainisierung der Politik', *Zeitschrift für Parlamentsfragen* 31/1 (2000), p.156.
4. Rüdiger Schmitt-Beck and David M. Farrell, 'Studying Political Campaigns and Their Effects', in David M. Farrell and Rüdiger Schmitt-Beck (eds), *Do Political Campaigns Matter? Campaign Effects in Elections and Referendum* (New York: Routledge, 2002), pp.16–17; Rüdiger Schmitt-Beck, 'New Modes of Campaigning', in Russell J. Dalton and Hans-Dieter Klingemann (eds), *The Oxford Handbook of Political Behavior* (Oxford: Oxford University Press, 2007), pp.753–7.
5. Bingham Powell, 'The Chain of Responsiveness', *Journal of Democracy* 15/4 (2004), pp.91–105.
6. Ibid., p.97.
7. Richard R. Lau and David P. Redlawsk, 'Voting Correctly', *American Political Science Review* 91/3 (1997), pp.585–98.
8. Richard R. Lau, David J. Andersen and David P. Redlawsk, 'An Exploration of Correct Voting in Recent U.S. Presidential Elections', *American Journal of Political Science* 52/2 (2008), p.396.
9. Lau and Redlawsk, 'Voting Correctly', p.586.
10. See Lau and Redlawsk, 'Voting Correctly'; Lau et al., 'Exploration of Correct Voting'; Richard R. Lau and David P. Redlawsk, *How Voters Decide: Information Processing during Election Campaigns* (Cambridge: Cambridge University Press, 2006); Richard R. Lau, Parina Patel, Dalia F. Fahmy and Robert R. Kaufman, 'Correct Voting across Thirty-Three Democracies: A Preliminary Analysis', *British Journal of Political Science* 44/2 (2014), pp.239–59; Sean Richey, 'The Social Basis of Voting Correctly', *Political Communication* 25/4 (2008), pp.366–76; Anand Edward Sokhey and Scott D. McClurg, 'Social Networks and Correct Voting', *Journal of Politics* 74/3 (2012), pp.751–64; Matthew A. Baum and Angela S. Jamison, 'The Oprah Effect: How Soft News Helps Inattentive Citizens Vote Consistently', *Journal of Politics* 68/4 (2006), pp.946–59.
11. For an exception see Rüdiger Schmitt-Beck and Patrick Kraft, 'Political Information Flows and Consistent Voting: Personal Conversations, Mass Media, Party Campaigns, and the Quality of Voting Decisions at the 2009 German Federal Election', in Bernhard Weßels, Hans Rattinger, Sigrid Roßteutscher and Rüdiger Schmitt-Beck (eds), *Voters on the Move or on the Run?* (Oxford: Oxford University Press, 2014), pp.193–216.
12. Lau and Redlawsk, *How Voters Decide*, p.16.
13. Lau and Redlawsk, 'Voting Correctly', p.586.
14. Ibid., p.585; see as well, for example, Michael Delli Carpini and Scott Keeter, *What Americans Know about Politics and Why It Matters* (New Haven, CT: Yale University Press, 1996); and for the German

context, for example, Jürgen Maier, 'Was die Bürger über Politik (nicht) wissen – und was die Massenmedien damit zu tun haben – ein Forschungsüberblick', *PVS Sonderheft* 42 (2009), pp.393–414.

15. Lau and Redlawsk, *How Voters Decide*, p.16.
16. See Lau and Redlawsk, 'Voting Correctly'; Lau et al., 'Exploration of Correct Voting'; Lau and Redlawsk, *How Voters Decide*; Lau et al., 'Correct Voting across Thirty-Three Democracies'.
17. Andrew Gelman and Gary King, 'Why Are American Presidential Election Campaign Polls So Variable When Votes Are So Predictable?', *British Journal of Political Science* 23/4 (1993), p.433f.
18. Ibid., p.435.
19. Ibid., p.433.
20. Lau and Redlawsk, 'Voting Correctly', p.591.
21. Gelman and King, 'Why Are American Presidential Election'; Kevin Arceneaux, 'Do Campaigns Help Voters Learn? A Cross-National Analysis', *British Journal of Political Science* 36/1 (2005), pp.159–73; Randolph T. Stevenson and Lynn Vavreck, 'Does Campaign Length Matter? Testing for Cross-National Effects', *British Journal of Political Science* 30/2 (2000), pp.217–35; Richard Johnston, Julia Partheymüller and Rüdiger Schmitt-Beck, 'Activation of Fundamentals in German Campaigns', in Weßels et al. (eds), *Voters on the Move*, pp.217–37.
22. Paul F. Lazarsfeld, Bernard Berelson and Hazel Gaudet, *The People's Choice: How the Voter Makes Up His Mind in a Presidential Campaign* (New York: Columbia University Press, 1944).
23. Pippa Norris, *A Virtuous Circle: Political Communications in Post-Industrial Societies* (New York: Cambridge University Press, 2000).
24. Ibid., p.18.
25. Ibid., p.318.
26. Gelman and King, 'Why Are American Presidential Election', p.435.
27. Lazarsfeld et al., *The People's Choice*.
28. Bernard R. Berelson, Paul F. Lazarsfeld and William N. McPhee, *Voting: A Study of Opinion Formation in a Presidential Election* (Chicago, IL: University of Chicago Press, 1954), p.183.
29. Ibid., p.183.
30. Hans Rattinger, Sigrid Roßteutscher, Rüdiger Schmitt-Beck, Bernhard Weßels and Christof Wolf, *Rolling Cross-Section-Wahlkampfstudie mit Nachwahl-Panelwelle GLES 2013* (GESIS Datenarchiv 2014, Köln: ZA5703 Datenfile Version 2.0.0, doi: 10.4232/1.11892).
31. Richard Johnston and Henry E. Brady, 'The Rolling Cross-Section Design', *Electoral Studies* 21/2 (2002), pp.283–95.
32. Julia Partheymüller, Rüdiger Schmitt-Beck and Christian Hoops, 'Kampagnendynamik bei der Bundestagswahl 2013: Die Rolling Cross-Section-Studie im Rahmen der German Longitudinal Election Study', *Arbeitspapiere des Mannheimer Zentrum für Europäische Sozialforschung* 154 (2013), p.11.
33. Lau and Redlawsk, 'Voting Correctly', p.589; for the alternative experimental approach see Lau and Redlawsk, *How Voters Decide*, p.54ff.
34. Patrick Kraft, 'Correct Voting in Deutschland: Eine Analyse der Qualität individueller Wahlentscheidungen bei der Bundestagswahl 2009', *Arbeitspapiere des Mannheimer Zentrum für Europäische Sozialforschung* 148 (2012), p.18.
35. Lau et al., 'Correct Voting across Thirty-Three Democracies', p.247.
36. Tatjana Rudi and Harald Schoen, 'Verwählt? Eine Analyse des Konzepts "korrektes Wählen" bei der Bundestagswahl 2009', in Bernhard Weßels, Harald Schoen and Oscar W. Gabriel (eds), *Wahlen und Wähler. Analysen aus Anlass der Bundestagswahl 2009* (Wiesbaden: Springer VS, 2013), pp.407–25.
37. Kraft, 'Correct Voting in Deutschland'.
38. Lau et al., 'Correct Voting across Thirty-Three Democracies'.
39. Kraft, 'Correct Voting in Deutschland'.
40. Lau et al., 'Correct Voting across Thirty-Three Democracies'.
41. Ibid., p.247f.
42. Angus Campbell, Philip E. Converse, Warren E. Miller and Donald E. Stokes, *The American Voter* (New York: Wiley, 1960).
43. See, for example, Lau and Redlawsk, 'Voting Correctly', p.589.
44. All analyses in this article were calculated as well once with the party identification instead of the candidate evaluation. Except for small differences concerning the level of the total correct voting amounts, all these analyses show exactly the same pattern of results.
45. To illustrate this complicated coding procedure, let us consider the following hypothetical example: a respondent is convinced that the CDU/CSU is most capable of solving the political problem he or she considers most important. The CDU/CSU is therefore assigned a score of +1.0 on this dimension whereas all other parties are coded as −1.0 (since they have not been mentioned by the respondent). Further, let us assume that the respondent's ideal point on the taxation/welfare issue is closest to the perceived position of the CDU/CSU, followed by the position of the FDP. The CDU/CSU is then

assigned a score of +1.0 on this dimension, the FDP is coded as +0.5. All other parties are assigned scores in descending order according to their relative distance to the respondent's own policy preference (e.g. SPD: 0; Greens: −0.5; Left: −1.0). Finally, a similar procedure is applied to the respondent's evaluations of the parties' leading candidates. Suppose, for instance, that he or she evaluates Angela Merkel (CDU/CSU) most favourably and Gregor Gysi (Left) most negatively. This leads to a score of +1.0 for the Christian Democrats, and a score of −1.0 for the Left, whereas the other parties are assigned scores in between, depending on where their candidates rank for this respondent (e.g. Greens: +0.5; SPD: 0; FDP: −0.5). After averaging across these three dimensions, it is obvious that the CDU/CSU is top ranked in this individual party ranking. Concerning the final coding of the correct voting variable, there are now three possibilities. If the respondent indeed wants to vote for the CDU/CSU, his or her voting intention is classified as 'correct' (code 1 on the resulting variable). If he or she aims to choose another party, the classification depends on his or her coalition preference. A vote for the FDP would also be classified as 'correct' if the respondent stated that he or she is most in favour of a black–yellow coalition. In contrast, a preference for any other party, or a preference for the FDP without a matching coalition preference would be classified as 'incorrect' (code 0).

46. Wording: 'And how interested are you in particular in the current campaign for the forthcoming Federal Election?'
47. Wording: 'And how important are the results of the forthcoming Federal Election to you personally?'
48. Wording: 'In the Federal Election, you have two votes: the first vote and the second vote. Which one of the two is decisive for the relative strengths of the parties in the Bundestag?'
49. See, for a similar operationalisation of indifference, Markus Steinbrecher, 'Are Alienation and Indifference the New Features of Elections?', in Weßels et al. (eds), *Voters on the Move*, p.270.
50. Reuben Baron and David Kenny, 'The Moderator–Mediator Variable Distinction in Social Psychological Research: Conceptual, Strategic, and Statistical Considerations', *Journal of Personality and Social Psychology* 51/6 (1986), pp.1173–82.
51. Lau and Redlawsk, *How Voters Decide*, p.210.
52. See Henning Best and Christof Wolf, 'Modellvergleich und Ergebnisinterpretation in Logit-und Probit-Regressionen', *Kölner Zeitschrift für Soziologie und Sozialpsychologie* 64/2 (2012), p.382f.
53. For example Lau and Redlawsk, 'An Exploration of Correct Voting', p.404.
54. Norris, *A Virtuous Circle*, p.18.
55. For instance see Lau and Redlawsk, 'An Exploration of Correct Voting', p.403.
56. In a more extensive analysis similar patterns can also be found for voters' exposure to the parties' TV ads. However, due to the fact that respondents were asked about TV ads only in the last month before the election (starting on 25 August, the date when they were first broadcast), the number of cases is too small to compare the results with other models. Still, it deserves mention that, first, exposure to televised party advertisements increased considerably in the course of the campaign, and that, second, exposure to party ads had a significant and autonomous effect on correct voting, too. Yet, in all likelihood as a consequence of the insufficient number of cases this effect is not robust and loses its significance if one includes the other mediator variables in the model.
57. Gelman and King, 'Why Are American Presidential Election'.
58. Powell, 'The Chain of Responsiveness'.

Index

www.ingramcontent.com/pod-product-compliance
Ingram Content Group UK Ltd.
Pitfield, Milton Keynes, MK11 3LW, UK
UKHW020352010325
455677UK00021B/409

9 780367 892401